BIRD DOG TRAINING

&

PROBLEM SOLVING

ROBERT PETTIT

BIRD DOG TRAINING & PROBLEM SOLVING

Copyright © 2016: Robert Pettit.

All rights reserved

DEDICATIONS

People I would like to recognize for their input and the encouragement they gave me in writing this book. First I must give credit to my wife Lilián for her perseverance in dealing with me while trying to master this complex machine called a computer. I'm short on patience when laboring with machines, whereas she exemplifies the cliché patience is a virtue, and she has plenty of both. My two sons Robert and Kevin gave me the inspiration and courage to finish this undertaking.

Another person who has since folded his tent and passed on to an eternal reward is Robert L. Jamison. He was my old hunting buddy; who constantly encouraged me to share my talents by writing a book about training dogs and fixing the unfixable.   Here it is, Bob!

FOREWORD

I met Robert Pettit in the early 1970s at a field trial at Beale Air Force Base in Marysville, California. If memory serves, it was for the running of the California Pheasant Championship. Bob offered a summer training program for bird dogs. Consequently, I was invited to spend many summers in Moses Lake, Washington at the Pettit Ranch. Since that time a bond developed and our friendship has grown over the years.

Spending time with someone on a day-to-day basis will give a person rare insights into an individual's personality, character, and innate talents. I felt I got to know Bob as well as anyone. I came to realize he possessed a certain mystique that I was unable to fathom. This characteristic was transferred into his training methods. Bob possesses a certain undeniable talent which enables him to take other trainers' washouts and make something out of nothing. This ability is not something one pulls out of page 29 of a training manual; one is born with it. At times, Bob was an animal psychologist which enabled him to achieve the desired results he was trying for.

Bob has a talent with a dog that many of us envy. Mystique or not, Bob gave me insights into more than just dogs.

Winner of 15 Championships both Open and Amateur, 8 Runners-Up and numerous Classic wins.

Ron Bader

TESTIMONIAL

I first met Bob Pettit in 2002 when my German wirehaired pointer developed a tail flagging issue, a major fault in field trial competition. A professional trainer who could not resolve this problem referred me to Bob who specializes in rehabilitating problematic dogs. I discovered he had that special innate ability to understand a dog's thought process and communicate that understanding back to the dog to obtain the desired results.

Using Bob's methods my dog's problems were fixed with no magic or stress involved, just common sense and logic. More importantly Bob taught me how to think like a dog and that opened my eyes to this new approach of training, something I hadn't learned even after years of attending dog training clinics.

Whether you are a first-time dog trainer, a seasoned trainer or simply struggling to solve a training issue, this book will guide you through the process of training your dog the smart way. It will provide you with the understanding of how a dog reasons.

Bob's teachings have been the foundation of my training program in the following years. Those teachings have helped me to win 10 field trial Championships, 8 Master Hunter titles, 1 National Championship win with 11 placements and 6 runners-up, including the #1 Amateur Gun Dog two consecutive years.

Meg Eden

Endorsement

Iv'e just finished reading this magnificent book written by Robert Pettit. I found it very interesting and it fulfilled my expectations. I met Bob more than 20 years ago when he judged my dog in the Mexico Shooting Dog Championship. It was an honor. He has vast knowledge of training and handling at the higest levels of bird dog competition. He's known for his abilities to analyze problem dogs and use their natural instincts to fix them.

Sr. Oscar Chavez

Jalisco, México

Author, competitor, and respected judge of American Field Trial Championships, as well as shooting and retrieving competitions in Mexico under Canófilo rules. Handler and trainer of pointing dogs and retrievers.

Endorsement

When talking about pointing dogs; Bob speaks their language. You can see the challenges of individual dogs through his eyes and the detailed instructions he writes, of how to fix problem dogs. This book will help people to make changes in their training techniques, not only for themselves, but it will also give helpful advice to other readers around the world. I can't remember how many books I've read about training dogs, and they all follow the same pattern. In this book Bob speaks to the reader as though they were having a conservation while sitting under a tree in the country. His words plant a vision in your eye.

Sr. Antonio Larre

México City, Mx.

Big game bow hunter, falconer, member of Mexicos Hunting Federation, and an owner/trainer of different breeds of pointing dogs. Acclaimed writer of hunting and fishing magazine articles. Speaker at Safari International Club.

Introduction

This book is full of sound advice and proven methods that have been amassed from over fifty years of experience training dogs while also instructing their owners, plus many years of hunting and field trial competition in three different countries. There are detailed explanations of how to cure supposedly incurable dogs, mostly by using unconventional training and problem solving procedures. These practices have stood the test of time and many dogs that were considered hopeless became productive gun dogs. Although written primarily for pointing dog owners, the training and problem solving techniques within apply to all breeds. The many field trial champions I've trained, the championships I won along the way, all began to diminish in importance when I discovered my abilities to deal with complicated training issues pertaining to problem dogs.

Throughout this book you will find stories of dogs that were given up on by trainers, both amateur and professional alike for one reason or another. Those same dogs after being rehabilitated went on to make an impact in the field trial world, or became first class hunting dogs. All dogs that man has ruined can be restored and turned into productive animals; if you have the know-how. This book will give you that knowledge although you will have to put in the time and effort. Preventing problems is well worth it, but if you do acquire a dog that's timid, gun-shy, bird-shy, blinks or bumps birds and has other serious problems, the solution is within these pages. It's all here, I've held nothing back.

I've incorporated stories of some of the more difficult training dilemmas encountered during my training career to make for better understanding of problem dog training. There is also is a Question and Answer section. These are questions submitted to me from hunting dog owners about common problems encountered while training their dogs. The remedies are offered in the answers. I've included the true stories of The Ghost Dog, The Reject and The Runaway for your reading pleasure.

R.P.

CONTENTS

Chapter I

Selecting the Puppy   1

Show dog vs. hunting dog, cost factor, the breeder, testing the puppy, transporting, kennel or house, health.

Chapter II

Starting Training   16

Noise introduction, voice, positive and negative training, discipline, hands, age and maturity.

Chapter III

Obedience Training   24

The collar, tying, jumping up, heeling, e-collar, sit, stay, down, come here or recall, teaching whoa.

Chapter IV

Natural and Force Retrieving   54

Caution on retrieving, natural retrieving, water retrieves, hunting dead, force retrieving, bolt collar vs foot squeeze, retrieving birds, preventing hard-mouth.

Chapter V

Field Training   76

Planted pigeons, electronic release trap, encouraging the puppy to point, shooting birds, honoring another dog, whistle, pattern training, and range.

Chapter VI

Finishing the Dog   97

Breaking to wing and shot, breaking with the e-collar, breaking with the check cord, stop to flush

Chapter VII

Problem Dogs   108

Problem dogs and examples of how they were rehabilitated, Mitzi, & Omar. Curing gun-shy and bird-shy dogs, feather shy, breaking the gun-shy/bird-shy dog.

Chapter VIII

Complex Problems   141

Hard-mouth, trailing, blinking, false-pointing, flagging, bolting, bumping birds, pointing fur.

Chapter IX

Common Problems   163

Sitting or lying down on point, digging, fear of thunder and fireworks, barking, learning to kennel, fighting, dominance, poison proofing at home-field, snake avoidance, porcupines.

Chapter X

Conditioning the Hunting Dog   184

Building muscle and endurance, pads, boots, proper food, eye care.

Chapter XI

Training Timid Dogs   190

Tricks, how and why to teach them to timid dogs, financial rewards, example of a timid dog, Molly, and how she was rehabilitated, Timing.

Chapter XII

Pigeons and Game Birds   203

Pigeons, Quail, Chukar and Pheasant, Callback pen.

Chapter XIII

Dogs Stories

Ghost Dog   211

The Reject   225

The Runaway   237

Questions and Answers   248

Recessive Behavior, Hard Mouth, Retrieving, Feeding of bird parts, Intensity, Rewards, Use of the bark collar.

Conclusion   256

Acknowledgements   257

Glossary   258

Chapter I

Selecting the Puppy

Selecting the puppy: When the moment arrives to select a puppy various factors come into play! They are all equally important such as the costs, color and temperament. I will assume anyone who is reading this book has already decided on the breed of dog they would like to acquire. Your breed selection should depend on what kind of birds you normally hunt. A quail or chukar hunter should consider one of the pointing breeds, whereas a waterfowl hunter would commonly purchase a retriever. It's always an exciting event getting a new puppy. You are thinking about your next great dog, and that helps a young man to gain enthusiasm for the work ahead, and helps the old man dream young again.

In selecting a puppy, one of the first things people normally consider is how much is it going to cost? The price, although relevant, is not the most important consideration, but you should buy the best bred puppy that is within your financial means.

You can order a subscription to The American Field magazine (542 S. Dearborn St. #650, Chicago, IL 60605) or the Pointing Dog Journal, (2779 Aero Park Dr. Traverse City. Mi. 49686) The puppies that are advertised for sale in these two magazines will give you an idea of what the asking price is for well-bred hunting dog puppies.

Show dog vs. hunting dog: The people reading this book are doing so because they are contemplating buying a breed of hunting dog puppy or already own one or more. In looking for a puppy make sure he comes from hunting or field trial breeding and not show stock. You could possibly get a useful hunting dog from show parents, but for the same money you can buy a field trial bred puppy with an extensive pedigree, one which shows how many field champions, and how many winners those dogs produced. Some breeds will have individuals that have acquired the Dual Champions (DC)

rating, meaning the dog has won both in show and in the field. English pointers for example have very few dual champions while in German Shorthaired pointers it's not at all uncommon. American Kennel Club (A.K.C.) holds hunt tests to award Junior Hunter (J.H.), Senior Hunter (S.H.) and Master Hunter (M.H.) titles to deserving dogs.

Your chances are multiplied for having a good hunting dog if you buy from a recognized breeder, one with a history. Usually but not always, English pointers, English setters and red setters are registered with The American Field; whereas Brittanys, German shorthairs, retrievers etc., are registered with the American Kennel Club. All hunting breeds can be registered with either registry, but this is the norm.

The cost factor: By buying an inexpensive puppy that's often times just what you will get. A Perazzi shotgun will cost more than an ordinary cheaply built shotgun. You can shoot birds with both of them, but you will be prouder of the Perazzi, take better care of it and take the time to learn to shoot it properly.

When you buy a well-bred puppy the same thing applies. Certainly the cost will be a little more, but you will take more of a personal interest in him, and will take the time to learn how to properly train that puppy. I will use the masculine gender (him, he, and his) throughout this narrative with the exception of when I'm speaking about a specific female. This is done in order to avoid confusion.

The Puppy: First and foremost look at how the puppy is bred and you do this by studying the pedigree of both the sire and dam. A lot of hunters are skeptical about buying a field trial bred dog owing to their concern the dog either will run too big or run away, and they won't be able to hunt with him. These are valid concerns, but while reading the suggestions offered within this book you will learn how to train your dog to handle, and he will learn to hunt with you. Those concerns will vanish when your dog is finished on game as they are no longer credible. You will have learned to trust your dog and he will have the necessary confidence in you. That will prepare you both to work together as a team.

SELECTING THE PUPPY

Columbia Basin Herald Photo

Field trial bred dogs have many generations of winners behind them which allow you to make an informed decision regarding their offspring. These are dogs which have competed against a wide variety of other winning dogs of championship caliber. It's important to bear this in mind when buying a puppy. If strict breeding standards are not upheld; in each successive generation the percentage of exceptional transmittable characteristics will become less.

Many knowledgeable dog owners prefer a line bred dog, a dog that's been bred within the same family. These dogs have been proven to have

more stamina, intelligence and more style. Robert G. Wehle of Elhew Pointer fame proved the line breeding theory many times over. I personally believe the breeding of the puppies to be one of the most important factors that should be considered when making a selection. Sometimes, however, there are exceptions to the rule.

We all want to be proud of our dogs and to brag about them. Nothing is quite as sweet to the owner's ear as having his hunting buddy tell him he would give his left arm, to own a dog like his. By following the suggestions offered within this book you will be able train your dog to a high level, so that he becomes a legend amongst your hunting friends. This also promotes your abilities as a trainer, if of course that's one of your goals.

As mentioned before it's all about getting the best bred puppy you can afford and hard work after that. If you would rather stay home and work with your dog than go out with friends for dinner, you are committed. Dedication is what it takes to develop a *good* hunting dog.

Now that you have selected the breed of dog, you must select a breeder. You want a sincere person who is always working to improve the breed, and preferably not a backyard breeder. I'm speaking about the type of individual who indulges in haphazard breeding practices in order to sell the puppies with no thought of genetics, physical or mental attributes. This is called backyard breeding. It's possible to get a decent hunting dog choosing that option, but this is an investment in time and money, and cheap doesn't always equal good.

Many hunters believe they have the best dog in the world, and of course if they're maintaining that animal he is the best dog to them. The professionals call this kennel blindness. Folks don't see because they don't want to see. Some of those same hunters haven't watched a real performance or understand what it constitutes, so in reality they have little to base their opinion on. It takes effort and investigation on their part to understand just exactly what qualities they should be looking for in a hunting dog.

The Breeder: Now that you've selected the breeder, and have made an appointment to see the puppies; you are on your way. When you arrive at the breeder's house and are looking over the litter, pay close attention to each and every puppy. Before you make your selection ask the breeder if you can take the puppies outside of their kennel. It's very difficult to make an intelligent decision about which puppy to pick while they remain in their kennel, which is their comfort zone. It's absurd for anyone to say that he can just look at a litter of puppies and pick the best one. There are many steps involved in picking the best puppy and one which will suit you.

See if the bitch and the stud dog are available for inspection and ask to see the pedigree of each of the parents. If no pedigrees are available for examination it should raise red flags. Be careful for the reason that any serious breeder will have the pedigrees of his dogs. The dam should surely be on the premises as a result of her being the mother of the puppies so closely observe her. Look at one or both dogs' conformation. What are their temperaments? Are they shy or aggressive? Do they move lightly, or are they heavy on their feet? Do they show any signs of lameness, especially in the rear quarters? This could be a sign of hip dysplasia (malformation). Check if both parents are straight in the front and not out at the elbows. The rear legs should have the correct angulation and not be cow-hocked. Cow-hocked means the back feet are turned out and the hocks are turned inwardly. You will be able to see this as the dog is moving away from you. While you are petting the bitch check her mouth to see if she has under bite or over bite. This is called malocclusion. The top teeth should slightly overlap the bottom teeth, much like your own. All of the faults mentioned are transmittable defects. These imperfections are hard to detect in a very young puppy, but not at all difficult to discover in an older dog.

If neither sire nor the dam are available for examination, recognize the fact that the puppy you pick will have both the best and the worst traits of each parent. For that reason it's worth taking a little extra time to study the pedigrees. Winners produce winners!

I recently trained a dropper, in this case an English setter crossed with an English pointer, for a friend of mine. He has a lot of expenditures associated with this young bitch, vet bills, medicine, training etc. Costs such as these can never be recovered. She's a really nice young bitch and is going to make a fine hunting dog, but that's the end of the line. Not being

registered and with no pedigree make it not worth the time nor the expense involved in breeding her as the puppies would have no commercial value. The money spent while raising an unregistered litter would be better spent on buying a well-bred puppy or two.

There are many good breeders available for any breed of dog. The price of the puppy is the cheapest part of owning the dog. You wouldn't purchase a new car with no title inasmuch as you can't license or resell it, so essentially it's worthless. Purchasing a puppy should fall under the same criterion.

Is the puppy litter registered? You can go online to get the information as to how it's done, either from the American Field or American Kennel Club. Don't listen to those old song and dances that the sire or the dam can be registered, "but my friend hasn't sent me the papers yet," "or," "they are registered, but he misplaced the papers." Walk away!

When the puppies are whelped they can be litter registered showing how many males and females are in the litter. The names of the sire and dam will be listed on the litter registration form along with their registration numbers. By the time you arrive wanting to buy a puppy, the owner should have the litter enrollment number available. If the breeder hasn't processed the paperwork yet give him a down payment and the final installment when you have the documentation in your hands. Some registries offer on line registration as well.

Have the puppies been wormed and have they been vaccinated? This will of course depend on their age and if they are weaned. Do the puppies have a pot belly? If so ask the owner when he last fed them. Sometimes an inflated abdomen indicates worms.

What do you see when you are observing the litter? Is one puppy the exact color you want? About color; dark dogs are harder to see against a dark background in the field. A light colored dog would be easier to spot, but don't make that the only benchmark when selecting your future prospect. Another puppy is the runt of the litter. Do you pick him? You've heard the old saying the runt of the litter makes the best dog. Does the one you want have a naval hernia? That can be repaired, but it's usually a genetic factor, it's hereditary and those defects are transmissible to his or her offspring. These examples do not necessarily mean a puppy will turn out to be worthless, but on the other hand you need to have as many factors in your favor as possible. When any of these puppies are picked make sure the good points outweigh the bad.

A lot of people pick a puppy based on color and they forget all other aspects. There again, you're not buying a new automobile whereby picking the brand of the car and the color you are assured it will be the same as any other car of the same make and model. You wouldn't buy a new car with a dent in the door, so why buy a defective puppy? Every puppy in the litter will be different in some manner from his littermates, and for that reason you can't always be satisfied with the color, but try to pick the best one. Most reputable breeders will offer a replacement guarantee which states if your puppy has a genetically transmitted defect they will replace it.

This trainer was once given a well-bred English pointer puppy as a judging gift. After a year of training, feeding, and vet bills, my suspicions were aroused when after a day's hunt he would be lame the following day. X-rays confirmed my worst fears when it was discovered he had hip dysplasia. The dog was euthanized and I no longer accept free dogs from anyone. When you pay for a dog you have certain rights if the dog is deemed to have a genetically transmitted defect. A reputable breeder will respect that.

Does the puppy have longer or shorter than normal hair? This could signify that the mother of the puppies had a suitor of questionable lineage when she was in season. A bitch can have a litter sired by multiple males. For example a five week old English setter puppy might have very little hair, but it will grow heavier with age. An English pointer puppy might show a little more hair than normal. This could be a weather factor or something else. Now with the advent of DNA the *Field Dog Stud Book* offers testing on all dogs. The problem will lie in the fact that if the sire

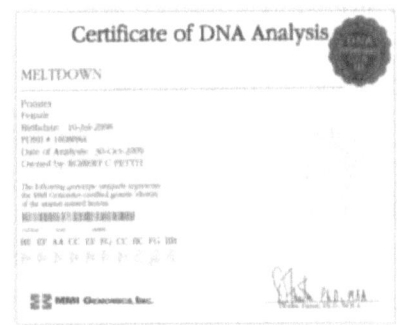

and dam haven't been tested, it won't be possible to check the puppies.

It needs to start somewhere so it's a good idea to have your puppy certified. If you decide in the future you want to breed you can test the bitch or the sire, whichever applies. Afterwards as long as both have been certified you can offer an ironclad guarantee that will go with the puppies you're selling, stating the sire and the dam are unquestionably the parents. This is a very inexpensive process, and you will usually get a better price for those puppies.

Look for an active puppy. When a puppy isn't watching you pick him up. Did he give an involuntary twitch or cry out in surprise or fear? It's been my observation this type of puppy will probably develop into a nervous and high-strung dog, whereas you will want a well-adjusted individual. The well-adjusted dog has a better attitude about accepting training as he tends to learn new things faster and with less effort on your part. This might not be a hard and fast rule, but after countless puppies and copious notes taken, I sure believe that it is.

Testing the Puppy: If anything is available that could be considered some type of obstacle course like a block wall or a fallen tree limb, you can use one or the other for a test. Separate the puppies you are interested in from their littermates. Take one or more of those puppies and put him/them behind or inside of the obstacle. Watch to see if any of them try to figure a way out. Pay attention to which puppies cry and eventually give up, lie down and go to sleep, and which ones try to find an escape route. In dogs, much like any other species, you have your slackers; and those contrast with other individuals which keep going no matter what kind of obstacles are in their path. Those puppies that persevere and try to find an escape route are showing a degree of intelligence and determination not demonstrated by their littermates. The age you can do this test is six weeks and older.

When I was raising numerous litters, I constructed a plywood maze that was used in helping me select puppies with the kind of character I valued, and wanted to keep. Much like what was mentioned before, this maze helped me to separate the whiners from the puppies which showed initiative. Those puppies that would actively search for the exit and then find their way out were marked for future reference. I equate that test to a level of intellect and persistence.

When speaking about pointing dog puppies take them into the yard and watch when they smell something interesting. *Usually* a low-headed dog upon getting a scent will go to the ground with his nose. A high-headed puppy will put his nose in the air trying to figure out where the scent is coming from. A good test is to put a piece of ham on top of any object six inches or so higher than the puppies head. Ham is a good meat to use due to its strong odor. Walk the puppies around this object until one or more catches the scent. Watch which ones put their nose in the air, and which ones look to the ground. Pay attention to the one or two puppies that throw up their heads while trying to figure out where the enticing aroma is emanating from. This is a test I've done for many years when raising puppies and I believe in it.

The reason you should look for a high-headed dog is easy to explain. When a high-headed dog locates birds, he winds them by their body scent and not foot scent. Dog's that hunt with a high head are not so prone to bumping or flushing birds by accident, whereas a dog that's hunting with his nose on the ground will constantly bump birds. I'm of course referring to a pointing dog and not a flushing dog. A flushing dog will follow both body and foot scent, and when close to the birds will flush them for the gunner. A pointing dog that follows body scent will be pointing birds where they are, and not pointing foot scent where they were.

Look for an independent puppy, one which is not afraid of getting away from his littermates. That would indicate self-reliance. Watch for the one which becomes curious about something and wanders over to check it out. That would demonstrate boldness. Take your time and be sure you are absolutely pleased with your selection, in that you're the one who will most likely keep the dog for the twelve to fifteen years of his life span. The veterinarian, the food bills and time spent training all add up to a large investment. The cheapest part is the actual purchase of the puppy. There's an old saying: *it costs no more to feed a good one than a poor one.*

If the new puppy is for you personally, then consider leaving the children at home. Whichever puppy you choose, the kids will be delighted with, but if

BIRD DOG TRAINING & PROBLEM SOLVING

they go with you, the puppy that's selected might be one they like and not the one that will best suit your purposes. Emotion shouldn't enter into your decision. Make a logical selection.

After picking your puppy the hard work begins, but the pleasure you derive from developing a young dog easily overrides the hours spent working with him. With the knowledge gained from reading this narrative you will be well equipped to train and finish your dog.

Transporting: Now that you have made your decision it's time to take your acquisition to his soon "to" be new home. Don't put him in a dog crate, the trunk or the back seat and start out. That's not a very good way to begin a long-term relationship. If possible have a friend go with you, so that person can drive. It will give you more time to bond with the puppy and for him to familiarize himself with your voice and smell. Put him on your lap, rub his stomach and massage his ears. By doing this he will be more relaxed. He's now your dog so start the bonding process as early as possible.

If you brought a collar with you, now's the time to put it on the pup. With all the new things happening, the puppy won't notice he's wearing it. Bring a bottle of water and a small dish with you, as well as a little treat. A nervous puppy will drink water and also chew on a small rawhide bone if it's offered. Your puppy has been jerked out of the only security he's ever known. It's time to let him feel that he's in a safe environment. This is a big ordeal, but you can lessen the trauma by following the advice being offered here. These small considerations will make your puppy eager to ride in your vehicle in the future. The puppy's first trip should always be a happy experience. The next time you want to take him for a ride in the truck or car, he's excited as he remembers it as something pleasant. It's always a good idea to stop every thirty minutes alongside the road in a grassy area to let him empty out, and have a drink of water.

To understand what the puppy is experiencing I will offer an example. You go to the orphanage to pick up your newly adopted son. You take the boy away from everything he's ever known, the friends, his room, the mother figure, and then put him in a box or the trunk of the car and head for home. Maybe stop to have a bite to eat on the way. You get the idea. The trauma associated with that experience could affect him for the rest of his life. The same thing applies to your new puppy. Upon arriving home you need to play with and make him to feel you are his best friend. By talking, caressing and spending a lot of time with him he will become attached to you and have absolutely no anxiety issues. This is called socialization. All of these things will help mold your puppy into the type of dog that is an absolute pleasure to train. You have an unwritten book in the form of your new puppy. How you write that book is up to you.

Now is a good time to introduce him to his name. Pick one you and the family has agreed on as this will keep everyone happy. Oftentimes the puppy will help pick his own name.

I once brought a puppy to Mexico City by air and the family picked me up at the airport. On the way home my young sons were playing with the pup in the back seat, and he was jumping around biting everything and causing havoc. My wife mentioned that the puppy was going to be a lot of trouble!

The boys immediately replied; "Let's call him Trouble," and that's how he got his name.

When the puppy is accustomed to riding in a car or truck you will be able to move him into a kennel or airline crate with a minimum of hassle. Everyone has seen hunting dogs that never get over their fear of riding in a vehicle. They vomit, defecate, tremble and show all the nervous signs of dogs that are stressed and not in their element. Upon the hunter arriving at his destination the dog is a quivering mess, and of course it will affect his performance in the field. This is not a pleasant experience for the owner or the dog and should never happen if only these preventive measures were taken. If you've purchased an older dog with these types of problems you will learn how to resolve them in *Chapter IX*.

Now that you're home with the puppy and he's had a few days to acclimatize, he's becoming accustomed to you and to his new surroundings. It's time to start playing a little rude with him. He's not at all fragile as demonstrated by the rough and tumble play he engaged in with his littermates. By the kids and yourself playing rudely with the puppy, you are teaching him to take the bumps and bruises he's going to encounter in his

world. This will also help overcome any shyness on his part. If the shyness is a hereditary factor you can help him conquer it by exposure to everything from noise, horseplay and strangers handling him. After he's been vaccinated, take him to the park, or downtown to let people pet and play with him. The traffic noise, the constant movement and the new smells will help him adjust to anything he may encounter. This is another good way to socialize the puppy.

Kennel or house: The old school way of thinking taught us that we should keep our hunting dogs in a kennel for the reason that by having them in the house they would be ruined. I personally believe it should be a combination of both.

When a young dog is exposed to the family, the kids pull his ears, step on his tail, and push him down the stairs. With that type of treatment he learns to accept anything that comes his way. Dogs kept in kennels don't have that socialization. Family interaction will help you with your future training, by having a dog that's easy to work with and eager to please.

Kids and puppys; an unbeatable combination.

Any training you start with your dog no matter how simple, always make sure it ends on a happy note. Petting, playing with, or giving an edible reward is something pleasant for the dog and will ensure the finish is as happy as the beginning. Your hands are one of the best training aids God has equipped you with. Hands that gently stroke an animal serve to have a calming effect, and to give him self-confidence as well as inspiring trust in you. Never forget this important fact. If you take this advice to heart, you will have a willing pupil for anything you wish to teach.

When first starting to train dogs I received the least desirable examples of dogdom to work with. Some clients gave me problem dogs to see what could be done with them, but more than likely trying to help me out as they weren't expecting much. A large percentage of those dogs were extremely fearful of people and lacked confidence. Whether this was a genetic factor or from them being isolated or both, I didn't know. Most, however, hadn't been socialized as puppies, and consequently were extraordinarily difficult to train. You cannot successfully train a dog that has no confidence in you and is frightened of everything. Read more about this later in the *Training Timid Dogs in Chapter XI.*

Health: You should have a veterinarian check of your new puppy as soon as possible. The vet will start your puppy on a vaccination program, and will keep a record of times to vaccinate and any other health issues such as parasite control. He will also explain to you why it's a good idea to microchip your pup. Every year during hunting season we hear about hunting dogs that tend to get lost or stolen. A percentage of those lost dogs can be recovered, if they have an implanted microchip. A responsible veterinarian will also call a week or so in advance and tell you when your dog is due for his next booster shot. This is an invaluable service for the dog's owner, because many people don't keep good health records on their animals.

Additionally, I would like to recommend that you also prepare a small medicine kit to carry with you when taking your dog on a hunting trip. The importance of this kit shouldn't be overlooked, as demonstrated by the next two stories.

The first incident happened many years ago to a fellow professional trainer and me when we were competing in a field trial near Los Banos, California. He was running a young English setter bitch and I was riding (these trials were conducted on horseback), along to scout. A scout's job is to help the handler find the dog if he's lost on point. On the breakaway the setter ran about one hundred yards in an open field when she suddenly stopped. It became apparent something was drastically wrong. She was

gagging and pawing at her head and mouth. When we rode up closer to the bitch we could see that she had something embedded in the roof of her mouth. It was a broken-off stick the size of your little finger. Where the stick came from in an open grass field and how it happened to become embedded in her mouth was anyone's guess. We were able to pull out the stick and relieve the dog of the extreme discomfort she was suffering, but neither one of us had a kit with antibiotics to prevent infection. Right then and there, I decided to put together a medicine kit with every conceivable tool or medicine that would ever be needed. In that way I would be ready for any situation which cropped up. This is why incidents such as this highlight the saying: *expect the unexpected and be prepared for it.*

The other occurrence happened to a falconer friend of mine in a remote region of Montana while hunting sharp-tailed grouse with his dog and falcon. The dog tried to kill a porcupine resulting in countless quills that were embedded both on the inside, as well as the outside of his head and mouth.

He had to drive sixty miles to a veterinarian's office to have the quills extracted. It ended up being a time consuming and expensive trip. With a little knowledge and a medicine kit, he could have given the dog a sedative, pulled out the quills and administered an antibiotic. It would have saved his dog discomfort and him a lot of time and money.

I have used my kit many times while training and competing with dogs in Canada, the United States and Mexico. It always goes with me and has saved many a dog from having any lasting effects from an injury. The vet can advise you as to what you would put into the kit, and also give you rudimentary knowledge of how to make an incision, stitch up a wound and give an injection.

To list a few items included in my kit: Karo syrup for possible sugar deficiency, Nutra-Cal and needle nose pliers for pulling out porcupine quills; lidocaine to deaden an area, syringes, antibiotics, vitamin k for suspected poisoning. A hair brush for taking out burrs, a box cutter knife, alcohol, tape, hydrogen peroxide, stitching needles, scalpel, thread, cotton pads, Q-tips and a small squirt bottle for eye flushes. A porcupine quill stick should be included as well. This will be explained in *Chapter IX*.

Take my advice and put together a medicine kit and learn how to use it. You will be happy that you did.

Chapter II

Starting Training

Painting by, Edgar Alcántara

Learning to read your dog: *Successful* trainers have learned how to read dogs or they would fail at their profession. All dogs communicate by using body language or their voice. You have learned your dog wants to be fed by him jumping around, or barking and howling. You know when his tail is tucked or his eyes are opened wide, he's probably scared. If his ears are flattened he's feeling threatened, or if they are cocked forward he's attentive. *Watch and observe.* You will be a better trainer for it.

Noise introduction: If you're going to have a productive hunting dog obviously he can't be gun-shy. Let's take a few simple steps to prevent this from happening. After the puppy has been brought to his new home and accepted his unfamiliar surroundings, it's time to start with noise introduction.

When you or your family members are around the puppy everyone should begin making loud noises. You are not doing him a favor by keeping loud noises away. The puppy sees you going about your business while all this noise is happening and will begin to realize he has nothing to be frightened of. At feeding time strike his food pan against the wall, bang the garbage can lid and drop noisy things on the floor, all while he is eating. He learns that he lives in a noisy world. If at any time the puppy shows nervous behavior during any of these proceedings, do not console him. By doing this you are indicating there's something to fear, but you are there to protect him. A word of caution! Be careful you don't accidently drop anything on him while you are introducing loud noises. That could set you back with your training.

Any time the puppy leaves the food bowl while you're making noises, take away the food and let him miss *a* meal. When he's really hungry reintroduce the noise program again. No healthy dog will starve himself no matter how strong his concerns are. Problem dogs, however, will refuse to eat for four-five days or longer when confronted with their fears. I have never seen nor heard of a healthy dog that would actually starve himself to the point of dying when food is available. You can use hunger as a tool when curing many types of problems associated with dogs. When the puppy has become accustomed to all the noise that's constantly around, it's time to introduce the gunshot.

For this you should enlist the help of a friend or a family member to fire the gun. Always start with a .22 caliber blank pistol. If you don't have a blank pistol you can use any revolver with any brand of .22 blank. Oftentimes blanks are difficult to find. If that's the case you may use the type of blank used to drive nails into concrete assuming, your pistol is in good working order. Always use the lightest load available, and when you've finished firing a round, check the barrel to make sure the wadding has cleared. This can

save you from a nasty surprise. These types of blanks have more powder in them, are more powerful and make a louder report.

Put your assistant around the corner a good distance from the puppy. The puppy shouldn't see him, but your helper needs to see you. As the puppy starts to eat, give a prearranged signal and at that moment, your accomplice fires the pistol. If the puppy takes notice of this and leaves his food bowl, immediately pick it up and start the lesson again the next day. Don't feed him until the next day when you're ready to continue with the gun introduction again. Start the next lesson by putting your friend farther away. The puppy will be famished by then, and when he begins to eat, your friend should again fire the pistol.

Anytime you see a problem starting to develop like the puppy being scared of noise or a gunshot, stop and resume the lesson next day when he's hungry. When he does eat, don't let him get fully satiated. The idea is for him to be a little hungry when he hears the shot. After he's eating under gunfire, start shooting a few seconds before he begins to eat. In this manner the gunshot becomes the dinner bell.

You can also purchase professionally recorded gunshot sound effects to acclimatize the puppy to the noise of the shot. The puppy can be introduced to this noise at any time, but preferably as soon as possible, while he's still very young. If you've done your homework with the noise makers, it would be a rare occurrence for something like the preceding incident, of him leaving his food bowl, to happen. By now he's learned the noise of the shot means its dinner time, and he looks forward to hearing it. All animals respond to food when used as a training aid, especially when they are hungry. A hungry dog is a cooperative dog. Maybe with your puppy's temperament some of these preceding steps won't be necessary, but it's always better to be safe than sorry. At this point you are able to move forward without creating additional problems you will have to deal with later.

We've all heard the stories of hunters who get their new puppy or even an older dog and take him to the field to see if he's gun shy. Why is anyone surprised to learn that, "Yep" he's gun shy. You can imagine on the puppy's first outing where everything's new and different, when suddenly he hears a loud bang. He's startled never having heard anything like that before. Next comes the fear and suddenly he's heading for a safe place. If he comes to you for protection, the problem is easier to resolve than if he runs away and goes back to your vehicle. By coming to you, it indicates that he trusts and recognizes that you are his safe haven, and there the puppy knows he will be protected.

It's always difficult for me to believe dog owners make their dog gun shy for no reason, when a few precautionary measures would prevent this. It's all about common sense. Later we will get into introducing shotgun fire using live birds under field conditions.

Positive and negative training: There are two kinds of training, positive and negative, and you will use both. Anytime you do something negative, immediately follow it with positive reinforcement. An example of this would be when you give your dog a command he knows, but doesn't follow it. Let's say you are in the field and he finds a bird, but instead of pointing, he flushes it. You gave the command "Whoa," but he ignored you and bumped the bird anyway. You are now forced to make a correction, in as much as he didn't heed your order, and that correction needs to be given immediately. That's negative training. You would follow it with a positive action such as giving him another bird to point and then killing it for him. In this manner the dog learns to follow an order that's been given, in that when he does something positive happens, like you killing a bird and giving him a piece. That was an example of negative training with consequences, but it was followed with positive reinforcement.

Bad choices were made when you were young, and those choices had ramifications, but you learned something. If it was followed by positive reinforcement the positive aspect stayed embedded in your mind, and the negative aspect in most cases was forgotten.

Words of caution: Before you start with any serious training of your dog, it's important to bring to your attention a few of the mistakes you don't want to make. First, I would like to talk about hunger and how it applies to dog training. When speaking of hunger; and I will speak about it often, I wish

to clarify exactly what's meant. I'm talking about something like the puppy missing a meal due to him leaving his food when he heard a loud noise. After missing a meal, he will more quickly adapt to whatever it is you are trying to teach. When he's hungry he will be more amenable to accepting training in order to appease his stomach.

I will make it crystal clear! A puppy that misses a meal won't be affected by it; but never let him miss too many meals in a row. You would never have a reason to do that with a growing puppy. That would constitute abuse. An older dog can miss quite a few meals and no harm will be done, but a young puppy doesn't fit into that category. As stated before, when dealing with older problem dogs that are stressed, oftentimes they won't eat for four or even five days. Food then becomes a training aid which will speed up a cure.

Voice: One of the most important warnings I can give you is; "Never" scream at your dog. I use the word scream, because it implies using a more forceful tone, than the word talk, or shout. It's important to remember this. If by accident or design you get too vigorous in disciplining your dog during a training session, there will probably be no harm done. If you screamed while physically making a correction, you have set his training back and consequently that negative lesson won't be forgotten. Your voice will do more to get your dog to cower and show fear, usually by putting his belly on the ground and showing submission, than any other action by you, his trainer. This seems to be one of the most important facets of training many dog owners bungle. I just can't emphasize this enough. Sometimes in the heat of a training session you might tend to lose your patience. It may cost you in the long run, by your dog not having confidence in you and by him cowering or running away. Running away would be the worst possible scenario. No one wants to see a dog that's been intimidated, as it's a reflection on *you* as the dog's owner/trainer. It would also reflect poorly on the dog.

Imagine if you lose your temper and scream at your wife and kids. It makes it harder for them to forgive you, than if you had just kept your anger in check and talked to them about the point you were trying to make. It's no different with your dog. Dog's intelligence levels are defined by nature as to just how much they can grasp, so you can't apologize as you would to a human. So always keep your ire in check and your voice in control.

Hands: Hands that stroke the dog and pet him are the best training aids you have and should never be used harshly. Never hit the dog with your hands, and consistently use them in a positive manner. You do that by stroking and petting. Using your hands in a positive manner gives the dog self-confidence. You will see me write about the importance of your hands at various times throughout this discourse, as they can be a soothing and confidence-building tool. Never use your hands for anything but good. The only exception to this rule is when two dogs are getting ready to fight and that will be covered later in *Chapter IX*.

Discipline: When training a dog a certain amount of discipline is needed. What methods, how and when to use them, can make or break a young dog. There's a big difference between discipline and punishment. The word punishment is usually associated with harsh treatment, while discipline can be interpreted as bringing the dog into a state of control by his training, and the restraint you exert over the animal. You will use discipline while training your dog, but you should never use punishment, which is abuse. Any correction needs to be administered immediately after an infraction, but it should always be followed with positive reinforcement. Keep your temper under control while you're training so your finished product will make you proud. You don't want your dog to be scared of you, but you will need to earn his respect.

Always make sure any correction that you administer to the dog fits the crime he's committed. Make the correction when needed, but don't over correct! An example: Your dog knows the command to "Come Here," but refuses to comply. You are then justified in using more forceful methods such as jerking him to you by using a force collar and check cord. If your dog doesn't know what the command means; then you should be teaching it. One is calling for a correction while the other is calling for instruction.

Tools: The tools that may be used when training can be a flushing whip, slingshot, choke chain, force collar, e-collar, check cord, pulley, or a whoa

BIRD DOG TRAINING & PROBLEM SOLVING

strap. All of the above should be used with logic and used humanely. Never discipline a dog until he cowers in fear. A dog's tail and his eyes are the barometers by which you are able to judge how far you can go with any disciplinary measures. A tail that's tightly tucked tells you that you went too far, while a tail that's down and only slightly tucked means the dog got the message. Eyes showing fear are a warning signal. With any of these tools you need only to get your point across and no more. I will speak about this again throughout this narrative.

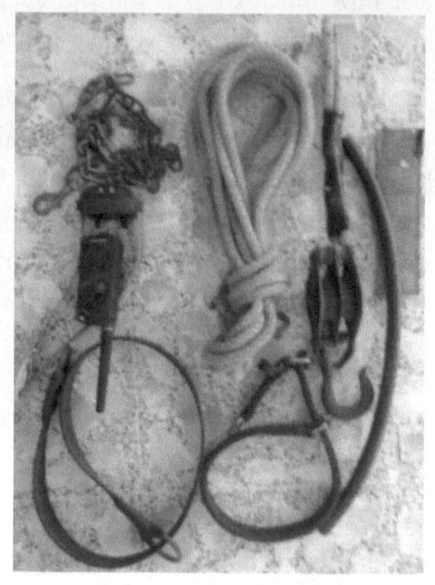

"Tools of the trade"

Age and maturity: The age we start a young puppy on obedience training is dependent upon several factors, but mostly his level of maturity. You wouldn't start a kindergartener on a course of trigonometry and the same principal should apply to the puppy. Most dog owners realize a puppy is capable of understanding and even absorbing some very simple training procedures at six or seven weeks of age. Any interaction you have with your puppy is considered training. Something as simple as housebreaking or teaching the command, "Sit" or "Come Here" is training and can be taught at a young age. Read further before teaching "Sit" to a pointing dog puppy.

The first thing you need to consider is how are you and your new puppy bonding? When you arrive home from work does he stop what he's doing and come bounding toward you, or does he look at you and continue with whatever he was fixated on? When he comes running to you, it means you and the puppy have a good rapport and simple obedience training can start at any time. If he doesn't pay any attention to you, it means you have a small problem. Don't let it become a bigger issue. You want to be the puppy's brother, sister, mother and father all rolled up in one. Start this by showering more attention on him by playing or feeding treats, until he would rather be around you than away from you. The rapport you have with your puppy will serve you later at the start of advance training.

It's important to take him to the field at least two or three times a week so he can run and play before beginning to work on obedience. After running ten minutes or so, offer a drink of water and let him cool down before starting on his lessons. This field work helps in two ways. One is the expending of his surplus energy, and the other is expediting the learning process by him chasing small birds and starting to use his nose to find them. The new smells he encounters will hasten his education as to what is desirable and what is best avoided. Generally speaking he will also learn to pattern by staying in front of you, and that is an important aspect of his training.

German Wirehaired pointer puppy. Meg Eden photo

Chapter III

Obedience Training

Obedience: Just exactly what is obedience training? It entails more than just "Whoa, Heel, Sit, Down" and "Come Here." Obedience training is teaching a dog to become a good citizen. When you train your dog to be an obedient and mindful member of the family, it will keep everyone happy and he will become an asset rather than a liability. This is applicable whether he's a kennel or house dog.

Collar: The first thing you should start is breaking the puppy to the collar and this should be done as soon possible, if you haven't done so already. I'm speaking about his regular collar, not the electric collar, hereafter referred to as the e-collar. Put the collar around his neck, but leave it loose enough so that you can place one finger underneath. When he's an adult you should be able to slide two fingers underneath, although in both cases it needs to be tight enough to prevent the dog from slipping it. It will probably irritate the puppy for a short while. He will scratch his neck and try to get rid of the irritation, but in two days he will forget it's even there.

Here is a recommendation about which type of collar to buy. For a rapidly growing young puppy it needs to be at least three-quarter of an inch wide and have a D-ring. For an adult dog, use one that's wider, with a D-ring and an O-ring in the middle of the collar. This O-ring gives you an extra place to attach your lead or tie out too. Now you have two places to hook a swivel snap. A wide collar won't be so prone to twist when the dog is spinning around. For a mature dog many professionals prefer the one inch wide, orange for visibility, nylon collar with webbing inside. These collars last forever and are not easy to break. Electing to buy this type of collar for your growing puppy, you might have to trim it assuming you're not able to find one that's small enough. Pay attention to the tightness as the puppy grows, because a nylon dog collar won't stretch.

In mid 1970s while competing with a young English pointer in a field trial held on the Blood Indian Reserve in Alberta, Canada, he became lost. The dog was wearing this type of orange nylon collar at the time. After becoming frightened and losing his bearings, he turned as wild as a coyote and the people on the reserve started calling him The Ghost Dog. They would see him occasionally, but he would always run away and hide. Although efforts were made to capture him, he wouldn't let himself be caught. He lived in the wild for nine months through a severe winter and when he was eventually trapped, he still had on his orange nylon collar. At the end of this book you will find the extraordinary story of the Ghost Dog.

Tying: After three or four days of having the puppy at home and he's thoroughly familiar with his new surroundings, it's time to teach restraint by using a light chain. This training can be done on the same days you are introducing gunfire from the .22 caliber. Work on the tying in the morning while it's cool and gunfire in the evening at feeding time. The type of tying chain you should use is the kind that doesn't kink easily when twisted. A chain will serve your purpose much better than a cord due to its weight which precludes it from wrapping around the puppy legs, when he's twisting around.

To tie him select a low overhanging tree limb or any object no more than six feet off the ground. You can attach a tie chain with a swivel snap on both ends so that the puppy can't choke himself. One can never have too many swivel snaps on a chain, because if one snap fails you have a backup.

Over the years I've seen more than one dog almost choked to the point of death by a faulty swivel snap on a chain. A dog will never choke if he's attached to a chain with one or more functional snaps. Let me caution you about the quality of swivel snaps. Not all snaps are created equal. Some have small lumps or burrs from the casting process and those don't spin freely. The way to test this is to grab the top of the snap with one hand and the bottom swivel part with the other. Now pull the top against the bottom. It should still spin freely even with the pressure you are exerting. I've had

good luck with the brass snaps. They spin around freely and don't break easily.

It's better not to attach the puppy to a stake in the ground until he learns to tie, as more than likely he will get twisted up and possibly get injured. Attach the swivel snap on the chain to the D or O-ring on the puppy's collar so he can jump, run around in a circle and flip over, but cannot get wrapped up, or get the chain twisted. That means just enough slack to permit him to lie down, but no more.

The puppy will howl, bark and do anything to attract your attention, but ignore him. Go get a drink of water, read your newspaper, only stay close enough to where you can keep an eye on the youngster. When he's first hooked up, step away so that he doesn't associate you with the discomfort he's going to feel. After ten minutes or so he will stop fighting the chain. You should then go and offer a drink of water. Don't pet or console the puppy. By giving him a drink you are putting yourself into the position of being his hero. Now walk away. Probably by now he's becoming thoroughly chastened and completely submissive to the chain. He might bark or howl, but usually the fight is gone, at least for that session. Wait until he's thoroughly subdued before he's disconnected. Take him off the chain so he can to go and play, but not if he's barking or howling. He will then think that when he complains, he gets out of prison. Repeat the lesson every day until the puppy is comfortable and is walking around while being tied. Now that the puppy has accepted the chain and is not intimated, he is starting to gain self-confidence. Let me offer a word of caution. Don't connect the puppy to a cord and drag him to the tie out chain. He is not broke to lead yet and you would be dragging him into a trauma situation. Carry him to the tie out.

Change locations of the tie out every few days so that he becomes accustomed to being tied no matter where he is. After he's thoroughly subdued and accepts the tie out you can proceed to the next step, which is to tie him to a stakeout chain. If the chain gets wrapped around his legs he won't fight it hard and will learn to untangle himself. Now you can begin leading the puppy around the yard and play with him while he's connected to the lead, or check cord in dog trainer terminology.

This is a good time to start rewarding your pupil for his good behavior. Put a hot dog sliced into many small pieces into your shirt pocket or fanny pack, whichever you prefer, and call the puppy to you. Call him by name and say Sam, "Come Here" or, just Sam, "Here" and then pull him to you. Immediately reward him with a small piece of hot dog. Let him wander off a little distance and call him again, meanwhile pulling him towards you. When he arrives, give another piece of hot dog.

Don't get forceful with the puppy at this stage of his training. Wait until the puppy is six months or older before you start applying a little pressure. Now that he's lead broke and starting to come when called, you are ready to start teaching him to become a well behaved member of the family.

Jumping up: When your puppy reaches the age of four to six months he will start to become a nuisance by jumping up on people. This is a simple fault to correct. If you like many hunting dog owners want him to jump up and deliver a bird to hand, you should teach him to jump up on command. This "Up" command is particularly advantageous for those older hunters who find it convenient not having to bend down to take a bird.

To teach him not to jump up on you and everyone else the best method is to nudge him with a knee in the chest when he does, but don't scold him. He begins to understand that whenever he jumps on you, he gets a correction. If at the time you didn't say anything, he doesn't equate the negative aspect of it with you. He believes that knee jumped up by itself, and when that happens with everyone he jumps up on, this fault is soon corrected.

It would be a similar situation when using an e-collar on a dog chasing cows. If you shock him along with a verbal "No," then he realizes it was you who caused the pain and not the cow. When he's away from you he will chase cows again. If you didn't say anything but just nicked him, he believes the cow caused the pain and you have effectively cured him of chasing cows.

Let's go back to kneeing the dog. After he's been nudged in the chest two or three times he will be very leery about jumping up on you again. This habit of jumping up on people is an irritating one that needs to be addressed immediately. One day the mistress of the house will be in her going to town

clothes and the puppy will jump up on her with muddy paws. This tends to provoke women, so my advice is to tackle the problem while the puppy is still young. When grandma comes to visit she can be knocked to the ground if the dog jumps on her. That's another reason this needs to be addressed as soon as possible and not wait until the animal is fully grown. When friends come to visit have them execute the same maneuver. Tell them to call the puppy, but not by name. The name should always be associated with pleasure and not discomfort.

To do this effectively, have your friends make a big fuss over the pup, so he will jump up on them. Show them the process of raising the knee at just the right moment to bump him in the chest while saying nothing. After you

or your friend has nudged the puppy, he will stay away, due to being nervous about what just happened. Walk away from the spot where you made the correction, call the dog to you and pet him. The attention you show him will be positive, after the negative action of kneeing him. If you've moved from the spot where he got the knee, it won't be construed as you consoling him. After a number of times you or anyone else has done this, you won't have any more problems with the jumping up fault.

When you want to teach him to jump up it becomes a little more difficult for the puppy to understand. Previously, when he did it he had an unpleasant experience. He will be a little confused about why you want him to jump up now, whereas before he got the knee. Here's where it helps to have small pieces of hot dog or some other treat in your shirt pocket. Pick up his front feet and put them on you while giving the command "Up." Immediately give him a piece of hotdog and tell him what a good boy he is. Repeat this as many times as necessary until he has a firm understanding of exactly what it is you want. When he jumps up uninvited, knee him, but when he jumps up on command, reward him with an edible. Eventually you will be able to dispense with the treat and use ear massaging or verbal praise to get the same result.

Heeling: An important point to remember when starting with any type of training is; don't feed the dog before beginning work. You will get better results if the dog is a little hungry. At some point you might wish to compensate him for his efforts.

You will also make better progress with your dog if you spend a couple of minutes playing with him after each workout. This is the dogs happy ending that we all strive for when training. After those play times he will eagerly await his next training session.

"Heel" is a very important command for your dog to know. A good example of where this command can be utilized is when you have finished hunting a field. There's a big plowed field in front of you that's not going to hold any birds, but you have to cross it anyway. You should "Heel" your dog through the field as this gives him an opportunity to rest before starting to hunt again. Also give him a drink of water before continuing. Both of these actions contribute to the dog being able to hunt longer, as a result of being refreshed. Your dog will find more birds due to the fact; a fresh wet dog has better scenting abilities.

I was quail hunting at the invitation of a friend in the Mexican state of Veracruz on the Gulf Coast. My dog pointed eight coveys that morning and my friend's dog only pointed three. In between fields I kept my dog at heel to keep him from tiring himself. When the hunt was over my friend asked me why I always heeled and watered my dog every twenty minutes or so, when obviously he didn't need a rest or water. He told me that if his dog couldn't hunt three hours without water or resting, then he wasn't the type of dog he wanted. I asked him how many coveys his dog had found and how

many mine had found. As stated before, a wet and rested dog will find more birds than a tired dry dog.

Another important consideration is when you need to cross a busy road. If your dog is at heel he won't be in any danger. When he's under your control at all times a passing car won't hit him, and in the process you lose your best dog and hunting companion.

Most people are right handed, and they carry their gun in their right hand. That's the reason we teach the dog to heel on the left side. Exceptions to this would be left handed people. Dogs that are trained for falconers are usually trained to heel on the right side. The reason falconers generally carry their falcon on the left arm is; the right hand is used to hood and unhood the bird. During this process while the dog is at heel and out of the way, the falcon is also more relaxed.

Spike collar: I will show you two different ways of teaching your dog to heel. One method will be using the e-collar and the other by using a spike or pinch collar. Don't let the name spike collar frighten you. It's not a barbarous tool if used correctly.

A spike collar can be used gently on a cooperative dog or with more force on a hard headed dog. The best spike collar in my opinion is a J.A.S.A. named after José Antonio Sánchez Antuñano, a Mexican dog trainer who invented this collar more than seventy five years ago. It has been in constant use ever since. The collar itself is made of leather and the spikes are about one quarter of an inch long having dull points. This type of collar can be reversed and used as a choke or pinch collar. These force collars can be purchased at most hunting dog supply stores. You can also use a metal spike collar with links, which can be adjusted to the size of your dog's neck by adding or removing one or more of those links. Collars such as these can be bought at any location that sells pet supplies. I personally don't use these collars, as the links are always separating and over time the spikes get bent and become difficult to work with.

Let's get started: When heeling your dog pull him into your left side with a short four to five foot lead while telling him to "Heel," as you are walking.

Keep moving and every time he drifts away, repeat the command while pulling him into your side. When the dog surges ahead of you, turn to the right, pull him in and continue walking. This is easier for the dog than having to back up. As stated before, the spike or force collar can be used as lightly or as harshly as the situation demands. Obviously when the dog hasn't yet learned what a command means, it should be used lightly. Once he learns the command and doesn't want to comply, then you're justified in giving the cord a sharp jerk which will give you an instant response.

While heeling, his head should be even with your left knee. Sometimes he will fall behind and when this happens, pull him up into position while again telling him to "Heel." If he starts riding your left knee with his head, bump him by raising your knee, but say nothing and continue walking. Always start by walking with the leg closest to the dog. As stated before when starting heel training, continue walking, as this is easier on you and your dog. Whenever you are teaching a new word, be sure to repeat it often.

Stop walking after a while, and when you start moving again, slap your pant leg on the left side as you start off. The reason for this is, after he's learned to heel you won't have to say anything, only slap your leg and he will automatically start off with you. The dog also learns when the leg closest to him moves, he moves with it, but when the opposite leg moves, he stays. The "Whoa" command will be taught a little later, but it sure doesn't hurt to begin familiarizing him with the word. He begins to understand that when he hears the word "Whoa" you both stop. Whenever you work your puppy before he's six months old, five or ten minute sessions are enough. Be liberal with your praises and treats, and be sure to spend a few minutes playing with him after each training session. That way you always end on a good note and the pup will have a positive attitude when you start the next day. After you've heeled him six or eight times in different sessions, he will be walking beside you. At that point you're able to dispense with the cord. If he doesn't heel correctly then you need to go back to using the cord.

Whenever you advance to teaching the "Whoa" or "Stay" commands whichever one applies, you'll start off with the right leg. Tell him "Whoa" and he will stay. After so many lessons you won't have to say anything, just walk away while raising your right hand with the open palm facing the dog.

He will learn that signal means he must stay there. This will also come into play later when he's pointing. You won't have to verbally caution him, just raise your hand and he will remain in place. We will learn about "Whoa" training later on.

You can use this open hand many times when bird hunting. Late in the season when the birds are spooky, you will never have to verbally caution your dog. The dog will see you as you approach, and when you raise your hand, that means "Whoa." The birds won't hear your voice, won't be as nervous and will normally sit tighter. We as hunters know wild birds are not accustomed to hearing a human's voice. Consequently they equate it with danger and oftentimes flush prematurely or run away before we arrive on the scene. Anyone who has hunted with a person who's continually cautioning his dog knows how irritating it can be, besides being counterproductive.

E-collar: Teaching the command "Heel" by using the e-collar is pretty much the same as the force collar; however, you should put it on and take it off the dog numerous times prior to its use. Do this for at least three days before it's turned on. This familiarizes the dog with the e-collar before you actually use it. This is to help ensure that he doesn't learn that the e-collar is the source of irritation. The professionals call this collar wise. Before it's used make sure the collar is on the lowest setting. You can always go up in intensity, but if you start with too much current, you might create a problem and that's what you are trying to avoid. I would advise against using this method on a very young puppy, even though it's an easy way to teach heel. Some brands of collars are hotter than others while on the same number. The way to test this is by holding the two contact points against the palm of your hand. Start on *number one* and press the nick button. Gradually increase the intensity, until you are no longer able to bear the pain. Now you know how much current you can give your dog. It affects animals in much the same way it affects you, so test it on yourself and not the dog. If you have a heart condition you may want to disregard this last recommendation.

You should have the transmitter in your right hand and a short leash in your left. The leash is then hooked to the e-collar and *not* the regular collar. Connect the e-collar so that it's loose enough to be able to spin freely on the dog's neck when you pull on the cord. If the e-collar is loose and the electrodes are short, it will easily spin around and those electrodes will be on the bottom left side of the neck, as you are pulling from the dog's right side. As long as you have a little tension on the lead it will remain in the same location. Again, start by using the lowest setting on the transmitter. The idea is to create an irritation on the left side of the dog's neck by using the e-collar on constant stimulation while walking away and pulling him into the heel position. It's easier to be walking forward when starting this exercise. Tell the dog to "Heel" and pull him in while pressing the continuous button and as soon as he's in the correct location immediately take your finger off the button. For all other training situations you will want the receiver on the bottom of the dog's neck.

The dog is now learning that when he's away from you he feels an insect biting him on his neck, but when he's next to you that insect is gone. When the dog surges ahead it's easier for both of you to turn to the right while pulling him in. It's simple yet it's effective. As the dog progresses and is heeling well, in all probability he will automatically start correcting to your position.

Sit, Stay and Down: We will walk through these three commands, but first I would like to offer an opinion. I feel that a young pointing dog doesn't need to learn these three commands and here are the reasons why.

The most important word a pointing dog needs to know is the command "Whoa." That command along with "Come Here" supersedes all others. If you have taught the commands "Down" *or* "Sit," the first thing the dog will do is either sit or lie down when you add pressure to finish him. In a field trial, you would be disqualified if your dog did either. With hunting dogs, no one wants to see the dog sit or lie down when they are pointing birds. If at a later date when the dog is broke, and you want to teach the commands "Sit" or, "Down," you won't have the same problem of him sitting or lying down when pointing birds. I have finished many dogs that the owners have taught

to "Sit," and it makes the job that much more difficult. You first have to teach the dog to stand up on the "Whoa" command. *It's easier to put em down, than to get em up.* Whether to teach any of these commands to your pointing dog will be a decision you have to make.

Sit: This is probably the easiest command to teach. Both 'Sit" and the "Down" commands are taught by using a short check cord or leash. If you give the dog a treat and hold it above waist level, he will jump up a few times, and then will sit and wait for you to give it to him. If every time the dog sat for any reason and you told him "Sit" when he completed the action, in a few days he would be sitting on your command. The best way, however, is to teach your dog those commands while he's learning to "Heel."

Bring the dog into the heel position and when you stop, tell him "Sit." If you are agile enough, pull his head up and push down on his rear end with your right foot behind your back. This is really easy after you've practiced it a few times. If that's not convenient, bend over at the waist and push the rear end of the dog down while pulling up on his neck cord. Then again command him to "Sit." After a week of teaching this he will have it ingrained in his mind. When he knows the command and doesn't want to-do it, then you will have to get more insistent, and that's where the force collar will come into play.

Stay: When your dog is sitting, step in front of him with the off leg. Do not step out with the left leg as he's been taught to walk with you when that leg moves. Keep the leash or cord in your left hand. Raise your right hand palm toward the dog exactly as you would on the word "Whoa," and say "Stay." Of course he will want to move, so make him "Sit" again and repeat the command.

When teaching the command "Stay," walk a couple of steps in front of the dog to begin with. A few days later start walking a few more steps in front, as well as walking around behind. Normally he will move when you start walking behind. If that happens put him back into position. Most dogs will do this due to them wanting to see what you're doing back there, *or* this might be a confidence issue and if it's a matter of trust, only you can resolve the problem. A dog only has a 240° field of view, and as a result of that he has a blind spot. He's unable to see directly behind without turning his head and with the head usually goes the body. That could be one reason for him to be wary about having you back there. Only time coupled with trust and a lot of handling will fix the problem. If your dog has confidence in you, there is no limit as to what you're able to achieve.

Again, use your hand with open palm facing the dog. Always repeat the "Stay" command after he moves and as you put him back into place. If in a few days he doesn't want to "Stay" where you made him to "Sit," spin him around in a tight circle with the cord. Then put him back in the original position. Do this maneuver three or four times. Dogs don't like being spun around, and it helps you to get your point across faster.

Down: This is most easily taught from the heel position as well. Make the dog "Sit," take one step out in front of him with your right foot and pull down on the cord until he's in the prone position. This is best done by using a series of small jerks, until the dog complies. The more times you repeat this new word the faster the dog will learn it. Always repeat the word as you are pulling the cord down. For the most part a dog will lift up his rear end, as you are jerking his front end down. If his rear end is up, push him flat while holding his neck down with your hand on the check cord.

A more practical method is; when you command him to "Down" step on the cord close to his neck, hold tight on the other end and push your foot to the ground using the same jerking motion. He will probably try to resist at first, but will go down as the cord is tightening. If he gets up from the down position make him to "Sit" again before pulling him down. You can stroke the dog after he's been in the

down position for thirty seconds or so. This is all the praise he needs at the moment; in as much as, he will jump up if you start verbally praising him.

When you have done this in two or three training sessions, it's time to start moving away from the dog. Put him in the down position, tell him to "Stay" and move a few yards away. You should walk behind him as well, while gradually increasing the distance until you can go as far as you feel comfortable in doing. You can also tighten up the regime by rotating the force collar so the spikes are on top of the neck instead of the bottom. If he doesn't want to "Stay" jerk down with more force, as he's trying to get up. Now that you've made your point and he's remained there for a moment, come back to his right side, slap your pants leg and start walking with your left foot while telling him to "Heel." Give him a word of praise.

I will have to interrupt this narrative to mention a humorous incident that happened while obedience training a Labrador. This event occurred while showing an owner the commands his dog had learned. This owner explicitly told me that if I ever told anyone about this he would kill me; his words not mine. I told him if I ever wrote a book I was definitely going to include it.

After working with this dog for about three weeks, the owner, we'll call him Mike, was called to come out and see how his dog was doing. He was a local man, so he was able to come out that very afternoon. Walking down my driveway while the dog was at heel, I began to go through the commands of "Sit," "Stay" and "Down." Mike saw that when I stopped, the dog stopped and sat down. He was shown that when I stepped in front of the dog and gave the command "Down," the dog then lay down.

Now it was my client's turn to work his dog. He started with the dog heeling and was doing great. When he stopped the dog stopped and sat down.

I then said to him; "Now step in front of the dog and tell him "D-O-W-N." I spelled it out so the dog wouldn't lie down when he heard me give the command.

The client stepped in front of his dog and spelled "D-O-W-N" just like I had done. I started laughing and then it dawned on him what he had done.

He told me, "I thought you taught the s.o.b. how to spell." The telling of this story has amused a lot of dog fanciers over the years.

Come Here: Now that the dog is a little older it's time to work harder on the "Recall" or "Come Here" training. Attach the check cord to his collar and give the order Sam, pause "Come Here." It's always better to kneel or squat when giving this command especially with a timid pup. When you are in this position, you are not as intimidating. After your dog is complying with the "Come Here" command, you can shorten it to Sam, pause "Here," and stand up while giving the order. By now your puppy is probably six months or older and you can be more demanding with the suggestive commands he's learned up to now. When the dogs occupied with something give the command, and if he doesn't respond immediately give the cord a jerk, pull him to you and then give a reward. It's convenient to have a fanny pack with a zipper to wear on the front of your waist. After giving the dog a treat you can easily close the zipper, so that when you bend over the remaining treats won't fall out. The noise the zipper makes when you open it will keep the dogs attention riveted on you, as he's anticipating a reward.

This food based reward system works best on problem dogs, the ones that don't want to look you in the eye when you start working with them. If a dog won't look at you, you're not going to be able to get the best out of him. Dogs should always look at your face, but especially your eyes while you are training them. If they do, it means they're anticipating a command and reading from the same page you're on. I am not speaking about a dog confronting you by forcefully looking directly into your eyes. That can be construed as a challenge. There's a big difference between these two scenarios and I will get into the dominance factor in detail in a later chapter. You will find that all your training sessions will go easier if you have a food reward to give to the dog for his good behavior.

Some dog owners say their dog obeys because he's loves them. Personally I feel annoyance when I hear this as I believe the dog respects the owner as his leader and will show affection based on that alone. Dogs are pack animals, and in every pack there is a leader and the leader has to be you. We could also label that affection as the dog kissing up to you to get a

reward, or to be recognized. Once the dog is obeying commands you can gradually stop giving treats and go to petting and verbal praise. At any point from now on when you call the dog, you have to enforce the command whether or not he wants to comply. It is a command! You are not asking him to "Come" if he feels like it. You are ordering him to "Come" and if he doesn't respond, yank on the cord and drag him to you with a series of sharp jerks, while repeating the command to "Come Here." Praise and/or reward him when he does. In this manner you will always end on a good note.

Come here using the e-collar: When teaching the dog the command "Come Here" by using the e-collar, the same method is employed that was used when teaching "Come Here" and "Heel" with the check cord. Unlike the loose e-collar that spun freely around the dog's neck when you were teaching heel, have it fitted snugly with the electrodes underneath the neck. You are still going to be using a check cord, only now you are going to be introducing stimulation. The check cord is attached to his regular collar, not the e-collar. Always start with the lowest setting on the transmitter. As stated before, you can check this by putting the two contact points of the collar on the palm of your hand while pushing the constant button on the transmitter. On the lowest setting you will barely feel a tingle. You can never go wrong by doing this. Once again I will stress that the e-collar needs to be on the lowest setting. Remember, it's effortless to increase the amount of stimulation when necessary, but if you start on too high of a setting you might be heading for a wreck.

Use a longer check cord of twelve to fifteen foot length, and take the dog for a walk. Again, the cord is connected to his regular collar not the e-collar. The dog will begin to show interest in something and leave your side, and when he does call him by name, Sam, pause, "Come Here." He should respond immediately, but if not press the continuous button on the transmitter while pulling him to you. You are not giving him stimulation on his name; you are giving it on the command. The name is used to get his attention, not to enforce a command. He has learned to "Heel, "so he will naturally pull into your left side. At that point you should give him the command "Heel," and start walking. You've killed two birds with one stone by doing this. You are teaching him to "Come Here" by using force and also reinforcing the "Heel" command, one he already knows. The heel position is comfortable for you to have the dog in when he's close. You won't be tripping over him when he's by your side.

Most retriever owners want the dog to deliver the bird on their left side and remain there while they are walking. Many pointing dog owners also like the dog to heel in to their left side as well, but that's a personal preference. That is the long and short of it. Sam, hesitation "Come Here" and then pull him in to you while using the continuous stimulation button. When he's where you want him to be, take your finger off the button. It's the exact same thing as calling him to heel when using the force collar and check cord.

Now let's talk about what to do when the dog knows the command "Come Here," but doesn't respond to it. This will happen so it's better to be prepared. You won't always have an e-collar or a check cord connected and he will know it immediately. So how can we enforce the command when the dog decides he has other more interesting things to do, and coming to you is not on his agenda?

Slingshot: Buy yourself a simple slingshot or catapult, one that doesn't have the wrist brace, or if it has one, take it off. The slingshot should easily fit into your back pocket. You will need the slingshot and also a sack of round gumballs. Don't use rocks or marbles due to the chance of injury, especially accidently hitting an eye. Practice with the slingshot on a target until you are reasonably proficient with it, usually in a couple of days. Most of us when we were children had a lot of practice with a slingshot and we could hit what we were aiming at. That skill will return rapidly. It's effortless to carry the slingshot in your back pocket and some gumballs in your shirt pocket. This method besides being practical has the added advantage of you being able to chew on the extra gumballs while training your dog.

Take the dog to an area where he's easily distracted and let him wander around with no training aids, such as the force collar, e-collar or check cord attached. This is the moment that you will teach him to respect the "Come Here" command, anywhere and at any time. He will remember it for the rest

of his life. When the dog is running around investigating something and has forgotten about you, call him, and if he doesn't respond forthwith, pop him in the rear end with a gum ball. As soon as the ball hits him, repeat the command. You will find this will immediately get his attention and he will come to you in an instant. When he arrives you should pet him, but don't do anything that could be interpreted by the dog as consoling. It's his job to come when called and you should expect it. He might come sheepishly, but that negativity is immediately followed by the positive action of you petting him. You are giving him praise for coming when called; you are not consoling him because he got zapped. Two or three times of getting hit with a gumball on two or three different occasions, will give you the results you want.

The nice thing about the slingshot is the dog never learns when you have it on your person, and he doesn't know its effective range. Your dog realizes when he has the check cord connected, and many also learn when they are wearing the e-collar. I prefer using the slingshot to any other form of correction. It produces the same results, but with less trauma to the dog. You aren't physically disciplining the dog, as it's done from a distance. Something simple yet effective, with the added advantage of the dog never forgetting.

Teaching Whoa to Pointing Dogs: As stated before, all pointing dogs need to know the command "Whoa" and instantly respond to it. There are many ways to teach "Whoa" to a pointing dog, but I will explain methods I have used successfully. You should wait until the puppy is at least six months old and preferably eight to ten months old before starting seriously on this command. The command "Whoa" overshadows all others including "Come Here." This order could save your dog from injury or death by the dog responding immediately when he hears it. Once your dog has learned the command "Whoa," he can be stopped at any distance for any reason.

I have found that when teaching your dog this command, one of the easiest methods, and the one I prefer above all others is called the "Whoa Post." In constructing the post you may use an overhead rafter, tree limb or any other reasonable substitute that will support a little weight.

I'll never forget the late trainer Tom Schwertfeger who called and told me he had found the most wonderful way to "Whoa" break a dog. Of course he was talking about *the* "Whoa Strap." I had been using that system for some time, but didn't have the heart to tell him so.

If you decide to use this method you will need to make a "Whoa Strap." That strap consists of a two inch wide piece of stiff leather about thirty six inches long with a small o-ring on one end and a larger O-ring on the other. See photo in the equipment section. It's important the small ring easily passes through the larger ring and forms a loop that slides back and forth freely, and tightens when pulled on.

Pulley: Many trainers prefer using a double pulley capable of handling two cords. The reason for the double pulley is so you can control both the back and front end of the dog. Tie the pulley to a tree limb or on the garage rafters and pass a stiff nylon rope about twenty five to thirty feet long through it. The length of the rope depends on the height of the pulley. The rope or ropes need to slip through the pulley easily. They also have to be long enough so that you can walk a distance of at least twelve to fifteen feet in front of, and around your dog when the tension on the cord is loosened. The first time you do this, walk the dog under the apparatus, stop him and pass the leather strap around his waist. Pass the small ring through the larger ring and connect it to the swivel snap on the end of the stiff nylon rope. The strap is now around the dog's waist. Command him to "Whoa" and take up the slack as you walk away. Hold the end of the rope in your hand. Most of the time the dog will try to follow you when the rope starts to tighten, but when that happens pull on the end of it until he slides back into his original position under the pulley. He will naturally struggle and move around. There's no need to lift the dog off the ground as in the manner put forth he learns the command "Whoa" with less trauma.

The strap tightens when he pulls against it and it's a little uncomfortable. When he's directly under the apparatus, slacken the rope. The strap will not physically harm the dog, but it is troublesome. Say "Whoa" in a firm voice when he quits struggling. Tighten the strap if he moves again, and when he's finished moving around, again tell him "Whoa" and loosen the strap. This is

a similar to what's called a flank strap on rodeo stock. It's attached to the flank of a horse or bull, to make them buck harder.

If the dog tends to kneel down in the front or to lie down completely then you should use the second rope that's threaded through the double pulley. You will attach that rope to the collar of the dog. If he's kneeling down in front, pull on the rope that controls the front end. If he's sitting down lift him to a standing position by using the rope that's connected to the waist strap or you can use both ropes simultaneously to get him standing up straight. Immediately slacken both ropes when the dog is standing up correctly. This double rope has the advantage of him learning that "Whoa" means stand up and stand still. Each time you nudge him with the strap repeat the command. After two or three days of being connected to the strap, he will stand still, but will be a little nervous. By using the double ropes the dog will learn the command faster.

Whoa used as a warning: I would like to caution you about how to use the command "Whoa." You need to use it as an order and not as a warning. I have heard this word used as a warning so many times by amateur and professional trainers alike, with no consequences to the dog when he disobeys. Used as an order it sounds like "**Ho**!"

An example of this would be: You warned your son that he had better empty the trash can, but two hours later the trash can still hasn't been emptied. Your son didn't obey, so you took away his Nintendo for a couple of days. The next time you tell him to empty the trash can, he will obey immediately. The same thing applies to a dog. You order the dog to "Whoa," but not by using a warning tone. When you give the command and he doesn't comply, there have to be consequences. Normally when people give a command in a warning tone, there are usually no ramifications. A warning tone would sound something like *"Whooa."* There is a big difference between a curt "Whoa" and "Whooa," and the dog will detect it instantly.

One of my longtime customers was an English setter man who truly loved his dogs, and always had a truck full of them. During one summer at dog camp in Saskatchewan, I finished one of his male setters called Patch. I took the dog home at the end of the summer and killed some birds for him. He was well broke when he was sent back to the client. This customer who like many others, believed once a dog was finished, that's all there was to it. Animals are not like a car the mechanic certifies as repaired. The car you can drive away and have no more problems with it, whereas the dog owner needs to spend the time to learn how to handle his dog and to keep him fully trained.

A year later this client brought the dog back to me saying in an accusatory tone: "You told me this dog was broke, but every field trial I enter him in he breaks and chases birds."

At the time I happened to have a flight pen full of pheasants that were destined to be released on my hunting club. I caught a couple of those birds and planted one in an alfalfa field. This dog hadn't seen me in a year or more when I pulled him from the truck. Patch smelled me for a couple of seconds, and then he was released, unhampered by either check cord or e-collar. He immediately found and pointed the bird. I didn't even bother telling him "Whoa," but just raised my hand which he knew the meaning of. I flushed and killed the pheasant and then sent him for the retrieve by calling his name. The work was flawless.

Upon returning to the truck with the dog, my client after some hem hawing around said that he would like to give that a try. I drove to a different alfalfa field and planted another pheasant so he could have a go at it. The client turned Patch loose and within two minutes the dog found the bird. As I'm typing this I am visualizing that tri-color Setter standing up so tall

and beautiful on point. When my client approached to flush the bird, I started hearing "Whooa Patch, Whooa Patch." One of his mistakes was that he used the dog's name, which was supposed to be called when the dog was sent to make a retrieve. He was also using a warning tone to "Whoa" him. Here is my client warning the dog he better not move, while saying his name, which was used to release him. What he was saying in essence was "Stop," "Fetch" and the "Stop" was said with a warning tone. I was getting a little confused at that point to say nothing of the poor dog. I'm sure you've figured out what happened next. I saw my client flush the bird and away went Patch chasing like a puppy. Five minutes later when the client returned to the truck with the dog, he told me the dog obviously knew the difference between him and me. I agreed with him.

I had previously worked many dogs for this gentleman and he had been taught the commands and how they were used. Why he would continue using the wrong commands in the wrong way was a mystery to me. Obviously the dog hadn't been disciplined for infractions and realized he could do as he pleased. It was very evident the dog had no respect for his owner.

Back to the strap: Don't concern yourself with hurting your dog with this strap in as much as I've used it on countless dogs, and none were ever injured by this process. The dog will come to understand that if he moves the strap tightens. When you've done this a few times and he's steady on the hookup, continue to nudge him with the cord while walking all around, and each time you nudge him say "Whoa." Take off your hat and throw it on the ground, kick it around a few times and try to create distractions. All the while make sure he stays there in the same spot and doesn't move. The longer the rope the farther you can step away from him. A few days of this and he won't want to move any longer, and that's when you can begin stroking him.

This is what I call the sweeting up period. If perchance he tries to move again repeat the previous steps, but this is the time to start putting your hands on the dog. When you are stroking him it starts to become a pleasant thing, even though he's connected to the strap. Nothing you can do takes

OBEDIENCE TRAINING

the place of caressing the dog with your hands. Always when caressing him run your hands in the direction that the hair lays from front to back. Start at his muzzle and finish at the tail. This is more soothing to an animal than going against the hair.

When you give the dog his next lessons don't hook him to a check cord and drag him under the strap. This would constitute dragging him into a stressful situation. Neither should you call the dog to you, in order to hook him to the strap. Calling a dog should be for something pleasant, not for something that's uncomfortable. You should pick him up bodily and stand him under the apparatus.

On the first day of your dog learning this command, and after a training session you will have to release him from "Whoa." Physically pick up the dog and drop him a few feet in front of you saying Sam, pause, "Alright." This is the manner by which he learns he's not permitted to move until he's physically moved by you. After you've done that a number of times on different days, lift him slightly by his collar while simultaneously tapping him on the head and saying Sam, pause, "Alright" to release him.

You will read more about using the dog's name and the practicality of using it when you advance to the chapter on retrieving. This can be used in any number of situations, such as releasing him to complete a retrieve. Later on in his training, and when he's completely finished on game, you can start verbally releasing him from "Whoa" by calling his name such as Sam, pause, "Come Here." You can do this by either calling him to you or by letting him continue to hunt by saying Sam, pause, "Alright." If he tries to anticipate the release, "Whoa" him, walk to him and jerk on his collar a few times while repeating the word. This system of releasing him verbally will come in handy if there's an obstacle between you and the dog, and it's difficult to go and physically release him. I prefer this method of teaching "Whoa" above all others. A dog that's "Whoa" broke with the strap never forgets it. In my opinion it's one of the easiest ways with less stress on the animal due in part to the hands on stroking. As expressed before, this command is the most important one.

After seven or eight lessons and the dogs thoroughly accustomed to the "Whoa Strap" it's time to start walking him around the yard with the check

BIRD DOG TRAINING & PROBLEM SOLVING

cord attached to his collar. When you stop tell him "Whoa;" he should immediately stop, but if not, loop the cord under his waist and nudge him with it. By doing this he will quickly get the idea, and when you walk away drop the end of the cord onto his back. He will think he's still hooked to the strap. When he's responding promptly to the command you can dispense with dropping the cord onto his back.

Now is the time to let the dog run freely around the yard dragging the cord, and when he passes close to you step on the end of it. Tell him "Whoa" when he's jerked to a stop. Make sure the end of the check cord has a knot in it, otherwise it will slip under your foot and it might fail to stop the dog. Catch him if he doesn't want to stop, and then take the end of the cord and pass it under his waist giving it a sharp jerk while repeating the command. You go to the dog, do not call him to you to do this!

When he's performing well and stopping on command, it's time to get in

front of him, rattle a few bushes and kick the grass like you would if you were flushing a bird. This will help in his later training by accustoming the dog to you being in front of him while he's actually pointing birds. Remember the word "Whoa" is a command and it doesn't mean take a step or sit down, it means stop completely and stand there until you his trainer release him.

Another simple method of teaching "Whoa" is by walking with the dog beside you at heel, and when you stop he stops. At that point you say "Whoa" and when he moves, set him back in the original spot and make him to remain there. Gradually you should start walking around the dog, and every time he moves put him back and tell him "Whoa." As time goes on you will have to do a lot of putting your pupil back into position before he understands that you won't accept any movement on the command. You may also loop the end of the check cord under his waist and tighten it while giving the command. As soon as he's standing again, loosen the cord. This method is using the same technique as the "Whoa Post," but has the added advantage of you being able to use it wherever you go. Let him drag the cord around when he's advanced enough, and again stop him by stepping on it.

Now let's review what's been discussed. You've been successful in teaching the command "Whoa" to your dog. You can stop him anywhere on the command, and he stands like a statue. When someone walks by him, or another dog runs alongside him, he's considered "Whoa" broke if he doesn't move. Congratulations, you've done a good job. However, if he's failed any of these tests, he's not totally "Whoa" broke. If that's the case back up and reinforce what he should already know.

Teaching Whoa using the e-collar: Another method of teaching 'Whoa," is with the e-collar. This is not my preferred method, but it's used by most trainers today, as it saves time, and time is money to the professional. I'm old school on this! I believe that if the old time professional trainers who came before me could properly finish a dog without the e-collar having been invented yet, then I could do it as well. Electronics certainly have their place in dog training today, but there are limitations such as instilling confidence in your dog. To my knowledge that cannot be done with electronics.

You've learned that by lightly putting your hands on the dog in a gentle stroking manner it imparts confidence, and when he's broke he shows it in his attitude while pointing game. You as the owner/trainer can use this modus operandi as well. It takes more time, a lot of patience and repetition, but you will have immeasurable pride in the finished product. Not only will the dog gain from these hands-on methods, but you will also. These techniques will teach you how to become a better trainer, if that's your goal.

You will be rewarded for all the hard work you've done when the dog stands up like a bull while pointing game, and doesn't shrink or let down

when you walk in to flush birds. That dog has confidence in you and in himself. Those same hands we talked about earlier can also instill fear and anxiety if used improperly, and you need to be fully aware of that.

Look at pictures of guide dogs on clubs or in videos published on You Tube, of people training or hunting their pointing dogs. What you see is a percentage of those dogs are wearing e-collars, tracking collars and their regular collar. Makes me think we need to breed dogs with longer necks to accommodate all those collars! What does this tell you? The dog that's been finished properly doesn't need to be wearing an e-collar. Will he make mistakes? Of course he will and so will you, but when he makes a mistake, lay down your gun, "Whoa" the dog, and go to him and immediately make a correction. Usually a sharp jerk or two on his collar, and a verbal reprimand will be all that's needed.

The e-collar can be used on the neck, the waist or used on both, to teach the command. Read through this "Whoa" breaking by e-collar, so you can make an informed decision as to where on the dog you want to use it. By placing it on the dog's neck it can be used successfully for three different commands, but by using it on the waist you have reduced your options to only one. It takes more time for the dog to master the command when its attached to the neck, but it takes away the necessity of having two collars, or having to switch one from neck to waist or vice versa.

Some people use one collar on the waist and one on the neck. Both have different color straps, and the one on the neck is used for "Come Here," and the one on the waist to "Whoa." Both are operated using the same transmitter, but are often confused when the waist collar is used for "Come Here," and the neck collar to stop the dog. There is absolutely no need for something like this to happen. You don't need two collars; you just need to learn the correct method of using the one you have. If the dog happens to make a mistake when you have two collars attached, and the wrong button is pushed at the wrong time, the result will be a confused dog at best. You may have created a problem at worst.

Neck: By continuing to use the e-collar on the neck, here is what you will have to do. The dog has already learned two commands using the e-collar "Come here" and "Heel." Now we will teach him "Whoa." You will start teaching the command by nicking him, or using momentary stimulation with the e-collar. What I recommend at this time is using it only for the "Whoa" command. The reason is you don't want to confuse the dog. When you start using the collar live, he will want to come in and heel to you, and that's due to the fact he hasn't yet mentally separated the nick from the continuous stimulation. This process will take more time and a little patience, but once the dog understands it he will easily separate the nick from the continuous.

For this exercise don't turn the e-collar on because the temptation might be too great to use it. At this point you don't want to move too quickly. Strap the collar on his neck like always and hook a short cord to the ring or guide on the e-collar. If there's no ring you will have to improvise. Many new collars have a plastic collar guide, and as that's unsuitable; you will have to attach a metal D or an O-ring. The important thing is to make sure when you jerk on the e-collar the box with the electrodes stays on the bottom of the neck.

Start heeling your dog and then stop him by saying "Whoa" coupled with a sharp twitch on the cord. You stop promptly as well. This helps the dog to learn the command faster, as he learns to imitate you. What you are trying to do is simulate the nick of the e-collar, but without the juice. That means you can't jerk too hard, just a short twitch. Stand there for a while and then tap him on the head to release him, and start heeling him again. Do that ten or twelve times for the first four or five sessions, but on different days. Then using the same methods don't give the command "Whoa," but stop him with just the twitch on the e-collar. When he responds to that twitch, the e-collar can be turned on. Be sure it's attached with the blinking light facing forward. This helps you to determine whether the collar is actually working, as the blinking light is visible when the dog raises his head.

Turn the transmitter on the lowest setting, and do exactly the same thing you were doing before. Now you're nicking him with a tap on the transmitter button at the same time that you twitch the cord. It's extremely important the nick and the jerk (twitch) are done simultaneously. Five days

of nicking him on the lowest setting, it's safe to discontinue the jerking and only use the nick. If he's not responding, go back to doing the previous method another three or four days. He should definitely be stopping by now, but if not you will have to increase the amount of stimulation. This of course depends on the temperament of the individual dog. Advance one number on the transmitter and go back to the accompanying jerk. If the dog shows *any* apprehension on the higher setting, go back down immediately to the lower. The dog when stopped should show no concern, but if he's acting confused go back to jerking the cord simultaneously while nicking him. You are the judge on how the dog is handling the pressure. Take your time. If it takes two weeks or more to get it done, so be it.

When the dog is showing no anxiety about stopping with the stimulation, it's safe to start walking around him. He now understands what the single nick means and will stop anytime you use it, with or without the verbal command "Whoa." The dog is coming to you when called, so in all probability you won't need to use the constant stimulation again. You will find this to be an easier system by having the e-collar on the neck rather than the waist, but it does take longer for the dog to learn.

In any training session where the dog is acting confused, always go back one step. Don't keep advancing or things will start to unravel. The dog's tail and how he's carrying it is the best indicator of how the animal is handling the pressure. The tail is down, but relaxed you are fine. If the tail is tightly tucked, stop what you are doing and go back to working with something he knows and praise him when he does it well. You've heard me say back up various times throughout this discourse, so please take it to heart. You can't hurry when building trust and confidence into a dog.

Moving too fast when training a dog would be similar to pouring wet cement for the footing of your house. You can't advance with building the house before the cement dries and hardens, or it will sag and probably fall apart. The same principal applies to the dog. Make sure the cement has hardened, or the lesson has been learned before you advance.

Sometimes in our daily lives we are pushed for time and don't spend that extra few minutes playing with the dog after his lessons. This is a mistake! Playtime is very important as it gets the dogs mind diverted off of any confusion, or trauma he might have experienced during the training session. Play with him for a few minutes and then put him away and start again on another day. You will have a happier animal, one that anticipates the next day's training session with eagerness.

Waist or flank: We are now going to teach the dog to "Whoa" by using the same e-collar, but by putting it on the waist or flank. As mentioned before, I'm not a fan of this approach; however, most professional trainers use it. I prefer the neck method, although as was stated previously, it does take longer for the dog to learn. The location you select to use the collar is entirely your decision based on what's convenient for you.

Strap the e-collar snugly around the dog's waist but don't turn it on. He's

not going to be very comfortable and probably won't want to move. Connect a check cord to the collar on his neck and lead him around the yard for a while. Once he's starting to move freely, connect a three foot long cord to the e-collar on his waist. Make sure when you jerk upwards on the waist cord the electrodes stay directly underneath the dog's stomach, and not off to one side. The cord should be long enough so that you can hold it in your left hand, but not so long that it interferes with the other hand which has the longer cord. While you're heeling the dog and want to stop, hold onto to the waist cord and give it a sharp twitch while saying "Whoa." Every time he stops you stop as well. This is a case of monkey see, monkey do. A few days later turn on the e-collar. Start on the lowest setting and when stopping him with a tug of

the cord, simultaneously tap the button giving him a nick. The sharp jerk you give him coupled with the nick will start conditioning him to the command "Whoa" while using the e-collar.

After four or five days, try stopping the dog with just the nick of the e-collar. If he stops he's made the association, but if not go back to using the e-collar cord. If he's responding well you can take away the short cord attached to the e-collar on his waist. Continue walking him around by using just the check cord attached to his regular collar. Order him to "Whoa," and simultaneously tap the button to give him the nick. When he stops, you stop promptly as well.

Now that he's stopping with the nick you can start walking away from him, but if he comes with you it means he's confused and doesn't yet understand the command. Go back one step with your training. You've heard me say back up many times in this narrative. Problems are created with the dog when you don't heed the warning signals. After a few days of him responding to the nick he can be turned loose in a controlled area without a cord. "Whoa" and nick at the same time to see if he immediately stops, but if he doesn't, back up and go with the cord again. Pretty soon you will be able to stop him by just using the nick from the e-collar without saying anything. You will be able to use this method if you decide to finish the dog steady to wing and shot using the e-collar on the neck or the waist.

Any program that you use to teach your dog "Whoa" is not important, but what is important is teaching the dog that command. All pointing dogs need to learn how to stop on command no matter what word you use.

Now we have taught the young dog how to "Heel," to "Come" and to "Whoa." We've introduced him to .22 caliber gunfire while he's busy eating. At times no matter how well you've trained your dog, you will need to have refresher courses to keep him tuned up. Dogs are similar to children in the respect that if your kids learn a foreign language, but it's never used, they will eventually forget it or make a lot of mistakes when speaking it.

With all the survival skills your young dog has learned, such as coming when called, stopping when commanded too and not jumping on your spouse, kids and grandma, he's now on his way to becoming a good citizen.

If he's a renegade and doesn't have the manners necessary to cohabitate with the family unit; they will want you to find a new home for him. That is a heartbreaking experience when you are attached to your dog, so it's worth the effort to help him in becoming an integral part of the family.

Pointing quail in Morelos, Mexico   Photo by: Jaime Lopez

Chapter IV

Natural and Force Retrieving

Painting by Edgar Alcántara

Caution on retrieving: Before we get into retrieving whether natural or by force, I would like to offer the following advice. All hunting dog owners want to start their new puppy retrieving and rightfully so, but there's one thing you should think about before beginning. Simply put, don't overdo it. This always concerns me due to most first-time hunting dog owners taking it to extremes, and later the dog becomes soured on retrieving and doesn't want to play the game any longer.

I have just finished force breaking a Labrador who retrieved when he felt like it, but most of the time he didn't feel like it. The owner told me that members of his family were always throwing objects for his dogs to retrieve. One of his older dogs was faster than the Lab and it was that dog which always made the retrieves. Later the Lab just gave up and wouldn't bother trying to compete with the older, faster dog.

Obviously you don't want to make the same mistake as this man did, so make sure your young dog never competes with an older, faster dog. You want your puppy eager to make retrieves. By throwing a dummy just a few times and stopping while he's still energetic, he will develop into a top-notch retriever when mature. As the puppy gets older you can add a few more retrieves to his retinue and increase the difficulty of each of those retrieves.

Natural retrieving: When introducing the young dog to the retrieving game (a game it should be) it's recommended that you start at a very young age. The reason I say this is, if you're not successful in getting your puppy to retrieve, or he's a sometimes yes, sometimes no retriever, force breaking will be the next step. Most young dogs love to retrieve if you approach it as fun and games with the correct attitude. Make it a game, but be sure not to carry it to extremes. A new puppy is a novelty and it's easy to create a problem by asking him to retrieve more and more. An example: The neighbor comes over to see your new acquisition and the puppy has just finished two or three retrieves. Don't send him for any more. Ask your neighbor to come back and see the puppy retrieve another time, after he's rested.

The majority of dogs I have force broken were dogs that had been soured on retrieving. You probably enjoy going to the sports store now and then, but if you had to go ten times a day you would soon become discouraged about going at all. It would be the exact same thing for a young pup having to constantly retrieve.

When the puppy is very young start throwing a wooden dowel wrapped with a soft cloth, or a couple of old cotton socks folded over to form a dummy and secured with electrical tape or cotton string. You can also use his favorite toy, or a small retrieving dummy, but never a ball that's so small

he can swallow it and choke. Don't allow him to play with a homemade dummy wrapped with string or tape, as he will chew it and possibly ingest some of the tape. A piece of swallowed tape or string could cause intestinal problems. From now forward I will refer to your choice of retrieving objects as a dummy for the sake of clarity.

On a young puppy attach a light rope or check cord to his collar. Tease him for a few seconds with the dummy before you throw it, and when you actually do, don't throw it very far. He will run to pick it up with the cord dragging behind. Hold onto the cord, but be sure there's enough slack so he isn't brought up short. When he gets it in his mouth, call him and pull him back gently to you. Make a show by scratching his butt and rubbing his head, but do not take the dummy immediately. Fifteen or twenty seconds later and when he's *facing you*, take the dummy away by putting your index finger in his mouth behind it, and gently removing while telling him "Give." A dog can't close his mouth on your finger while it's behind the dummy. Now pet him again so he understands that he did a great thing by bringing you that wonderful prize.

You don't want to jerk the dummy away or fight him for it. That's a mistake. Pretty soon you will be playing keep away, or tug of war instead of the puppy delivering it as he should. Teach him to release it after bringing it to you. Now praise him again. Do this, two or three times every day, but stop while he's still excited about playing. The puppy is young and you are trying to build that desire to retrieve into an inexperienced youngster, and if done correctly you will have a dependable retriever when he's older.

Many people think that some breeds of pointing dogs are poor retrievers and that's certainly the case with some of them. It's a result of no one spending the time to make them into good retrievers. In teaching a dog to be a good retriever you fill two needs with one deed. Not only is the dog learning to retrieve, but he's also learning how to hunt for dead and/or crippled birds. This is a skill that you should be teaching your puppy from the beginning. You will shortly learn why that's so important.

Why is retrieving so important in a pointing dog? I just spoke with a friend who has English pointers about retrieving. He told me retrieving wasn't important to him in that if he shot a quail and it fell in the bottom of a canyon he didn't mind going down after it. Going down is one thing, but climbing back up is another. People whose dogs won't retrieve will tell you stories like this, but if you want the complete package you should teach the dog to retrieve. This same friend is in his early forties, but he might change his mind when he's in his late sixties as the canyons get much deeper with age. The time and energy spent descending to the bottom of a deep canyon, looking for the bird, and then climbing back up again is better spent on more hunting. A dog could make that retrieve in three or four minutes, whereas it will take a person at least fifteen to twenty minutes of hard work searching for the bird, and then climbing back up.

Water retrieving: What is the need for a pointing dog to retrieve out of water? If I've heard that question once, I've heard it a hundred times from pointing dog owners who also own retrievers. They say they hunt upland birds with their pointing dog and waterfowl with their retriever, so why worry about their pointer making water retrieves. I'll tell you why!

Practicing water retrieves with English pointer -Holland- Lake Chapala, Guadalajara, Jalisco, México

You're hunting pheasant and your dog points a rooster that prematurely flushes and flies over a body of water. At that moment instinct takes over

and you pull the trigger. Down goes the bird thirty yards from shore. Your dog starts to make the retrieve, but when his toes get wet that's as far as he's going. Where's your retriever now? You shot it, so protocol dictates the bird needs to be retrieved. It's time to shed your clothes and swim out to retrieve the bird. This could have been avoided by teaching the dog to retrieve in water when he was a puppy.

All hunting dogs should know how to swim and make water retrieves. A dog that will retrieve anywhere at any time in any medium whether land or water, is a valuable asset. Some breeds of pointing dogs are quick to adjust to water retrieves, while others don't adapt so easily.

Any dog can be taught to swim including pointing dogs, although many hunters fail to see the need to teach their dog the basics of water retrieving. Most retrievers I've trained were very quick to adapt to water retrieves even though they had no prior experience. They were bred for just that thing, whereas pointing dogs were not, so sometimes it takes a little more effort to entice the puppy into making water retrieves.

To start a young puppy retrieving in water you should begin his lessons when the water is warm, usually in spring or early summer. If you bought your puppy in the winter months or you live in a colder climate, wait until early summer when the water warms up. Let him run around for a little while, and when he starts to get heated take him to a shallow pond. The water heats up faster in shallows as compared to deeper water which takes longer. Start him retrieving the dummy in a couple of inches of water and gradually increase the distance of the retrieve, and the depth of the water over a period of a few days. If the puppy is nervous about making a retrieve in water use a clipped wing pigeon, (feathers removed from one wing) *if* he's retrieved them before. Restrain the puppy and throw the bird in shallow water where it will have to make its way into deeper water, while trying to get away from you and the dog. It will flop and struggle while attempting to get airborne. Obviously pigeons can't swim, but their frantic action will excite the young dog, and when you release him he will plunge into the water. To keep his focus on the bird his head will have to be down at water level, and that prevents him from dog paddling. Now he's swimming. One or two retrieves the first day is sufficient. Don't over tire the puppy; let him work into the process slowly.

Gradually increase the difficulty and the length of his retrieves and by summers end you will have a competent retriever on land, and in the water. Now you won't have to shed your clothes and go swimming after a downed bird that fell in the water

Back to land retrieves: When your puppy is retrieving well on land, throw the dummy while holding onto his collar until the dummy hits the ground. Let go of the collar, call him by name and then say, 'Fetch." An example: Sam, pause, "Fetch" with emphasis on the "Fetch," at which point you release your grip on his collar. As he's approaching the dummy say, "Dead," "Dead" and as he grabs it say "Fetch" again, and then "Come Here" or just "Here." Eventually you will only have to use his name when you release him. If you still need the check cord to get him to come back to you, go back to using it. Don't let him take the dummy and play with it. This is a bad habit, and it will get worse as time goes on if you don't stop it now. He should rapidly bring it back at this stage in his training.

Let me explain the reason why we use the dog's name on a retrieve. Many hunters enjoy hunting with two or more dogs, and if you are one of those hunters you will encounter situations in the field where one dog is pointing and another one or two dogs are backing. Let's say you are hunting over finished dogs and you kill a bird. The dog that found the bird should have the prerogative of making the retrieve. Saying: "Fetch" at this time will release all of the dogs and that can get complicated real fast. That's the reason why we use the dog's name to retrieve.

After a week of play fetching he should be bringing it to you promptly, but if not, are you jerking it out of his mouth as soon as he returns with it? Maybe you're not letting him hold it long enough before taking it away. In his mind it's his, in that he has possession. When the puppy comes back to you, is he turning his rear end toward you? If so he doesn't want you to have the dummy, and if this is the case go back to using the cord. Pull him in facing you and massage his ears, but *never* take away the dummy if the puppy isn't facing you. Take your time about taking it away, and repeat the command *"Give."* Release him for another retrieve by saying Sam, pause

"Fetch," there again with emphasis on the "Fetch." When he's close to the dummy, say "Dead," and "Dead." Repeat the "Fetch" command when he picks it up. Over time and in successive training sessions, you will be able to drop the "Fetch" command if you so desire, and just use the dog's name when you send him for a retrieve.

Let's assume there's a vacant lot near you that's full of weeds. Throw the dummy in the weeds for him to retrieve. Restrain the puppy until he's absolutely crazy trying to go and get it. After five or six seconds has elapsed the puppy will have lost his mark, and will have to use his nose to find it. Release him. By doing it in this manner you've accomplished three things. First you're teaching blind retrieving; secondly you're giving him more desire to retrieve by restraining him, and thirdly he's learning how to hunt "Dead." It's a simple matter to go from retrieving a dummy to a bird, but first let me caution you about something of importance. *Never* let the puppy fail on a retrieve. If he's been searching for a short while and can't find it, go to him before he gets discouraged and gives up. Help by going to the exact spot where the dummy fell while acting excited and pretending to search for it. Doing this puts the puppy in direct competition with you, and as you're searching keep repeating the word "Dead" over and over again. He is learning what the command "Fetch" means and now he's also learning that the word "Dead" means something is there.

A good way to do this is by bending over while sweeping the grass with your hand. He will be curious and come to you while trying to figure out what you are doing. If the pup still needs help, move the dummy with your hand or foot, and when he finally finds and picks it up; run back to your original spot. The puppy will be running behind you. Upon reaching that spot turn around and start petting him, but there again let some time pass before you take away the dummy. He's proud of himself and he's showing this by his attitude, so let him have his few seconds of fame before you take the dummy. When you advance to the point of killing birds it's the same principal. A dead birds down, but the dog didn't see where it fell. Take the dog to the area and say "Dead," "Dead," and he will immediately start looking for the bird in order to bring it to you. He will remember what was taught to him in his yard training.

When you progress to hunting you should still take an extra few seconds to praise your dog when he brings you the bird. Don't take it away from him immediately, as he believes it's his bird. He found it, pointed it and then retrieved it. I've seen many instances over the years of hunters snatching the bird away from the dog immediately upon him returning with it. Then they resume hunting without a kind word or a pat on the head to acknowledge the dogs work. That dog hasn't been paid for his efforts, and invariably it will come back to haunt the owner in the form of a fault like hard mouth or lazy retrieves. We will get into the feeding of a bird head as a reward a little later in this text.

As the puppy matures, you will see a big change come over him if you have followed the previous suggestions about rewarding the dog with a pat on the head, praising or giving an edible reward. Let your dog decide when he no longer needs praise or a reward when delivering the bird. The biggest change will be the speed of his retrieve. He will immediately go back to hunting after giving you the bird. He won't have time for your caresses or you telling him how great he is, as by now he's all business. You should be proud of yourself; you've done a good job.

Hunting dead: Teaching your dog to hunt "Dead," can and should be started at the beginning of his training. Introduce the word "Dead" in the yard before you advance to the field. It needs to be started early in the training process. You began introducing him to the word "Dead" when he was looking for the dummy, but now you're going to pick it up a notch.

In these days of limited wild bird areas many sportsmen will be hunting on clubs or game bird release areas. Hunting on a club is expensive and the price per bird is usually calculated on the number of birds released, not on the number of birds that are harvested. If you are paying for ten birds to be freed and only four are delivered to bag, you're not getting a good return on your investment. Any bird shot by the hunter, wounded or dead should be found and retrieved. Assuming your dog has been trained to hunt "Dead" and is persistent in his efforts, he will return most if not all of the birds

you've shot. You will have an effective dead bird retriever that finds and retrieves dead or crippled birds to you and that dog is a valuable asset.

Teaching the puppy to hunt "Dead:" The puppy by now is retrieving well and starting to hunt "Dead", so it's time to get serious about this aspect of molding him into a complete hunting dog. Without your puppy going with you, go to an area with short grass, or weeds and drop the dummy. Then go and get the pup and return to that area while you and he start searching for it. Of course you know where the dummy is, but you are pretending otherwise. Start saying "Dead," "Dead" when you are within a few yards of it and act like you are looking for something. He will soon get excited and start searching as well. Your hand scent is on that dummy and he knows from his other retrieves this is what he's looking for. Back away and call him to you when he finds it. I've mentioned before, that sometimes it's necessary to actually move the dummy with your hand or foot in order to get his attention, but when he sees or smells it he will pick it up. Some puppies learn this fairly rapidly, while with others it's a slower process.

A quicker way to teach a dog to hunt dead is with food. Assuming you haven't, or you're not going to, poison-proof your dog, hot dogs are great for this. Go to wherever you are going to teach this and throw three or four pieces of hot dogs around the area. This is best done in short grass to begin with, as it will be easier for the youngster to find the pieces. Remember where each piece landed, and then go and get the puppy. Bend over and rub the grass with your hand near the meat while repeating "Dead." The puppy will come over to you, smell the meat and eat it. Go to each piece of meat until the puppy has found and eaten all of them. By now he's really excited and looking for more. Keep doing this on different days until you can take him into any area to search for whatever it is that you've dropped on the ground. After a while you won't have to bend over to get him interested in finding the hot dog pieces, you will only need to go to an area and start saying "Dead" over and over again. He will immediately go to work, and in short order will find and eat every piece.

When switching from meat to a dummy or to a bird, you should restrain him as mentioned before. I would suggest using a different field so he doesn't associate the new place with finding meat. If you don't do this he will be searching for hot dogs and not a dummy. You have to turn the switch from find and eat, to find and retrieve.

Get him excited with the dummy before you throw it and when you do launch it, throw it so that he sees it flying through the air, but not exactly where it landed. Release him so he can go and find it, meanwhile saying "Dead" over and over again. By now he's getting the idea what "Dead" means, so he will find and retrieve whatever it is you've thrown, or hidden as it will have your hand scent on it. This could be a coin, a corn cob or a dead bird. I will talk later about making the transition from a hand thrown object to a bird that you've shot; one that doesn't have your hand scent on it. As the dog matures you won't have to repeat the word "Dead" continually as once or twice will suffice. "Dead" is not used as a command per se, it's an invitation for the dog to find whatever it is you're looking for.

By instilling in your dog the desire to hunt "Dead" with a subsequent reward, he will find the bulk of your dead and crippled birds. Now, when you are club hunting you will get the most bangs for your buck. The majority of the released birds will end up in your game bag. If you can drop em, he can find' em.

Force retrieving: You should wait until your puppy is at least a year old before introducing force retrieving. In this case we *do not* use the dog's name when commanding him to retrieve. The reason for this will be explained a little later. To force break your dog and make him into a dependable retriever, I will point out various techniques. It will be up to you to make a decision as to which method you wish to employ. My first choice is to use a bolt collar I designed. You can make the bolt collar and use it many times for force retrieving on different dogs. Having finished force breaking your dog to retrieve by using this method, you have only to remove the bolt to have a serviceable collar. I will tell you how to make and how to use it, after explaining other methods.

Another technique is to use the foot squeeze. You squeeze the foot or paw until the dog cries out in pain. He will then open his mouth and allow you to put in the dummy. Many trainers prefer this method. They will put the dog on a long table. When he's elevated enough it's easier to work with him. The dog is able to walk the length of the table from one end to the other while carrying the dummy. Usually a cable is running the full length of the table and that cable is fastened about four feet above it. The dog is then connected to the cable by means of a short chain. The dummy is introduced to the dog in the same manner as mentioned before. As the dog progresses the dummy is thrown to the other end of the table and if the dog refuses, the foot squeeze is applied. This is a very effective method, but the decision is yours as to which one of these techniques you wish to utilize. The next choice, and by far the simplest, is to let the fingernail on your left thumb grow out a little. Put your left hand under the dog's collar with the exception of the thumb. Lay the dog's ear on the collar with your right hand, and then squeeze the inside tip of the ear against the collar by using your left thumbnail while commanding the dog to "Fetch." The dog needs to be standing or sitting in the heel position to accomplish this maneuver. The inside tip of the ear is a very sensitive area and no matter how often you have to press his ear using your fingernail or the bolt collar, you will not injure him. Following are the instructions on how to make the bolt collar if you so desire.

Bolt collar: Use a leather or stiff nylon collar. Leather is preferable as it's usually stiffer. A stiff collar will give you more control and prevent the dog from turning around and snapping at you or trying to get away. Never allow a dog to snap at or to bite you. If he tries to turn around and gives any indication that he wants to bite, he hasn't accepted the fact you are the leader of his pack, and he needs to subject himself to you. You are the leader!

If this happens, immediately stop, grab his collar with both hands and hold onto the side of his head while staring into his eyes. Start scolding him with an authoritative tone of voice. It really doesn't matter what you say as

RETRIEVING

he won't understand you anyway. Never blink or avert your eyes until he does. If you blink or look away you've lost the battle, and in addition the dog has lost respect for you. He's accepted that you are the leader when he wants to turn his head away or tries to avoid looking you in the eyes. I will explain this and various other methods of how to deal with serious issues like alpha dogs and dominance in *Chapter IX*.

Take the collar that you've selected and punch a one quarter inch hole directly behind where the buckle will be when it's attached to the dog's neck. Allow enough room for your four fingers. The buckle is the heaviest part on the collar, so it will always tend to ride down and end up underneath. Into this hole, put a quarter inch bolt about one-half of an inch long. Make sure the head of the bolt is on the inside of the collar. You should use a round headed bolt that won't irritate the dog's neck if you leave it on for a few days. Fasten a flat thin nut on the outside of the collar and tighten. Ideally you want about one quarter of an inch sticking out. You don't want a point that will puncture when you lay the dog's ear on it and press down.

The bolt collar should be loose enough to permit four fingers to slide underneath, but tight enough so that it allows you to maintain control of the animal.

Make a retrieving dummy if you don't already have one. You can make one out of a one inch wooden dowel about ten inches long. That extra length is needed, so that you can hold it comfortably in your hand and still have five or six inches extra for the dog to grab. Wrap the dowel with two layers of old cotton socks or soft clean rags and use

electrical tape, or cotton string to secure them. If you have access to corncobs, they may be used as well. It really doesn't matter what you use, but the retrieving dummy should be soft and clean. Personally I use a dowel that's wrapped with soft cotton rags. After using the dummy for a few days I remove the dirty rags so they can be washed, and then they're rewrapped on the dowel, using electrical tape or cotton string to secure them.

Now let's talk about the most important factor when force breaking a dog. No one wants a dog that cowers, or shows fear in as much as it's a reflection on you as his owner/trainer. We all want a dog that will follow any command happily and speedily. I will explain how we get that when we are using negative training methods.

First and most importantly it's your voice. Always keep your voice in control and don't yell at the dog. When you give the command "Fetch" use a firm, but not aggressive tone. When the command has been complied with, then comes the stroking or petting, which is the positive. You can get by with murder when training a dog, if you keep your temper in check and don't scream. When starting this force retrieving program and while the dog is holding the dummy in his mouth, stroke his head with your hand to convince him he's doing the right thing. That's the positive, but don't get carried away with your praise just yet, as the dog will think everything's done, so he can drop the dummy.

I believe this is the appropriate time to tell you about a gentleman whom I met while running dogs in California thirty five years ago. This man had been operated on for throat cancer, which left him unable to communicate by using his voice. He was competing with a dog that was completely and beautifully broken on his birds. He was also winning. This story should give us pause when we think it's necessary to get raucous when training, or handling our dogs.

Time to get started: Put the dog on a somewhat elevated platform such as a stable box, or at heel whichever is most comfortable for you. Attach a check cord to the D-ring on the collar and slide four fingers under the bolt collar with your thumb out. Use your left hand if you're right handed, and then using your other hand lay the tip of the dog's ear on the bolt. Now press down and say in a firm voice "Fetch." Depending on the character of your dog as to how hard you will have to push. The dog will automatically open his mouth and cry out.

Place the dummy in the dog's mouth and hold it there. Immediately release the ear pressure when the dummy's' in his mouth. Let me stress this: Dummy in, pain off. He's going to try to spit it out, but you have to hold it in. Pay attention so that his upper lip (flew) is not pinched by a canine tooth against the dummy. After fifteen or twenty seconds you may gently take the dummy out of his mouth by using the command "Give." Now massage his ears and repeat the process. This is called negative training. The only positive thing he gets is the head stroking, and the ear massaging. The reason for massaging his ears is; we don't want the dog thinking that every time we reach for an ear it's going to get squeezed.

All dogs love to have their ears massaged or scratched, but if not you should check to see if there are ear mites. You will be able to determine if there are mites by inspecting the ear canal. You may discover bumps like black coffee grounds or reddish brown waxy secretions. If the ears are encrusted inside, or they are painful to the dog while you're massaging them, they need to be treated.

He's not going to be happy about this force retrieving process for a while. The idea is to make the dog understand that when the dummy is in his mouth, he has no discomfort. When he spits it out before the command "Give," he suffers the consequences. You will find that after a few days he accepts the dummy in his mouth and holds it. You do not have to teach him the command "Hold." He learns to hold it on the command "Fetch" until you tell him to "Give." Probably he will not try to take it just yet, but this depends entirely upon the dog. By working him twice a day for ten minutes, he will learn faster than if you work him once a day for twenty minutes. Most dogs will hold the dummy in two to three days, while many will do it on the first day.

Where you do this doesn't matter. I once force broke an obstinate dog in the living room while watching television. The temperature outside was freezing, so it was opted to do this in a comfortable environment both for myself and for the animal. The dog was worked when a commercial came

on. In two weeks he was a competent retriever, and once the retrieving was moved outside he adjusted rapidly.

Going back: When the dog starts to open his mouth and tries to take the dummy, that's the time to begin holding it a little lower. The dog will then have to bend down to grab it. Any time in the future when he refuses the command "Fetch," put on the ear pressure. At this point if he's on an elevated platform, move him off, because soon he will have to pick the dummy off the ground. After he starts picking it out of your hand when it's a few inches above the ground, it's time to put it on the ground.

Now it becomes a different ball game. I've trained dogs that have been force broken in less than two weeks, but also had some older dogs which had been soured on retrieving, that took me almost two months.

When you put the dummy on the ground you will have to forcibly take the dogs head down to it. The reason for this is, an animal will bend to pain. If you are hurting his ear he will naturally try to put his head up to relieve the pressure. Most of the times when you push the dogs head to the ground; you will have to put the dummy in his mouth for the first few days. He will start biting at it due to the discomfort you are inflicting, but will soon grab it. This will be the most difficult part of the transition, but you need to follow through.

By now you will notice that the dog is trying to anticipate the command. He will try to grab the dummy when you put it close to him. Don't let him! Keep him under control and go through the process. By letting him grab the dummy without the ear pressure, you won't have a finished forced retriever. The dog should now be picking up the dummy immediately on the command "Fetch" and holding it until the command "Give."

Keeping the check cord attached to the dog, start walking him around with the dummy in his mouth. He will probably drop it as soon as you start to do this. Grab his ear when this happens and make him pick it up. He will soon realize that he can't drop it until you command him to "Give." While he's walking with you and has the dummy in his mouth, pull him to you on the command "Come Here" and take the dummy from him when he's directly in front. Training any of the retriever breeds, you may wish to bring them into the heel position before taking the dummy.

"Congratulations," you have accomplished the hardest part. Now, start throwing the dummy a few feet in front of you. Keep the check cord attached to the dog when you are working with him, or he might decide it's permissible to wander away. By having the cord connected, he will realize he's under your control. During this time if he decides not to pick up the dummy, go to him and make the correction by pinching his ear. Then take him to the dummy on the ground and command him to "Fetch." Always remember that once the dummy is in the dog's mouth instantly release the ear pressure. You shouldn't  get confused about that. Walk back to the original spot. He now realizes that he has no option other than to retrieve, whatever it is you've thrown.

Start throwing the dummy out ten or twelve yards. He should retrieve it promptly. Go to the ear again should he refuse. If this happens, walk him to the dummy while applying ear pressure and make him pick it up. Use the check cord that's still attached and pull him back to where you started the process, while using the "Come Here" command.

At this point in his training you should start giving him praise when he brings you the dummy and ear pinching him when he drops it. We are now starting to get away from the negative training and going more into the positive aspect. This is the time to start praising him and giving a treat, but

BIRD DOG TRAINING & PROBLEM SOLVING

don't let him drop the dummy to get it. Make him give you the dummy first before you actually give the treat. By now the dog's attitude is changing from Oh no! I have to do it, to, Oh great! I can't wait to do it.

Let me bring to your attention something mentioned previously that you might be confused about. Back in *Natural Retrieving* section, I advised using the dog's name when sending him for a retrieve, and I explained the reason for it. The reason you command the dog with the word "Fetch" when force breaking is, during this process there is discomfort involved. That precludes you from using his name. His name always needs to be associated with something pleasant.

Starting on birds: Now is the time to start retrieving birds. Use a freshly killed dead pigeon with its head tucked under the wing and with wings taped or tied to the body, so that it makes a compact unit. Throw the bird out a short distance and give the command "Fetch." Repeat the ear treatment if the dog refuses to retrieve the bird, and he will soon realize that if you throw a lighted cigarette it has to be retrieved. Getting rough with the bird at this point is perfectly normal. This is him taking his frustrations out on the bird since he can't take them out on you. Not all dogs will do this, but some will. After a number of retrieves the problem will disappear by itself and you will have a soft mouth retriever.

I remember a client who came to see his dog at this stage of training. The dog was chomping down hard on the birds and this naturally concerned him, as he was worried about having a hard mouth dog. I told him he didn't have to pay me if the dog finished being hard mouthed. That sent him away happy. The dog finished as a soft mouth retriever and I got paid.

Once your dog is retrieving all the dead tape-wrapped birds you have thrown, it's time to advance.

The time to kill a live pigeon is when he's successfully retrieving all dead ones you have thrown. That's assuming he's broke to the shotgun. You don't have to set up a big production like it's your child's birthday, you only have to throw a live bird, shoot it and send the dog for the retrieve.

Fire the .22 caliber blank over him if he's not yet broke to the shotgun. First kill the bird by hand and then throw it at the same moment you fire the blank. Oftentimes the dog won't bring it back. The reason for this is the bird that you have just killed either by hand, or with the shotgun, won't be taped and tied into a compact unit like what he's become accustomed too. The wings will be flapping and the head will be flopping, so it's a different sensation in the dog's mouth. If he refuses the retrieve, go to the dog; do not call him to you. Get a good hold on his collar, pinch his ear while saying "Fetch," and take him to the dead bird. When he finishes the retrieve throw the bird one more time, and he will bring it back without fail.

Do not get exasperated with the dog if he's rough with the bird. As I've said before, this is normal. Don't scream at, or discipline him if he's gnawing on the bird. This always makes the problem worse. The dog will stop that unwanted behavior as soon as he's relaxed and retrieving well. During this type of training, it's imperative you have control over your dog, and that means a check cord has to be attached. Don't forget this important item as this could set your training back. Now and in the future when you shoot a live bird over the dog, and after he makes the retrieve it's time to start feeding the bird's head as a reward. The feeding of heads is his reward for a job well done. *It will not encourage him to eat the bird.*

From this point forward it's safe to start the dog on the retrieving of any species of game bird. Frequently when changing birds, say from a pigeon to a pheasant, the dog won't make the connection that although the bird is bigger and different; he still has to retrieve it. You won't have the bolt collar on him when you are hunting, but your fingernail will do just as well. If he refuses a retrieve, go to him, grab his collar and take him to the bird while pressing on the ear as you are moving. I have force fetched a handful of dogs using the thumb nail on my left hand and the method is very effective. I would suggest leaving on the bolt collar the first few times that you take him hunting if you don't have any fingernails.

After this force fetch training you have a dog that is more responsive, behaves better and has become more attached to you. That's because the negative training on force retrieving is complete and now it's all positive.

You have become his leader and he respects you. When you give an order he obeys. You will notice his retrieves are faster and tender mouthed.

Some folks are advocating no pain force retrieving, or what's called a conditioned retrieve. That looks good on paper, but if there is no discomfort to the animal it can't be classified as force. Putting the dummy in the dog's mouth and making him hold it will work fine until one day when the dog is cold and wet, he will refuse a retrieve. That's due to the fact he wasn't force broken properly. It can't be considered force training if no force is involved. Force, just like the word implies is making an animal do something against its will.

I will now get into the theory and the practice of giving heads or bird parts to your dog upon completion of a retrieve, so please read on. The rewarding of bird heads, legs or intestines, speeds up the dogs retrieves, and with a tender mouth. It also makes the dog hunt for dead or crippled birds with more enthusiasm as he learns there's an edible reward at the end of the retrieve.

Preventing hard mouth: My definition of hard mouth is a dog that chews on, maltreats or eats a bird he's been asked to retrieve. The bird then becomes unfit for human consumption. This type of dog is said to be hard-mouthed. Most hunters are aghast when they see me give the dog pieces of a bird I shot, or in some cases I give them the whole bird. Why? To prevent or cure hard mouth whichever is the case or simply as a food reward after the hunt is finished. Numerous hard-mouthed dogs have been cured using this system.

My client was a physicist working at a nuclear facility in Washington State. He was watching me train one day, finishing an English pointer bitch for an owner in Mexico. The bitch pointed a quail which I then flushed and shot. She brought it back to me without ruffling a feather. Then ripping the bird into pieces, she was given each piece. The physicist became highly agitated and asked me what I was doing? He told me that I wouldn't be able to make a hunting dog out of her in that she would learn to eat the birds.

Now admitting that I don't know anything about the nuclear energy field, but I do know something about dogs and how they reason. Working that same bitch on another planted quail, I waited for it to fly out a little farther before I shot, hoping for a wounded bird. I got my wish by seeing in the manner by which the bird fluttered down it was only wing tipped. I then sent the bitch for the retrieve. We could both see the very much alive bird struggling in the dog's mouth as she was approaching. I gave the head of the bird to the bitch and the physicist was strangely quiet. I'm guessing he had

just witnessed something he was trying to process mentally, as to why that bitch didn't eat the bird. A friend once told me never to bet a man at his own game. The physicist hadn't made a bet with me, but I think he began to realize this was my game.

Every dog you finish whether field trial or hunting dog, should be rewarded with the head of the bird you've killed. A dog needs to be paid for his work. You don't make good bird dogs by not shooting birds. I've always believed there is no substitute for developing a good bird dog other than killing birds.

Six years of conducting a summer training program in Canada where by law you aren't allowed to kill game birds during the training season, it was time to move operations back to the United States. I started a summer training program at the home kennel. That summer program consisted of me killing an average of twenty to thirty birds per dog, depending on the individual. Most of those birds were bob-white quail because of the covey factor, costs and easy obtainability; however, some pigeons were used in problem dog rehabilitation.

The concept behind this system is uncomplicated. When the dog retrieves the bird, the heads torn off and given to him as a premium. The dog begins to understand that when he returns with the bird he's compensated with a tangible reward. You are programming the animal to perform an easy task and when he accomplishes the task he's compensated. It's that simple! Any hunter you ask will tell you that by giving bird parts to the dog you will make him hard-mouthed, and soon he will be eating the whole bird. They will tell you his premium should be in the retrieving of the bird. Don't listen to the naysayers.

I feel there are a whole lot of holes in that hard mouth theory and will explain why by using this illustration. Your boss gives you a check for ten thousand dollars and tells you to go to the bank, and deposit it into his account. You will of course do it as that's your job, and you've been trained, or programmed, to follow orders. What reward did you get out of that? You did the job as your boss ordered you to do and when it was finished he told you thanks. That's equivalent to a pat on the head for a dog.

Now let's change this scenario. What if your boss told you to take a check for ten thousand dollars to the bank, cash it, and put nine thousand into his account and the other thousand into your account? What just happened? The boss just gave you a piece of the bird, in the form of a thousand dollars and that's your reward. From receiving that unexpected compensation your attitude improved, and now your tasks are performed faster and with more pleasure.

In a dog's mind he tries to find dead or crippled birds with more enthusiasm, as he's eager for the end result. The end result is his thousand dollars in the form of an edible reward. I've taught some professional trainers and many amateur owners this practice, and after learning it they are firm believers in the system, although it does have some detractors.

This retrieve and reward system is based on the logic of how the dog reasons, and it has never failed me. We always have to be conscious of the fact that a dog works to satisfy his stomach, and a retrieve doesn't feed his stomach, whereas a bird head does. Rewards are generally more effective than discipline when training a dog. The understanding of just what makes a dog tick is based on the recognition of just how intelligent the dog is. Do you think with the dog's limited reasoning ability he's able to understand that if he brings a bird to you he's only going to get the head? On the other hand if he runs away with it he can eat the whole bird at his leisure. Folks, a dog just can't reason things out like that. The dog only knows that when he delivers the bird he gets his reward. It's as uncomplicated as that. I will get into exactly how, step by step, to cure the hard mouth dog in *Chapter VIII*. It's not a difficult fix.

Soft-mouthed retrieve of a pigeon

Chapter V

Field Training

Use of planted pigeons: Starting a young dog in the field requires ample size acreage where you can walk freely with your dog. A field of at least twenty to thirty acres (ten–twelve hectares) is necessary, although larger is more desirable. Your puppy will learn about new smells, chase little birds, and encounter holes, ditches, trees and a myriad of other things. He can only learn about these through exposure. The field should have abundant cover as well.

This is the time to introduce him to birds and the shotgun. You will have to furnish your own birds if there are no wild ones in the area. Pigeons are the best to start with, easiest to find and cheapest to buy. They will be called planted birds.

Probably one of the first professional trainers in America who pioneered the use and the training of pointing dogs with planted pigeons was Er M. Shelley. In his book (Bird Dog Training Today and Tomorrow) Mr. Shelly claimed to be the first trainer in the United States to train dogs with pigeons. He freely admitted, however, that people in Europe had been training their dogs on pigeons for some time before he started the practice. Er Shelley was one of the most accomplished trainers of his era, and recognized the need to start using planted birds as early as 1900, but especially the use of pigeons. He realized he could get more training done in less time and with less effort by using planted birds. It was more effective than walking around for hours trying to put different dogs on wild birds.

Shotgun: When introducing your young dog to the shotgun use a lighter gauge gun, preferably a .410 caliber. I'm assuming you have done your homework and your pup has been broke to gunfire from the .22 blank. From there it's a simple matter to fire over him while he is actively chasing a bird.

By this, I mean fire in the air so the young dog learns to associate the bird with the noise of the gun. This gunfire will begin to represent something good for the dog. I will emphasize again; you should always start the young dog in the field with the lightest caliber shotgun that can be found.

Starting the puppy: By holding a pigeon with the wings folded back against its body you won't have a wing slap on the puppy's nose. That wouldn't be a good start for a timid young dog although with most puppies that wing slap would get them excited. Tease the youngster with the tail of the bird by rubbing it back and forth in front of his nose, until he becomes really frantic. Release the bird, clap your hands together and make a lot of noise, which will encourage the puppy to chase.

I will suggest that you don't fire a gun on the first bird or two. You need to observe just how resolute the puppy is in his desire to catch the bird. A halfhearted chase suggests that you need a more committed attempt before you fire. The next time pull the primaries from one wing of the pigeon. The primaries are the longest wing feathers on the end of the wing. That will make the bird fly off balance and a little slower, and will encourage the puppy to chase even harder. This is the moment to fire one shot while he's actively chasing. Sometimes a timid puppy will notice the shot, and if that happens immediately release another bird. Clap your cupped hands together and shout to encourage him to chase. That will get his mind off of his previous preoccupation. The preceding scenario about him noticing the shot would be unlikely to have happened if you've followed the guidelines offered earlier. Now that you have fired over your puppy and he's oblivious to the shot, you can start planting birds.

The chasing is going to continue for a while. As the puppy grows older you will notice that he only chases a few steps and then turns away to hunt for more birds. This can happen anywhere from six months to a year and a half of age, and it applies to a pointing dog as well as flushing dogs. It will of course depend on the breed, how much exposure he's had, and his degree of maturity.

Planting pigeons: With planted game your dog won't learn how to go to objectives which might hold birds, nor learn to hunt correctly, unless you

plant birds in those objectives. For example, if you always plant birds in a patch of grass, or a clump of bushes, that fact will be fixed in the dog's consciousness. He will recall where he's found birds in the past, and subsequently it's where he will hunt in the future.

On the other hand if you want a close working dog that will quarter, keep it in mind when planting the birds. Training the dog to quarter you would plant the birds in an alfalfa or similar field with no visible objectives in sight. There they can be planted in a zig zag pattern. With a puppy that doesn't know what a bird is; take along a bag of five or six pigeons. I personally like to use a game bird bag which is built somewhat like a woman's purse. It has an over the shoulder strap and a spring loaded gap on top that stays closed, but is easily opened by you. The birds can't open it themselves and escape. This type of bag will hold one pheasant, three-four pigeons or five-six quail. They are very durable and don't wear out easily. You can purchase these bags at any gun dog supply house. Any bag will do assuming it has sufficient ventilation which will let the birds breathe without suffocating, but the ones with the over the shoulder strap are certainly more convenient.

To plant a pigeon, dizzy the bird by holding it with its head facing outward, and its wings tucked tight against the body. Start swinging the bird around in small circles until the head is extended and starts to flop around. Immediately tuck the head under one wing and lay it in the grass, head side down. The pigeons head should be pointed in the direction of the oncoming breeze, as it will tend to stay there longer if the wind is not ruffling its feathers. The dog will scent it when he's brought around behind the bird and into the wind. If done correctly the bird should remain there for about ten or fifteen minutes. The down side to this maneuver is the pup can catch the bird unless you have him under control by the use of a check cord.

Working a dog using this method is best done with the help of an assistant. While you are restraining the dog, your helper needs to kick around the weeds close to the planted bird, but not to flush it. Make sure the puppy is facing into the wind so that he can detect the birds scent. Don't let him get too close, or you will have an accident. Sometimes this kicking action will encourage the puppy to point, or to make him stauncher, if he is pointing. At other times it will encourage him to try grabbing the bird. Use common sense when determining just how long you hold him in place. If the puppy is jumping around trying to get to the bird, flush it, as you gain nothing from holding him there for an extended period of time. Have your helper flush the pigeon directly away from the pup and then release the check cord, so he can chase.

You can make a timid young puppy bird shy by flushing a bird directly into his face and if you fire at the same moment, you might end up with a bird shy and gun shy young dog. Anything can be fixed, but prevention is the key, and it's a lot easier not causing those problems in the first place. Only shoot while he's actively chasing, but at this stage you don't need to kill the bird. You're only demonstrating to the puppy the bird and the shot are tied to one another.

All young pointing dogs will chase birds and you should not discourage them from doing so, as it has two advantages. The first advantage is that after the puppy has chased so many birds he begins to realize he can't catch them. He will then start trying to sneak up on the bird, and shortly after the sneaking comes the point. The second benefit is; the chasing of the birds builds a desire in the puppy to find more birds to chase. This is one of the things which helps make a good bird dog. That desire will serve you well in the future when the dog's tired, but won't quit hunting. When the puppy or young dog starts pointing birds it will be time to start killing them. I realize all first time pointing dog owners want to see if their puppy will actually point. Read on and you will see how to satisfy yourself on that count.

As far as flushing dogs go, the chasing of birds also builds the desire needed to forge an enthusiastic hunting dog. When the flushing dog learns he can't catch them, he will begin to shorten his chases, and in that manner he won't unintentionally flush other birds by running wildly all over the field.

String method: Another manner of planting pigeons, and a much more practical technique at least from my perspective, is using the string method. No one wants a young pointing dog to catch the bird, for the reason that if he catches one, he thinks he can catch them all. Using the previous

BIRD DOG TRAINING & PROBLEM SOLVING

mentioned method (the pigeons head under its wing) can result in a caught bird if your assistant isn't vigilant enough.

You can use the string method either on homing pigeons that are return birds to your loft or on cull pigeons you are intending to shoot for the dog.

This method will only work with pigeons. Attach a light (smallest diameter available) nylon grass trimmer string to one leg of the bird by making a loop with a slip knot. The string needs to be about thirty inches long. By using the lightest trimmer string you'll find it's much easier to work with and usually won't come off the leg as long as there is a little tension on it. Again, make sure you attach the loop to only one leg of the bird. Pull it tight and go to where you want to plant the bird. Wrap the end of the string twice around one finger. If you don't do this the line can easily slip through your fingers before you're ready, and then you've lost the bird. Let the pigeon fly while holding onto the end of the string, and when it hits the end of the line, gently jerk it back. Every time it tries to fly away, jerk it back. Don't jerk so hard you pull the birds leg off. This will take a little practice before you become proficient at it. You may have to do the bird flying and you jerking back operation ten times, or possibly more. Pigeons that have been used numerous times before will require more jerking back than birds which are used for the first time. The pigeon will always try to fly away at first, but the more times it tries, the more its jerked back. The bird soon realizes there's no escape, so it starts trying to fly into the ground to hide.

Hiding on the ground is an unnatural thing for a pigeon to do, but they will do it after a number of times of them flying and you jerking them back. Let the bird go to ground, but continue holding on to the string. The pigeon now realizes it can't escape by flying, so will try walking away. Don't let it! Leave a little slack in the string and try moving the bird with your foot a couple of times to encourage it to make another flight attempt. If it does, jerk it back. The bird will soon stop trying to fly or to walk, and when that happens, drop the string and step away. This sounds a lot more complicated than it is. With practice you can accomplish this whole maneuver in three minutes or less, from tying the string to planting the bird.

Plant the string pigeon in light cover so if the dog tries to catch the bird it can easily make its escape and fly away. The dog will be able to see the bird and this might encourage him to sight point it, but it might also embolden him to try catching it. Planted correctly and not in heavy cover, the pup won't be able to catch it, even if he charges ahead at full speed. If the bird was planted in dense cover it won't be able to get untangled from the weeds fast enough to make an escape. I've planted birds using this method that have actually walked and fluttered up on a rock to better see what's going on, and still wouldn't fly until the dog was approaching.

This technique of planting pigeons is preferable in that you are simulating wild bird conditions. The young dog sees or scents the bird and when that happens, he will usually try to catch it. Using this method the bird sees the dog long before the dog is aware of it, and when the dog tries to catch the pigeon it flies away. The bird will not let the dog get too close, due to recognizing him as a predator.

A bird that perches somewhere before flying back to the loft won't get tangled due to the strings rigidity. In the evening when you feed the birds, they are unharmed and easy to catch in order to remove the strings. By using any other type of flexible string, if the bird decides to sit in a tree it will probably get tangled. It could then end up dangling by one leg. The neighbors tend to get a little irate when they see a pigeon hanging upside down from a tree branch or an electrical cable. I learned that from experience! This is the reason why you should only use the lightest trimmer string.

Cardboard method: Another means of using pigeons to start a *very* young puppy is attaching a light nylon string about two feet long to one leg of the bird. On the other end of the string connect a small piece of cardboard approximately four by eight inches long. The pigeon when released into a field will fly about fifty yards before it alights. That will happen when the cardboard starts whipping around, and the bird thinks it's being chased by a falcon. It will then go to ground. After the initial flight it will usually attempt another, but won't fly nearly as far.

Take the puppy into the field and let him find the pigeon. When he smells or sees the bird he will probably try to catch it. The pigeon won't let the puppy get too close before it again fly's a short distance. If done correctly the youngster won't be able to catch the bird. This is a productive means of starting a young puppy to initiate his desire to find and point birds. If after two or three flights the puppy points the pigeon, you should kill it. You will only be able to do this in an open area with no trees or electrical cables, and it should be done in a field of short grass; or something on the order of short wheat stubble. If not, you run the risk of the bird getting hung up and not being able to get airborne. Then of course it's easy for the puppy to catch.

Electronically controlled bird release traps: I've discussed other methods of planting birds and will now explain the techniques that are used by some trainers today. Most professionals and many amateur trainers have bird launchers that they can operate remotely. The results will be the same. You insert a pigeon or game bird into the release trap and when ready, push the launch button on the transmitter. Some models of traps have a door that opens while the trap itself remains closed. This is a convenient means of introducing a bird into those traps, while with others you have to put the bird in when the trap is open. This is usually a little more troublesome.

First acquaint the puppy with the trap without a bird in it. Most of these traps make a fair amount of noise and jump up a few inches when they spring open. You don't want to frighten your puppy by hearing a sudden and unfamiliar noise that's associated with a bird. Another thing you should be aware of is the strength of the springs on these traps. Heavy springs are needed to throw the bird three to four feet in the air. These springs can make your puppy bird shy if he gets hit on the nose when the trap opens, and heaven forbid you fired at the same moment.

This happened recently to a friend's timid young English setter puppy. This puppy had never pointed a bird in a release trap before. When my friend tripped it, the trap jumped up a few inches and startled the youngster. The puppy didn't get hit, but the noise and the movement spooked him. He then called me for advice, as the puppy blinked the next bird that he put into the trap. Keep in mind Murphy's Law! If something can go wrong, it will, and usually at the worst moment.

Imagine you are sitting at your grandmothers' kitchen table smelling all those wonderful food odors and you decide to help yourself by reaching across the table for a biscuit. Your grandma then smacks you across the nose with her cane. You probably will not want to sit at that table again, and you sure wouldn't reach across it if you did. This would be the equivalent of your young pup smelling that enticing bird scent and then getting hit on the nose with the release trap.

You can familiarize the youngster with the noise and the movement of the trap by tripping it without a bird in it. Trip it when he's some distance away, and at the exact moment the trap opens, hand throw a pigeon near it and let him chase. Do this a couple of times before you actually let him point a bird in the trap. This will acquaint the puppy with the sound and movement the trap makes when it springs open, and in the future he will identify the sound with a flying bird, and that makes it good.

I have cured a few bird shy young dogs brought to me for training after they were unintentionally slapped on the nose with the release trap. Don't let this happen to your puppy. In most cases after that incident the youngster will blink a trap holding a bird, but not necessarily blink a bird which is not planted in a trap. They quickly learn the difference.

Encouraging the puppy to point: I've spoken many times about young dogs chasing birds, but all pointing dog owners want to see if their puppy will actually point a bird.

I understand this very well. The first question a prospective puppy buyer will ask you is; "will he point?" You can train a Fox Terrier to point, so that's certainly not an obstacle when dealing with a pointing dog. It's much more important to build up the desire in your puppy, and that's done by him finding and chasing birds. Pointing can come later; however, I will explain a technique in order to satisfy yourself that your puppy will actually point. Most puppy owners do the fishing pole routine with a bird wing tied to a string, and that's fastened to the end of the pole. In this manner they can assure themselves their pup will point. The wing is flipped on the ground and the puppy will start to jump on it, but it's jerked away so that he's unable to catch it. By flipping it away a few times he will soon start to point the wing. All artificial training methods have their limitations, so don't overdo them. That will include this next technique.

English pointer puppy owned by Oscar Chavez, Guadalajara, Jalisco, Mexico

Start your young dog off right by letting him build up his desire by finding and flash pointing birds and then chasing. If he wants to bump and chase that's o.k. too, because as mentioned before, a young dog builds up that tremendous enthusiasm by finding and then chasing birds. The most important thing you can do for the puppy and for yourself is to let him develop in his own time. There's a big difference in training and developing.

Refrain from pushing him to point birds before he's ready. It's much more important to let him explore, learn how to handle and the pointing will come when he's ready. This can make the difference between you having a marginal dog or a good one.

In Horace Lytle's book "How to Train Your Bird Dog," first published by Field & Stream in the year 1927, he tells the story of a well-bred English setter bitch that he owned. He states it took almost five years before he and other trainers could get the bitch to point and handle birds. He mentioned the fact that if he had foreseen then it would take five years to get her pointing birds, would he have considered it worthwhile. He answered that with a resounding "YES!"

Most hunters wouldn't have the patience to wait that long for a dog to develop into a productive gun dog, and I'm probably one of them. Thankfully most well-bred pointing dogs of today have a highly developed pointing instinct, which help the owner/trainer to finish the dogs at around the two year old mark.

With that being said I will explain how to encourage a puppy to point birds. It should take the pressure off, wondering whether or not he will point at all. If you have an assistant take him along. Have a bag of fifteen or twenty pigeons with you when you go to the country. Leave the birds in your vehicle. Walk the pup until he's starting to get a little tired and then double back to your truck. Give the youngster a drink of water and let him rest for a short time. Having a helper for this next maneuver will help you to get the puppy pointing staunchly.

Take the puppy and the bag of birds into the field. Remove a pigeon from the bag; bend over while holding it in your hand close to the ground. When the pup comes close to investigate, release the bird. He will chase and when he comes back, have ready another bird in your hand and repeat the

previous step. Every time you release a bird you should say "Whoop." He comes to understand that word means birds, but it also means caution, and it will eventually mean stop as well. He will chase the birds for a short distance and then come back looking for the next one. This is also a good time to fire a light caliber gun in the air while he's actively chasing.

The pup will start sneaking back to you wanting to point after so many birds have been liberated. He will be looking for another bird to fly out of your hand. After he's chased a dozen or more birds he will point the next one which you are about to release. Some dogs will point the first one they see in your hand, but more than likely it will take ten or more birds. That will depend on the age and maturity of your pup. Don't release the bird until he takes a step. Having a helper to release the bird will allow you to come up beside the pup and start to stroke him. He's pointing staunchly now, so push him lightly from the rear. He will start to push back and become even more rigid. Don't let him get any closer than ten or fifteen feet, or he might be able to catch the bird at the moment it's released and just getting underway. At this point you should hook him to a check cord. When you are confident the youngster will remain there pointing, have your helper slowly lower a dizzied pigeon with its head under the wing to the ground. Hold onto the check cord and be sure you have control of the dog. Have your assistant kick around a little and then kick out the bird. Release the puppy. This action of kicking around the bird sometimes serves to tighten up the young dog and to make him point with more intensity. Immediately flush the pigeon if the dog moves.

It's a bad habit to bend over too many times in front of your dog while he's pointing. He could then start bowing down in front, as he's anticipating the flush. This method is only used to satisfy your curiosity about the dog's pointing instincts and nothing more. I repeat: make sure you have a check cord hooked to the dog. You don't want him catching the bird. Be aware of what's going on. If the dog looks like he's going to break, instantly flush the bird. Now that he's sight pointing the pigeon on the ground, it's not a big leap for the dog to find and point a bird after this exercise.

FIELD TRAINING

This is a good time to start killing birds, if you so desire. You should always wait until your young dog is pointing staunchly before killing a bird. Continue using the word "Whoop." Once he learns that word he will always respond, no matter how far away he is. He's learned the word means to be cautious and to stop and point, as there are birds close by. That word is a good thing for him to know and I will tell you why.

While hunting, your dog runs by a covey of quail with the wind coming from the wrong direction and some birds flush. The dog never scented nor did he see them. You shout "Whoop" and the dog is going to stop and go on point. At that moment you would tell him "Whoa," and try flushing some stragglers. He's pointing now because you told him there are birds there. Often this will give you an opportunity to shoot a laggard from the covey. As mentioned before, it teaches the dog when you shout that word there are birds in close proximity.

I had a good pheasant dog who didn't know what a quail was if it sat on his nose. He was two and a half "years" old and completely finished on native pheasants, but he never had the opportunity to find or point a covey of quail. I brought the dog to Mexico to be my personal quail dog. The first time I took him hunting he ran right through a covey of quail, paying no more attention to them than if they were sparrows. Calling him back to where they had flushed, I began whistling like a bob-white quail. He immediately started searching for birds and luckily a sleeper quail flushed. The dog stopped on "Whoop" and I was able to kill the bird for him. From that moment forward he knew exactly what we were hunting. He never passed up another covey and turned out to be a superb quail dog.

A dog is running full speed in the field and you want to stop him; to do that shout "Whoop," pause, and then "Whoa." The first "Whoop" is to get his attention by telling him there are birds close, and the second word "Whoa" is said as a command a few seconds apart. The dog should be focused on his job of finding birds and his attention is on his work. That's why it takes a warning coupled with a command to switch his mind back over to you. The easiest way to "Whoa" your dog at this early stage of his training and have him stop on point, is to throw a pigeon when you shout "Whoop." He will stop and point after you've done this a number of times,

but be careful not to overdo it, as then the dog won't have his mind on hunting. He will be waiting for you to throw another bird. This method can also be used in teaching stop to flush which we will discuss in *Chapter VI*.

Shooting birds over a point: You have accomplished the starting of the puppy on planted birds. Assuming he's around six months or more of age, it's now a good time to introduce him to finding and pointing wild birds. Of course if you're one of the lucky ones that have access to wild birds or a working call back pen, your dog will be well advanced. Wild birds are entirely different than planted birds. Having worked your dog primarily on pigeons, he will be hunting for them and not game birds.

A boy and his dog

Oftentimes you will have to help direct the pup to birdy locations. Some dogs naturally have these instincts and will go to these areas to find birds without any help from you. Others will have to learn by experience to go to those birdy places. You can help them by turning and walking toward a field that looks like it would hold birds. At that time you are also teaching the young dog to pattern. This will prepare him to be mindful of your location as you are constantly turning and going to a different field in another direction. Finding or stumbling over wild birds will get the pup very excited when they fly, and you should encourage this by making a verbal show. A good method is shouting "Hey, Hey, Hey," and clapping your hands. This lets the puppy know these are desirable birds, and you are excited that he found them.

The puppy by now has found and chased a lot of little field birds and has realized that he can't catch them. The distance of his chases has been getting shorter. Now it's usually a brief spurt after the birds and then he resumes hunting. The same thing will happen after the puppy has encountered and chased a number of game birds. Then pointing instead of chasing will be on his mind.

Your puppy will know exactly what you are hunting for after finding three or four pheasants, and a few coveys of quail. He will want to chase these birds, and as stated before you shouldn't discourage this. It builds up his desire to find and point them in the future. A professional trainer can easily see which dogs have had a proper start and which ones haven't. The dog with a lot of desire, and isn't a quitter no matter how tired he is, was started properly. He will walk to an objective if he's too tired to run. Another dog when tired, one which doesn't have that tremendous desire will look for a shade tree in order to rest. That desire was partially created by finding a lot of birds as a puppy and chasing them.

The puppy pointing: You have already satisfied yourself that your puppy will point, so now let talk about encouraging him to point wild birds. As mentioned before, when he scents a bird or a covey of birds, start cautioning him with the "Whoop" when he's close too, or actually scents them. By having him hooked to a check cord you have the ability to restrain him for a short period of time, and if he's pointing, to stroke him. This serves to help

the pup to become more relaxed and encourages him to point with more intensity or to stay on point. If he doesn't want to establish a point, drop the check cord and let him chase, as he's still not sufficiently mature enough to begin pointing. He unquestionably still wants to try catching the birds. Now is a good time to start killing birds if you haven't done so already, but only if he's pointing them.

Having followed these previous guidelines your dog should be broke to the gun, has finished basic obedience and is starting to point. Don't worry if he still isn't inclined to point birds. When the time is right, he will. This type of dog still has more chasing to do as he hasn't yet learned that birds can't be caught. It's a question of maturity. Like humans, dogs mature at different rates. Females usually develop at a faster rate than males, both physically and mentally. Any dog that points planted birds will point wild birds as soon as he learns the game. By now you have done a lot of preparatory work on planted birds, so let's assume he's staunchly pointing.

On the first wild bird you kill you want things to go right. Not all dogs will want to retrieve that first wild bird you shoot. This is due to the fact your scent won't be on the bird and to a few young dogs this will be confusing. Some dogs will not pick up the bird, while others will pick it up and play keep away. This is normal behavior. If the dog picks it up, but is not force broken to retrieve, he will probably want to keep the bird for himself. In his mind it's his bird. He found it, he pointed it and now he has possession of it, so why should he give it to you?

If the puppy is playing with the bird, walk away and start calling him as you're walking. He won't let you get too far before he's following with the bird in his mouth. He will run ahead and when he does pick up the end of the check cord, call him and pull him to you. Don't take the bird away immediately. Pet him, caress him, tell him how great he is and then take the bird by inserting your index finger into his mouth behind the bird. Gently pull the bird out on the command "Give." Pet him again and you are on your way to building a good retriever. This is the time to start feeding heads if you've read the retrieving section, and believe a reward is called for.

When your dog doesn't want to pick up a downed bird; run to it in an excited manner. Pick it up, throw it a short distance and start racing the dog to it. He will want to get there before you as now it becomes a competition. You might have to do this a few times, but that's usually all it takes to make the young dog grab the bird. When he grabs it, pick up the end of the check cord, call and pull him to you. There again do not take the bird from the youngster before praising and petting him.

Dogs that don't want anything to do with a dead bird are usually a candidate for force retrieving. These types of dogs are a rarity, but they do exist. Wait until the youngster is at least a year old before you start that process. You can read about this procedure in the *Natural and Force Retrieving* section that we covered in *Chapter IV*.

Whistle, training to pattern and range: When training a dog to respond to a whistle you should select a whistle that makes the tone you want and stay with it. Personally, I don't use a commercial whistle for my hunting dogs. When wanting them to come in I give a shrill whistle using my mouth, and when birds are in close proximity I whistle like a bob-white quail. If you can whistle, you can do the same, and in time your dog will pull in and hunt closer when he hears that quail whistle. By using the bob-white whistle you've told him that birds are in the immediate vicinity.

When using a whistle in the field, a popular one is the Acme Thunder. It's a heavier plastic whistle that makes a deeper tone. It's confusing when shopping for a whistle due to the hundreds you have to choose from. Don't buy a metal whistle if you live in cold country; you might find it stuck to your lips in freezing weather. In field trials most handlers use a rolling sound for the dog to come in, or used as a contact whistle, and two toots for the dog to go out. That's pretty standard, but some handlers do use different tones.

To teach a dog to quarter or to pattern by using a whistle, you can use it in one or two ways. Connect your dog to a check cord and start walking. Whenever you make a turn, give the dog a sharp blast and turn in the direction you wish to go, while pulling on the cord. This will force the dog to turn with you. If he shows no inclination to turn, start walking at a faster clip. The fast pace will get his attention and make him pull with you while trying

to get ahead. Do this a number of times every day in training, and within a short while, he will be responding to the turn whistle and you can then dispense with cord.

To get the dog to return, use the same check cord and blow a series of soft rolling toots while pulling the dog to you. That's the "Come Here" whistle. Any variations of these whistle sounds will be your decision based on what's convenient for you, but always use the same tone for the same thing. The dog won't become confused as long as you don't change it.

If you have a responsive dog, one that is always concerned with your whereabouts, a check cord probably won't be needed. Walk the dog and every time you change directions, give a sharp blast on the whistle. He will see you make the turn, will equate the whistle noise with that turn, and will automatically pull in that direction. When teaching a dog to quarter, don't overdo it because your dog will be waiting for your whistle and won't have his mind on hunting.

Hand signals: Many hunters prefer to teach hand signals at this time also. That being your desire you can raise your arm and point in the direction you wish to go. If necessary use a check cord. While you're turning give a sharp blast on the whistle. Make sure that when you give a hand signal your arm is away from your body so the dog can see it clearly. When this has been done numerous times and the dog responds promptly, you will no longer have to physically turn. The dog has been programmed to turn on the hand signal and the whistle. By following these steps your dog will pattern and quarter exactly the way you've conditioned him to do.

Personally I don't see the need for hand signals to be taught to a pointing dog; however, some owners do want to teach them. That's a personal choice you will have to make. Any dog should learn to hunt in the same direction in which you are heading while staying in front of you. It's a natural instinct for the dog to always be in front. A retriever is a different case. By hand signals they learn "Back" and "Overs" and also how to "Stop" and "Sit" with the whistle.

Range: When speaking about how far a pointing dog should range in his quest to find game, there is always disagreement amongst bird dog men. Some like what are called shoe shiners. These are the type of dogs that naturally range close, or have been brought closer through force to what the hunter deems a suitable distance, which is usually quartering within gun range. If it goes against the natural instincts of the dog that wants to range farther, then he will probably have to be constantly hacked (shouted at) to be kept within those limits. This is detrimental to the animal due to him not being able to concentrate on his job of finding birds. It's also irritating to your hunting partner not to mention the human voice making game birds jittery.

Chukar hunters will most likely prefer a wider ranging dog; one which is capable of covering a lot of ground in a short period of time. The rolling hills where chukars reside is usually open country and semi-barren, with occasional patches of thick sagebrush. The type of dog that ranges wide will save the hunter a lot of steps. When the dog points it's quicker to walk from point A to point B in a straight line. It's not necessary for the hunter to cover all of the ground in between, as that's the job of the dog and he's already done it.

Grouse hunters who hunt the densely wooded areas where grouse are to be found prefer a closer working dog that's easily spotted while he's hunting and when pointing.

Hunters who pursue the sharp-tailed grouse and Hungarian partridge which live on the wide open prairies, will want a dog that doesn't let any grass grow under his feet. Visibility there is in miles, not yards.

So who's right? They are all right! A dog should hunt any terrain effectively, and the hunter should be wise enough to let the dog hunt at his natural range. The majority of dogs when given the option will remain close to the hunter while searching in heavy cover, but when hunting more open ground they will adjust their range accordingly. When a dog is finished or broke, he will handle and be trustworthy on game. At that point there is no need to be distracting him from his work by constant hacking or whistle blowing while trying to bring him closer. He's the bird finder, so let him adjust his range and do his work without hindrance from you.

BIRD DOG TRAINING & PROBLEM SOLVING

Honoring another dog's point: Most dogs will naturally honor or back after having had the experience of hunting with other dogs, however, some won't, and those that don't, we will discuss here. A backing dog is either pointing the other dog or the birds. Sometimes a dog that backs naturally will be soured on backing, if hunting with another dog which is continually false pointing. The natural backing dog, one that's never seen another dog pointing, stops because of seeing the other dog stopped.

How do we teach a young dog to back and what is the necessity of backing? Backing or honoring is what a finished gun dog does. It's important; a dog that doesn't back will frequently flush the birds of the pointing dog. Often times they will do this through jealously. Sometimes they will steal the point from the other dog, by virtue of having learned the pointing dog gets to the downed bird quicker. This often happens when someone is hunting two unfinished dogs together. That's why it's a good idea to give both dogs a reward whether they are pointing or backing. If your dog won't back it reflects on you the owner/trainer. It indicates your dog is not finished to the degree that lets you hunt with a sportsman who has the better trained animal.

There are various ways to teach a dog to back. Your dog should first know the order "Whoa." If you haven't taught that word to the dog, then back up and don't worry about teaching him to back until he learns the command. Without him knowing and respecting that command you are fighting a losing battle.

You may purchase an electronic pop-up pointer cutout if you deem it practical; although for a one dog owner the expense might not be justified. When the dog is running in the field, you touch the button on the transmitter and up pops the cutout. When the dog sees it he should immediately back. It's certainly a fine tool, but as you will only use it a few times, it might not justify the cost.

If you decide too; you can make a plywood cutout of a pointing dog and paint it white with brown or black patches. White with a contrasting color is easily detected by the dog, assuming it's not used in two feet of snow. When making the cutout, attach sharpened stakes to the legs so you are able to stick them into the ground. That way it will stand on its own. You can also put a heavy base attached to the legs if the terrain permits. The idea is to put the cutout in a place where the dog can see it as he's approaching from around a corner of bushes, or high weeds. When coming around that corner, he should suddenly notice the painted side of the cutout and stop.

The first couple of times you do this, it's nice to have help. Give your assistant a bag with four or five pigeons in it. Homing pigeons work great for this exercise, as they will fly back home and can be used again. Make sure you have the dog hooked to a check cord. With the cord you will have complete control. If your dog stops when he detects the cutout "great" he's a natural backer. "Whoa" him as soon as he sees the cutout, if he doesn't stop on his own. Have your helper go in front of the cutout and start a flushing attempt, and then have him release a bird. If your dog attempts to break and chase "Whoa," and calm him by stroking, and when he's standing again have your helper flush another bird. Your assistant then pushes the cutout to the ground and you will take your dog away. Two things have been accomplished. You've calmed your dog and prevented him from chasing, while also teaching him to back. You are starting on the road to having a finished gun dog.

I will explain another method. You will also need a helper for this, inasmuch as it's a force condition and is usually reserved for stubborn dogs that show no tendency to back. By now you have a bird bag of some sort that your helper can carry with him. For this method you will also use pigeons, by virtue of the fact they work the best. Again, always have your dog hooked to a check cord as with that you will have the control that's necessary. If you have taught him to "Whoa" by using the e-collar, you will use it again in this situation. If he doesn't stop on his own, nick him on a light setting as soon as he sees the cutout and tell him "Whoa." Anytime you use a force tactic with a dog it's always a good idea to kill a bird for a reward. Have your assistant flush two or three birds at different times, and if the dog is broke to the gun, he should kill one. Now that he's killed a pigeon, he should go pick it up and bring it back to the cutout while pretending to give some of that bird to it. He should stroke the cutout and tell it "Whoa" as well. Make sure your dog hears all of this, and that everything is visible to

BIRD DOG TRAINING & PROBLEM SOLVING

him. You've gained nothing if your helper is obstructing the dog's view. Have your helper push the cutout to the ground and come to the backing dog to give him his piece of the bird. What you have accomplished with this charade is showing your dog that when he honors another dog, he too gets a reward. As time goes on you can dispense with the e-collar after he's learned to back.

With the check cord you can mimic "The Whoa Strap," if you have taught him to stop by using that method. When you have successfully stopped him, fix the cord around his waist and restrain him from moving. This is one of the few moments in dog training where you will prevent a dog from making an error. As before, your helper will flush and kill the bird and deliver it to the dog. Over a short period of time the dog will slam into a back, as he's learned the end result which is a piece of the bird.

Photo by John Sullivan

Chapter VI

Finishing the dog

Painting by Edgar Alcántara

Breaking the dog to wing and shot: By having followed the instructions which are written in this narrative; your dog should be ready to break steady to wing and shot. His age and maturity level indicate he's prepared to advance in his training. He's finished all of his obedience training and has a lot of bird experience in the field with any number of birds killed over his points. You are very close to having a finished product due to the time and effort you have expended getting your dog to this point in his training. You have been successful, and I want to applaud your efforts.

The rewards that you receive from the dog being steady to wing and shot are numerous. He won't bump and chase birds like before, and if he runs into a covey by accident and some birds flush, he will stop. There's always a good chance remnants of the covey are still hiding there. As mentioned before, this is called *stop to flush*. When you shoot a bird the dog has pointed, he will learn to mark the fall better when he's standing, rather than chasing and losing sight of the shot bird.

I would like to write here about this current trend of breaking young dogs before they have had enough experience in the field finding and pointing birds. It seems like more and more people are doing this. In my opinion it will come back to haunt them at a later date. I've seen this happen in field trials where a dog is broke while still a puppy. By the time the dog is three years old he discovers it's more fun to self-hunt and to chase birds rather than point them. Then he reverts back to being a juvenile, and it takes more time and effort to get him back on track. The youngster needs to go through the puppy stage, just as humans need to have a childhood and acquire knowledge on their path to adulthood. Puppies should be building the desire to find and chase birds, and by doing so they learn birds can't be caught. If you take that away from the puppy and expect him to do adult work something is going to give and usually at the most inopportune time. Let your puppy be a puppy, and when he's had the necessary experience with birds and is mature enough, then finish him.

Many hunters will tell you they prefer a dog that's not broke. They say when the dog chases after the shot bird they won't lose a cripple. Their reasoning is the dog is on the bird faster. This may be true in some cases, but think about what was discussed previously when we were teaching the dog to hunt "Dead." A dog that's a competent dead bird finder and retriever dispels the theory about the animal needing to be on the bird faster. A percentage of these hunters have never had a broke dog, and due to that they lack the competency to make a judgment about what benefits there are to be gained by having one.

There is nothing more pleasing to you as a hunter, than having your dog hunt down and find a crippled bird that's run and hid. Through your training efforts and the dog's diligent work ethic, he will find and retrieve that injured bird. Many years later I still remember great retrieves.

By the dog remaining steady to the flush and shot, he won't put himself in danger of being injured or killed by an overeager hunter while chasing. We have all seen this almost happen. I've had some clients that have come close to shooting their own dog and me as well in a training session. I can't tell you how many times I have flushed birds for clients, and turned around to see a gun barrel pointed at me. I learned to hit the deck in a most undignified manner, but it probably saved my life on more than one occasion. It's not a pleasant thing to hear a shot fired over you in the location that your head was occupying a few seconds before. This tends to aggravate a person. A good rule to follow when training dogs is the gunner only puts one shell at a time in the gun. You know you are not going to get shot if another bird flushes and you have to jump in front of the shooter to make a correction on the dog.

Everything that you've done up to this point has been leading in the direction of having a broke gun dog. You are more than halfway there in the process and I would encourage you to finish it. Now that you understand the benefits of having such a dog, I will show you how to accomplish it. My recommendation is whatever method that was used to whoa break the dog; you now use the same method to finish the dog whether *check cord, e-collar* or *whoa strap.*

I would again suggest using pigeons for this process for two reasons. First, if you commit an error and put too much pressure on the dog at the wrong moment, you might create a blinker or another less severe problem. A dog that blinks a bird is one that knows the bird is there, but doesn't want to find it. He can pretend he can't find the bird, or if he does point, he might decide to leave it. How to fix this problem is covered in detail in *Chapter VIII.* The second reason I suggest the use of pigeons, is that you will never hunt them in the country. They don't live in fields and are not recognized as a game bird. You have to put a certain amount of pressure on a dog when you break him, and it's better for an amateur trainer to do it with a pigeon rather than a game bird. Usually mistakes which are made are more easily rectified when they are committed while using a pigeon. The cost of the bird is also a

factor. A quail can cost more than twice what a pigeon costs. This breaking process is best done with planted birds due to their availability and your ability to control any situation that may develop.

Let's start with pigeons for the reasons stated above, and by now I assume you have a ready supply.

Have an assistant with you this first time when you take a bag of pigeons into the field. I can't stress this enough by virtue of the fact, if you need an extra bird to make things right with the dog, you have one. It's better to have them and not need them, than need them and not have them. Plant a bird in the field using the string method or the release trap. Either of these two methods will work as the bird is not planted in a manner which will encourage the dog to try catching it. Your dog has been through this process a number of times. After you flushed the bird, he was allowed to chase to build up his desire and also for him to learn the birds can't be caught. The difference now is, when you tell him "Whoa" it's not a suggestion; it's a command he has to obey.

Breaking the dog with the check cord: With a dog that's been taught "Whoa" using the strap, connect a check cord around his waist while he's pointing the bird. He's had a strap around his waist many times before and probably won't even notice the cord is there, as he's intent on pointing. Have five or six feet of slack in the check cord and hold on tight. Stroke him and order him to "Whoa" as your helper flushes the bird. When the dog chases and hits the end of the cord, jerk him back with all your strength. It's *very important* that you get an *abrupt* stop of the dog, as it will make your job easier in the future. He will probably get spun around, fall down and get up confused. Take him back to the original spot where he was pointing. I always prefer to pick up the dog and carry him back to that spot. Stroke him and tell him "Whoa" with a firm, but moderate tone of voice. He's already mastered the "Whoa" command, but now is learning the order also applies to when a bird flushes. If this first job is done half-heartedly it will plague you and the dog later. You will end up having too much pressure on him when the pressure should have been removed. He will begin to show the continuous pressure in one form or another, and not in a good way. You can also do this with the check cord connected to the dog's collar. There again, when the dog hits the end of the cord, he needs to be upended and carried back to his original pointing position.

When the dog is back in position and has stood there for twenty to thirty seconds, have your helper fly another bird. A good trick for your assistant to use when doing this is for him to have a bird in his hand, and turn his back to the dog. While he's kicking around in the weeds pretending to flush, he drops the bird in front of him. The bird will flutter up and fly away. This way the dog doesn't realize the birds are coming from the hand and not the grass. This is more of a natural situation, and if the dog thinks there is always more than one bird in the bush, he will stay pointing with more intensity. Always have the birds released while the dog is standing, and not while he's moving around.

His next chase is going to be much shorter in length, and not as vigorous. Prepare for this by holding the cord shorter and with less slack, so you can react in the same manner as before. By now he's realized the cord is connected and probably will only take a few jumps, not an all-out chase. Put him back, tell him "Whoa" and stroke him. When you give that command keep your voice in a moderate tone. If the jerking to an abrupt stop was done right the first time, he might only take a small jump or no jump. Now is when the soothing hands come into play, so be sure to use them.

With most dogs, that's the end of their trying to chase on that particular day. Have your helper flush another bird, only this time he will kill it and bring it to the dog. Don't let the dog retrieve the bird. The reward needs to come from the hand. After giving the bird to the dog, release him from "Whoa" and let him carry it around a little while before calling him to you and taking possession. Give him the birds head if he will take it and call it a day. If you decide to follow this system of feeding a head, you will find it's easier to finish a dog steady to kill than to flyway. The reason is the dog learns when the bird is killed he gets an edible reward, so why get in trouble? Many people believe that it's easier to finish a dog steady to wing and shot when birds aren't killed, however, I disagree with that assumption.

I've broke many hundreds of pointing dogs and found it a much easier task when the dog was compensated for his work.

Let me caution you about killing birds. You won't hit all the birds you shoot at, and the dog never knows when one will be killed. My way of thinking is all birds need to be killed when first starting the breaking process. If you've missed the bird you can simulate the kill by walking out a reasonable distance, and bending over while killing a pigeon that you have in your hand. Then come back and give it to the dog. To him it's the same as if you had shot it.

When you're hunting game birds such as native pheasants, normally hens aren't allowed to be harvested. The dog learns that not all birds he points will be killed. If you are lucky enough to have a dog that only point's roosters, then you won't have to worry about this. I've had many people swear to me their dog would only point roosters, but I've never seen it happen. I've always wondered about the hen pheasants the dog didn't point. Did he blink them? I suppose if a person is club hunting in an area void of wild pheasants, and the club only releases roosters, then certainly this could be true. After countless dogs trained, I've never had nor seen a dog that pointed just roosters. All my dogs obviously weren't intelligent enough, as they pointed both sexes. I've never heard Santa Clause's reindeer prancing on my roof either, so naturally I'm a skeptic.

The next time you take the dog out you can probably do so without a helper, but if you have someone available by all means take him along. If you have access to another field, use that field over the one you've already frequented. Dogs have a great memory about where positive training situations transpired, but they especially remember traumatic incidents and the area where those occurred. By changing areas the dog starts off with a fresh perspective.

Plant the pigeon and get the dog on point. Don't expect the same frenzied chase as before. If you did your previous work well, that won't happen. You will use the same method which was used before with the exception that now the check cord with a knotted end is snapped onto the dog's collar, and not around his waist. Hold on to the cord with only a couple feet of slack, while you or your helper flushes the bird. Prior to the flush order him to "Whoa" with a moderate tone of voice, and if he chases as he probably will, jerk him back. At this point you should use some sort of tool to make a correction, be it a flushing whip or the check cord. You are disciplining him for not adhering to the command. A good method is to hold the dog by his collar and pick him up to where he's standing on his hind legs. You already have the knotted end of the check cord in your hand. Strike him a couple of times across his front legs and chest with the end of the cord. Put him down, and calmly say "Whoa." Be careful about this, as when you pick him up by the collar his air supply is cut off. Make sure his back feet are touching the ground and the dogs not completely suspended in the air while you make the correction.

Any discipline that you've administered to the dog must now be made right by rewarding him. While the dog is in his original stance, grab another bird from the bird bag and flush it from the same area as the first one. Kill this second bird and you or your helper bring it back and give it to the dog. At this time we don't let the dog retrieve. He will only get to retrieve when he does the job the right way, and this will come a little later. Same thing as before; let the dog hold the bird for a short time and then have him bring it to you, at which point you give him his reward. Do you recall that story about your boss giving you the thousand dollar payment for your account? That bird's head represents that reward.

Your wife who's watching television asks you to bring her a pack of cookies when you go to the pantry. You come back and give her the pack of cookies. What was your reward for doing that? Did she say thanks? That's equivalent to a pat on the head for the dog. You did what was asked of you, but you weren't rewarded. When she gives you one of the cookies, then you've been compensated. That birds head is a cookie for the dog.

During any training session you have with you dog always watch his demeanor, but especially the tail. This is a clear indicator of how your dog is accepting his training. You should also pay close attention to his eyes. Dilated eyes are showing fear, while flattened ears and lip licking are also signs of anxiety. When people run into trouble with a dog, it's often due to not paying attention to these warning signals, and they continue going down

the wrong path. Remember what was said about being able to read your dog. If he loses confidence in you, he becomes a problem dog! It's always easier to keep his confidence, rather than losing it and then having to regain it. Any time after this you can start using game birds in your training sessions.

Breaking the dog with the e-collar: If you started your dog on "Whoa, Heel" and "Come Here," by using the e-collar then you will continue its use when breaking the dog. The dog knows when he feels the momentary stimulation on his waist he stops, but when he receives the continuous on his neck he comes in and heels. This was done with the collar on the neck or on the waist, whichever place you had selected when starting this program. My advice is don't change the location of the collar from where you started. By changing locations you will only confuse the dog. The principle here is exactly the same, but you will be using stimulation coupled with some physical intervention to start with.

Plant the bird and go get your dog. I advocate using a pigeon for reasons stated. Again, use an assistant if one is available. I highly recommend a check cord in case all goes to hell in a hand basket. That cord should be hooked to his regular collar, not the e-collar. When you stopped your dog in the yard you were probably on one of the lowest settings on the transmitter, but now that a bird is involved, it's a different ball game. That being said; you should always start with the transmitter on a low setting, although the temptation to break and chase is now compounded due to the bird.

When your dog is pointing the bird, you or your helper tell the dog "Whoa" and flush it. Have the transmitter in one hand and the check cord in the other. The dog will try chasing when the bird is flushed and at that point you "Nick, Nick," and "Nick" him until he stops. If he only stops because of the cord, you will have to go up one number on the transmitter. I've had a few dogs that paid no attention to numbers one or two, and would only stop on number three. Most dogs will stop when you nick them with this much intensity, but will show by their demeanor they are concerned. In a case like this, immediately go back down one number on the transmitter. Keep in mind that all brands of collars have different intensity levels while on the same number.

You have to be very observant when you go to a hotter setting. By nicking the dog on too high of a setting you will see from his reaction you're treading on thin ice. Immediately drop down one or possibly two numbers. Remember the tail and watch his eyes. There's no better indicator than the dog's reaction to an outside stimulus, than the position of the tail and the concern he is showing in his eyes. You're not trying to create a problem, only trying to get a point across. It's not necessary to completely break him in one afternoon although with some dog's that can happen. The main thing is to keep the dog happy and with a good attitude. Most dogs that are collar broke will take two or three jumps after the bird, but upon feeling the stimulation they will stop. *As always, this will depend on how much preparatory work has been done.*

Whenever you make a correction and after the dog is standing, it's time to stroke him with your hands. As stated many times before, nothing takes the place of hands. Most training books you read will tell you to take the dog back to the original spot where he committed the infraction. I will do that in some situations like flipping him with the check cord, but not this one. Once he's stopped with the nick of the e-collar, its hands on time. As he progresses to being broke his jumps after the bird will become less frequent, until he's finally standing still. It's simple for the dog to learn that when he's standing he gets a bird shot for him, but when he's chasing he gets a nick from the e-collar. My feeling, and what I've learned from years of experience, is when the dog's standing; you should kill the bird and give him his reward.

While training with another professional trainer some years back, one of the dogs he was working was a problem dog. He couldn't get the dog to stand still after the flush. When this incident occurred the dog chased the bird about six feet and stopped on command. The trainer then made a correction. I asked him why he didn't shoot the bird. He replied that the dog broke and gave chase, and he wasn't going to reward him for chasing. He also told me he had been at this for quite a while and wasn't making much, if any progress.

BIRD DOG TRAINING & PROBLEM SOLVING

Mentioning the fact if everything that he had done up to that point hadn't gotten results, maybe it was time to change strategies. I told him what we were trying to teach the dog is when he's standing, he gets a premium. The dog was standing after that abbreviated chase, and the trainer still had enough time to kill the bird. This particular dog responded to the command "Whoa" after a couple of jumps, and stopped. What reward did the dog get for stopping? He received a correction with no reward. That was the moment when he should have been compensated with a kill. From the dog's point of view, he received a correction for stopping. The dog is not astute enough to decipher that he can chase the bird a few feet and still be rewarded. He only knows when he's stopped he gets his paycheck. When you kill birds the dog learns much faster, as the reward makes it fun and feeds his stomach. When one method is not getting the job done, it's time to change tactics. The dog ended up being perfectly steady after the summer's training. He knew that when he was stopped, the end result was a bird to retrieve and a head for his reward. By the way, this same dog went from being a problem dog to winning a field trial Championship later that year.

I will now finish with the instructions on how to properly finish a dog on game, by saying this. Many times throughout this narrative I've spoken about *hands* and your *voice* as related to giving the dog self-confidence and him having trust in you. No matter how many times you make a mistake, most of them can be rectified by talking softly and putting your hands on the dog in a positive manner. I'm not talking about a person abusing an animal and getting to the point of no return. I'm speaking about simple mistakes made in training, like jerking the dog too hard and the animal showing a little fear or confusion. That can be undone with your voice and the proper use of hands.

By following the recommendations that have been offered here, your dog will be about as perfect as any dog can be by the time he's between two and three years old. This will of course depend on the maturity of the animal and how dedicated you are. If you are a once a week trainer and can't devote the time that's necessary to work with your dog, you will be in for a rude awakening when you take him to the field. Nothing is more frustrating than an unbroken dog knocking and chasing birds all over the field on opening day of the bird season. This also tends to anger your hunting companions. They were expecting to see the great young dog you have been bragging about, instead of the wild uncontrollable youngster that's chasing all of the birds into the next county. This is certainly embarrassing for the dog's owner and need not happen.

Stop to flush: Just like the name implies; it means that when a dog is hunting and unaware of the proximity of birds and one or more flushes; he then stops and goes on point. This is a credible piece of work, and presents the gunner with the opportunity of possibly flushing another bird and shooting it for the dog. To teach this is relatively easy by hand throwing a bird and stopping the dog on command. When the dog is near you shout "Whoop" and then "Whoa" while launching the bird. Its best if he doesn't see it leave your hand. Drop the bird on the ground where it's not visible to the dog. The bird will immediately flush and fly away. After you've released so many birds by hand, the dog will stop and mark the flight of said birds. That's called stop to flush. Most finished dogs will stop on point due to anticipating another bird flushing, however, some dogs will master the technique of purposely flushing birds and then assume a pointing stance. Trainers call this bump to flush. This *is* a fault, and is covered later in the *Complex Problems* in *Chapter* VIII under bumping or knocking birds.

Chapter VII

Problem Dogs

Problem dogs: Most problems are man-made and not hereditary, but be that as it may, hereditary factors do play a part in the makeup of some timid or shy dogs. Timid dogs have more of a tendency to become gun-shy, blink birds, or present other difficulties. Most of these animals will develop into productive hunting dogs or field trial winners, if a little care is taken with their training. You will find dogs with this temperament are usually easier to train than hard-headed dogs. Hard-headed dogs like to do it their way. It's more difficult to keep them performing at a consistent level. A soft or timid dog will often respond to a jerk on the collar and a verbal castigation. Usually that will suffice. Most people expect the dog to adapt to their style of training instead of them adapting their methods to the individual dog. This can be a recipe for failure, especially with timid or problem dogs.

This is a good time to talk about why some people are so successful with one line of dogs, but have less favorable outcomes when working with others. A person that's short on patience and easily riled, usually has better luck working with a hard-headed dog, although anger has no place in dog training. A patient man can work with any type of dog and get the job done, but he will excel with soft or timid dogs. You will find that most dogs require very little discipline, but if they do, it should be administered not out of anger, but out of need. It's no different than disciplining children. First they need to understand what it was they did wrong and then the discipline that's necessary, but no more. Anytime you over correct the dog, you might be creating a problem.

I've trained and rehabilitated many problem dogs in my career as a professional trainer, and most of those dogs went on to become good working dogs that otherwise probably would have been euthanized. You will notice in the previous sentence, I said *most* of those dogs. The ones that didn't go on to become productive dogs was due in large part to their owners not taking the time to be involved in the dog's rehabilitation process. Those same owners needed to understand the root cause of the dog's problems and the procedures that were used in correcting them. By them participating in the cure, the dogs that went home wouldn't regress. That's why I started filming the techniques used in fixing these animals. The clients would then have a visual guide. Those same owners needed to know how to handle their dogs once they were returned to them. Much better results were obtained by the dog's owner due to that documenting. You can do the same thing by having someone film your dog while you are working with him. In the evening you can review the video, and you will be able to see things you didn't notice when you were training the animal. This will be very helpful.

You will be told many times by dog men who think they know what they are talking about that there is no way a certain dog can be cured of his problems. Like the old and tired cliché about thinking outside the box, that is exactly what you have to do when dealing with problem dogs.

The following two cases will highlight this, and also point out that any dog no matter how bad can be rehabilitated. Hopefully these examples will give you an idea of how to fix any problem you may encounter with your dog.

Mitzi: A German Shorthaired pointer bitch was about three years old and was one of the first real problem dogs I had ever booked in for training. I took her at no charge to the owner. My feeling was, if she could be successfully rebuilt, word would spread that the young professional could train and rehabilitate a problem dog. I would then receive more dogs for training.

The owner was a Canadian and a breeder of good German Shorthaired pointers, but this bitch was pretty hopeless, and how she got that way was only speculative. I was told she had been with various trainers. She, because of her age, had to be steady to wing and shot to be able to compete in field trials. When flushing a bird Mitzi was pointing, she would start spinning

backwards like a helicopter, whether or not she was connected to a check cord. While spinning she would move twenty feet or more from her original position.

In my youthful exuberance and ignorance I thought that if she could be taught the command "Whoa" well enough, she would never move. "Whoa" meant stopping and not moving for any reason. Four weeks of working with Mitzi primarily on that command, she would stop like you hit her in the head with a hammer. She wouldn't move no matter what distractions came her way. I was convinced that would be all there was to it. Boy was I ever wrong!

At the time I was training out of a kennel near Spokane, Washington and since there weren't many game birds in the area I drove to Lewiston, Idaho. Hunters had informed me there was a good population of native pheasants near a farming town close to Lewiston. After arriving and seeing a rooster pheasant run across the road and into an alfalfa field, I stopped, took Mitzi out of the truck and turned her loose. She found and pointed the rooster with style and intensity. I then "Whoaed" her. Man was I ecstatic, until the bird was flushed. The bird flew and the shot was fired. When turning around to face her, my heart sunk. Mitzi was spinning backwards so fast that if she had wings, she would have become airborne. At that point it was realized I had a really serious problem on my hands, with no available solution. Any of the dog men that I later asked about how to fix this problem would look at me with blank stares. Pretty much in unison they told me they had never encountered a problem like that before. Obviously I wasn't going to get any help from that quarter. In retrospect it turned out to be a good thing, as I had only myself to rely on.

All the dog training books I had ever read up to that point had also made no mention of this dilemma or anything remotely close to it, so now what? First I went back to square one. Is the dog worth trying to save? My answer was yes. This bitch was a really nice animal with tremendous stamina. She would run to the limits and find plenty of birds. No dog ever looked better on point. I had already spent five weeks working on what was thought to be an easy solution only to discover the surface of the problem hadn't even been scratched. How many people had tried to fix this bitch to no avail? Why was she doing what she was doing? That's what needed to be deciphered. It was time I learned to become a trainer.

When Mitzi realized she wasn't allowed to chase the bird and being a dog with overwhelming desire and determination, she expressed that desire to chase by spinning. It was just too much for her to stand still for the flush and shot which field trial etiquette demands. Starting her on a restrictive diet, I knew I would get more cooperation from a hungry dog.

Thinking about how to keep her from spinning, I was at a loss on how to get it done. I made a joke with the owner and told him that when she pointed a bird, I would get off my horse, mix some dry concrete with water, and then pour it on her feet. When the concrete hardened I would flush and shoot the bird. By doing so she would establish the habit of standing still at flush and shot, since she would have no other choice. He enjoyed the joke, but I was getting desperate for a solution.

That joke started the wheels whirling around inside my head, and the thought occurred to me there had to be a way to physically stop her from spinning. When being stopped became a habit and there was always an edible reward, I would be able to cure her of this fault. Stop moving your feet and there will be meat to eat! The solution like most was simple. How it was accomplished without the concrete of course, was by putting a harness on her and fifteen pounds of chain dragging on both sides of the dog. Mitzi was a forty pound dog, but with her desire to hunt and find birds, she would drag that thirty pounds of chain and never slow down.

I will never forget the day of her first find on a native pheasant hen while being hooked to the chains. I was running her from horseback when she pointed at the base of a little rocky knoll covered with sparse vegetation. The knoll had a few clumps of dried grass and a small stunted pine tree growing out of the top. At first I thought it was an unproductive as it wasn't a logical place for a wild bird to be. She was so intense you could have bounced a quarter off her back, so I dismounted and began to flush. When the bird flew Mitzi tried to spin, but got tangled up in the chains and was only able to make a three quarter turn and she then stopped. She didn't like those chains wrapping around and banging against her legs.

I was so happy I could have cried for joy. Only a three-quarter turn. "Wow!" I felt right with the world. This problem with Mitzi had become a very personal thing with me, and I sure didn't want to admit failure. I began to realize not many, if any birds had ever been killed for this bitch. That was the last bird she ever pointed for me that I didn't kill and feed her part of, or all of the bird.

On each successive point Mitzi made over a period of the next couple of weeks, she stopped trying to spin and her movements got to be less and less, until finally she stood perfectly still. She was never allowed to retrieve. A few wild quail were included in that total as well. Sorry about that Mr. Game Warden, a dog doesn't know when its bird season. They only know whether they get a reward, and the trainer should be aware enough to understand when they need one. This happened over forty years ago, so I can't be prosecuted as the statute of limitations has run out.

We were working mostly on planted quail and pheasant. Mitzi would get rewarded with a head or more after every kill. Next I took the chain off of one side and attached the other one to the middle D-ring on the harness. There again, when flushing birds in front of her she stood like a statue. Gradually I began putting on less chain, until she was down to dragging only a short light check cord, and then nothing at all. She was perfectly steady on her birds. After every successful piece of work done by Mitzi I also stroked her with my hands to instill confidence that she was doing the right thing.

Now I had to worry about her retrieving as she was eating pieces or all of the shot birds. The first thing was to pick up the quantity of food that she received. The next step was after a bird was flushed, she would be made to stand there for twenty seconds or so before she was sent for the retrieve. As I stroked her she became more relaxed. I would then feed a piece of the bird upon the completion of the retrieve. Inside of two weeks she was a very fast and tender mouthed retriever.

I called the owner and told him she was broke and he should come to see her. He wasn't able to come himself, but he sent a representative. After running Mitzi for a couple of hours with her having multiple bird contacts, the agent went back home and gave the owner a glowing report. A successful ending to a complicated problem!

This was the time I was getting interested in American Field trials with big running all-age dogs and cash purses. I told the owner I wouldn't be participating in American Kennel Club, or Canadian Kennel Club trials any longer. He told me that if I wasn't going to handle Mitzi in those trials I should see if a new owner could be found.

A very successful amateur trainer took Mitzi on trial. I told him about the previous problems she had and he said he would give her a good opportunity to prove herself. She proved herself to the extent that he asked me if I ever got another like her, to call him. One of his friends ended up buying Mitzi and left her with the trainer to run in field trials. He was able to win a few gun-dog stakes with her, but later she was forcibly retired due to losing a lung to spear grass. Mitzi then became a personal hunting dog.

Read further about a dog that was gun-shy, blinking birds, man- shy, and would bolt given the opportunity. While in the kennel he would hide in a corner when approached by anyone other than his owner. He wanted nothing to do with finding or pointing birds and was petrified of the gun. These statements are not exaggerated, they are absolutely true! This dog was completely ruined by man and was the sorriest dog that I was ever called upon to rehabilitate. He was finished steady to wing and shot, retrieved tenderly to hand, and in the process he gained confidence in himself and in me.

I started by teaching him simple tricks which helped him to gain trust in me. The amount of time put into the animal, and the hands-on approach were also contributing factors in his recovery. The more time I spent with the dog the faster he advanced. He turned out to be a fine example of his breed.

The story of Omar: Omar was a German Wirehaired pointer imported from Italy that belonged to a woman from Seattle, Washington. At the end of April she called to my home in Mexico and asked if I would take the dog upon arriving in the United States for summer training. She then outlined some of his problems. Gun-shy and bird-shy were only a few of them. The

woman then asked me if there was anything she could do with the dog in the interim. I told her yes; cut back on his food and put a live quail in his kennel. If he doesn't want to kill and eat the quail, then let him go hungry. Usually when you tell a client to do something like this it goes against everything they've learned about training dogs, and they rebel. This dog had been with other trainers and was an absolute basket case, so what other choice did she have?

She then told me the dog needed to be a tender mouth retriever if he was going to compete in field trials. I mentioned to her she would have to trust me if she wanted the dog to be cured of his problems. All her other options had been exhausted, so she decided it was time for her to change strategies. She finally agreed after me explaining exactly what it was that I did with problem dogs, and much to her credit, followed through. Also what helped her make that final decision was the recommendation of another professional trainer and the fact she agreed to the "no-fix, no-pay" guarantee.

Omar

When I arrived in Washington the first part of July to start the summer training program, the lady brought me Omar. What a beautiful animal, but a complete disaster. This dog was frightened of man, birds and guns. When I say frightened, let me change that word to *terrified*. It was obvious he had been ruined by heavy hands and unsound training methods. Later it was discovered Omar had been with two different trainers. I agreed to take the dog on the guarantee basis we had spoken about previously. That meant the dog had to be finished steady to wing and shot, retrieve tenderly to hand and be ready to compete in field trials, or the training was free. Mrs. X agreed to the guarantee, signed the contract and drove away.

Omar immediately climbed out of his kennel and it took me three days to trap him. He couldn't be caught no matter what subterfuges were used. He was only able to be captured owing to hunger, which made him a little less wary and helped overcome some of his fear. The hunger factor enabled me to bait him into a kennel. That particular kennel had a woven wire top which would prevent him from climbing out in the future.

After a few days of observation it was discovered that Omar was as close to being incurable as any dog that I had ever worked. That's quite a statement coming from me, as I have rehabilitated some of the worst. Capture a two and a half "year" old gun-shy, man-shy coyote, put him in a kennel and start training him. That's what I was dealing with; that was Omar! I began to think maybe I had bitten off more than I could chew, but if this quivering puddle of excrement could be fixed, anything could be fixed. That's exactly what he looked like in his kennel. He would lay there curled up in a ball shivering and shaking, and if you approached his indoor kennel, he made a hasty retreat to his outside run.

I have always believed whatever bad experiences an animal has suffered at the hands of one person; those bad memories can be alleviated by another. This is done by putting positive measures into play. The animal can then be reprogrammed, whether it's a horse, a donkey or a dog. By reintroducing training procedures in a positive manner you can correct any problem the dog may have. It's all about instilling self-confidence in the animal and him having trust in you.

Whatever trainers had ruined this animal, they did a very thorough job of it. Omar was a catastrophe. No trust in anyone! He wouldn't permit me to put my hands on him out of fear I would cause him grief. The dog wouldn't come out of his kennel voluntarily, would eat his small portion of food cautiously with both eyes fixed on me. If I was standing close by watching him he wouldn't eat at all. He was every kind of shy you could think of. He wanted nothing to do with any training scenario and was petrified of bird release traps, electric collars and especially any verbal command such as "Whoa" or "Come Here." Anything he saw in your hand caused him to panic, thinking it was a gun or disciplinary tool and he would make a quick exit to his outside run. "Come Here" meant run away as something bad was about to happen, and he would have run away too if I had permitted it.

So what can you do with an animal like this? When I get a problem dog in for training and am not able to handle him, the first thing I do is to reduce their food ration. I cut it by one half or more depending on the severity of the problem. Hunger is the great equalizer between man and dog. He's entirely dependent upon you for his survival, and this factor works in your favor, as you are in control.

I'm going to show you exactly how this dog was made into a problem free dog. By following the same logic and methods that were utilized on Mitzi and Omar, you will be able to fix any problem you encounter. **First and most importantly,** you have to gain the dogs trust, and I cannot emphasize this enough.

In my old kennel there was a television set located inside the feeding and storage area. In the evening Omar's inside kennel door would be opened, hoping he would come out on his own. I watched the evening news while sitting in my chair outside of his kennel. The first few days he wouldn't venture out and wanted nothing to do with me. After four days he was getting curious about what was going on, and I would feel a nose smelling around behind me. When you are sitting down and your back is turned to a dog, you don't represent a threat. Another factor was his hunger; his rations had been severely reduced and he could smell the hot dogs that were in a pan near me.

When he finally came and started smelling my back, I would put a few small pieces of hot dog in my hand. All my movements were slow so as not to frighten him. Curiosity and hunger eventually overcame fear and he would come behind me to take a piece of hot dog. Every time that he would grab a piece, it was back to his kennel at a dead run. No sauntering away for that boy. When he returned, I would call his name and talk to him. No orders only talk. I wouldn't look at the dog, but would recite the national news just in case he was interested. There was no touching of Omar or any eye contact until he finally approached and asked to be petted, and that took quite a while. I'm sure by then he was hungry enough to have eaten an old boot, if it was offered.

As I've said many times before; when you work with dogs like this, it's always productive to have them hungry. This is the fastest and easiest way of gaining their trust. Omar came to me; I did not go to him. In the same manner that he was fed pieces of hot dog in the kennel, the same practice was continued when starting his field training outside.

I have never trained a dog that wouldn't eat hot dogs over almost anything else, and they work exceptionally well when dealing with problem dogs. Remember, these dogs don't trust anyone, but especially a person who represents authority. To gain their trust, the fastest way is with food. Omar was also started on two simple tricks. I taught him that when a hot dog was placed on his nose, he couldn't eat it until he heard his name called. I would run through various names, talk about the weather until his name was finally called with emphasis. Then I would let go of his muzzle. He learned to flip the hot dog in the air and catch it on the way down. The other trick was learning to jump through a hula hoop. The great thing about teaching a trick to a problem dog is the dog can be rewarded immediately. This goes a long way in building up their self-confidence. He knows he did something right as a result of his being instantly compensated.

When teaching the hot dog trick to a hungry dog it obviously takes more time than it would with a well fed dog. By doing this with Omar we were in close contact. He was learning new things and was also gaining confidence in himself and in me. My hands were all over him during this adjustment period.

BIRD DOG TRAINING & PROBLEM SOLVING

The reason that in these problem dog stories you will see me place so much emphasis on trick teaching, food rewards and hands-on training, is because of the rapid results. I hope you will take this to heart if you are dealing with a problem dog of your own. It's about gaining the trust of the apprehensive animal and that is done quickly and effectively with food treats, hands and teaching tricks. Teaching a trick coupled with food treats is one of the simpler solutions to fixing a severe problem in a dog. Field training is much more complicated than learning a simple trick, and the rewards aren't instantaneous.

Let's get back to Omar. I started walking him around my driveway with a check cord and pulling him in a gentle manner toward me on the command "Come Here," and then rewarding him with a piece of hot dog. While working him on the "Whoa" command, I used a half hitch around his waist and would gently lift to exert a little pressure. When he was standing, I would stroke him and give a piece of hot dog. Normally a problem dog of this nature won't take food in a training session no matter how hungry. He's so worried about what's to come next; he won't accept a treat under any circumstances. When the dog does start to accept treats, it means he's beginning to trust you. This is why treats and trust go hand in hand.

Three weeks later Omar was taken out into a large field (always with the check cord) and I would "Whoa" *h*im. Every time this happened, he would turn his head away and not look at me. The action of him turning his head away indicated there was not enough trust between us. Until that complete trust was gained, I would not be successful in training him. A dog needs to look at you and be intent upon observing what you are doing, but especially watching your eyes. He should be waiting for his next command. I started to like Omar a little bit, so he was upgraded from a pile of excrement to pathetic.

Next I took the half hitch off of his waist and began walking him around a field. With the check cord attached to his collar I would then "Whoa" him. When he was stopped I rewarded him with a piece of hot dog. I then walked twenty or so feet in front of the dog and started flushing motions while making noises like I was trying to flush a bird. By clapping my cupped hands together it simulated a shot.

Omar would immediately lie down. He didn't like the direction this activity was heading. I would then unzip the fanny pack, and when he heard that unzipping noise he associated it with his treat. Now all of his attention was focused on me. Immediately I went back to him with a piece of hot dog in my hand, and when he stood up I fed and stroked him while repeating "Whoa." He had to stand up and face me to get that treat. When you are dealing with a problem dog always make the dog stand before he's given a treat. Never bend over to give the dog a reward. They have to stand up facing you. This will mentally prepare the dog to deliver a bird in front of you, while standing up, after he's made a retrieve.

Four or five days of this, it was time to advance his training. I put six homing pigeons in a bird bag and carried them with me while taking Omar to his place in the field. He wasn't real anxious about walking with me, due to the fact he could smell those live pigeons in the bird bag. He had no choice but to accompany me, as he was connected to a check cord.

When arriving at the area where he received all of the hot dogs, I would "Whoa" him. This was his comfort zone. Everything that was good had happened in that area. As stated before, this dog was terrified of birds owing to the unpleasantness they represented. He would learn that a dead bird was food, but a live one had spelled trouble in the past.

Homing pigeons thrown by hand from a distance of around fifty yards made him pretty nervous at first, but as he was in the security sector he stayed, although flat on his stomach. As mentioned before, I would clap my cupped hands together to simulate a shot. Going back, I would give him a couple of pieces of hot dog, but as always he had to stand up to get them. This involved a lot of walking back and forth, but it was necessary and something that needed to be done. The distance the flying bird was away from him was also a factor in keeping him in that one spot. If I had started releasing birds closer than the fifty-yard mark, he would probably have made his getaway.

Dogs that are bird shy and/or gun shy are not going to chase a bird. The farther there're away from the bird the more comfortable it is for them.

When the dogs are in their comfort zone, and are whoa broke, they will remain there without moving.

I'm now explaining the method used in breaking Omar steady to wing and shot.

Five days of this and Omar was gaining confidence in the proceedings and was starting to show interest in the flying bird. I then moved him to an area with higher grass. If he wanted to watch what was going on he had to stand up to see over the top of it.

I began throwing a bird and firing a .22 caliber blank pistol from the same distance of about fifty yards. When the bird flew and the shot was fired, I slowly started walking back toward him to give him his treat. This really made him nervous, but to his credit and the trust that was building between us, he was compelled to stay in his tracks, although on his stomach. He looked like a jack in the box, down and up. At this point I killed a bird by pulling off his head and fed Omar part of that bird. This dog was hungry enough to eat an onion if it would have been given it to him. He was beginning to look like he was on a hunger strike.

Omar's confidence in me was building to the point where I recognized the fact I was winning the game. It was time to upgrade him from pathetic to pitiful. After a week of this program he was starting to get more interested in the proceedings, and that's when the .410 gauge shotgun was brought into play. Staying at about the same distance of fifty yards, I threw a pigeon and killed it. I was very pleased that he had remained in his spot and hadn't moved, albeit on his stomach, but while walking back toward him he raised up to a standing position. I knew then that he was going to be cured of his idiosyncrasies within the allotted time frame.

Going back to the dog I parted out the bird and gave him the head and both legs. By now he had learned a dead bird was not a threat, it merely represented food. He was in his comfort zone and from past experience he knew that after the bird flew, he received a reward. Now with the gun noise it had changed from a hot dog to a piece of pigeon. I never allowed him to retrieve, but always brought the bird back to him. His reward always came from my hand.

By now, I could see the game was changing into one that he wanted to get involved in. From that day forward he couldn't get enough of the training. I continued to repeat the same process while gradually moving closer and closer until I was about twelve feet in front of him. By then he was standing on his tiptoes. It took about ten days to accomplish this. I didn't want to move too fast and undo the improvements that had already been made. Omar was licking his lips in anticipation, and at that point he was completely over his bird and gun fears.

He was now upgraded from pitiful to fair. He was getting into the habit of watching the bird fly, me shooting it, me retrieving it and then giving him part or all of the bird to eat. Sometimes, but not often, I would miss the bird. At that point he learned that no kill meant there was no bird head for a reward, only a piece of hot dog and hands on stroking with a soothing verbal tone.

Now was the time to start him pointing and retrieving. I attached a longer check cord to his collar and planted a pigeon on the ground about fifteen feet in front of him. It was planted in plain sight where the dog could see it. He immediately assumed a pointing stance, so I flushed the bird and killed it. Then I sent him for the retrieve by saying "Omar," pause, "Fetch" and tapped him on the head. There was quite a bit of reluctance on his part, and it took a little time to convince him that it was alright for him to go and get that bird. I literally had to walk with him.

You can imagine what thoughts were going through this dog's head. If I go to the bird am I going to be punished, is this guy going to hurt me if I pick it up? Who knows what abuse this dog had suffered? This was something different and it meant he had to leave his comfort zone. It was, make it "or" break it time for Omar. Walking with me, he went slowly to the bird as if expecting to get in trouble. When he grabbed it, I backed up and called "Come Here" while pulling him to me using the check cord. I took the bird away and began parting it out which wasn't difficult, as it had been run through a meat grinder. I then gave all of the bird to him piece by piece. Now instead of Omar having only one or two rewards, he had four or five pieces which constituted four or five payments for his good work. I still have

a scar on my right index finger from him biting it. Besides eating the bird it looked like he was starting to like the taste of dog trainer blood.

When feeding bird parts to a problem dog you can never punish him when he bites your fingers, they just happen to get in the way. In a case like this you have to suffer in silence. In most situations, the dog is not biting your fingers intentionally. That being said; some dogs *will* bite your fingers because they don't want you to have the bird. Omar was chewing that bird like a piece of bubble gum. The misery this poor animal had experienced with the gun, birds and improper training was the reason he was taking out his aggressions on the cause of his troubles. That happened to be the bird. In the past, every time he found a bird he got into trouble. His problems were then multiplied as a result of the wrong kind of pressure applied at the wrong times.

Now for those of you who are again wondering about the hard mouth, read *Chapter VIII* on curing hard mouth.

Every day it was the same thing. Take Omar to the field "Whoa" him and plant a dizzied pigeon. Flush it, kill it and send him for the retrieve. When he returned, and after pulling the mutilated carcass from his gullet, he was given the head and legs which were pretty well tenderized. Now I started picking up the quantity of dog food, so when his owner arrived to take him home, he wouldn't look like a dog with anorexia.

Over a period of the next couple of weeks, and after shooting numerous pigeons for the dog, he was flying back to me on his retrieves, but was still being a little rough with the bird. Twenty or more pigeons later, he became a super-fast retriever with a tender mouth. In his haste to retrieve the bird, he had no thought of chewing it. His entire focus was getting the bird back to me so he could collect his rewards.

It was at this point I decided it would probably be safe to switch over to quail. I would "Whoa" Omar, dizzy a quail and drop it in a bush about ten or fifteen feet in front of the dog. The bird would struggle while trying to free itself from that bush. When it was free it would walk around a little before I flushed and killed it. Omar had no desire to pounce on the quail even though he could see it struggling to get free from the bush. Not wanting to get in trouble, he had already figured out the end result of these exercises, which was a food reward. Every training exercise he had been through until now was stop, stand, the flush, the kill and eventually the retrieve. He would bring back the bird and it was parted out for him. Before the summer was over he wasn't showing much interest in eating birds. After retrieving a bird, he wanted me to plant him another. He didn't have time for me to part out the bird for him. By this time he was on a full ration of dog food.

Everything in this dog's life was now a positive experience. In the evening when the day's training was over, Omar was let to run loose around the kennel area inside or out while I watched the news. He was completely free and could have run anywhere on the ranch that he wanted to, and have untold acreage to hunt if he so desired. He didn't desire. He wanted to keep an eye on me as now the trust between us was complete. On occasion I would call him to me and pet him, and as you have probably guessed he received a piece of hot dog as a reward for coming. Two months before if I would have let him go outside he would have run away, but now Omar was perfectly content to hang out with me.

At this time he was also taught to shake hands and play dead. This was done more for my own amusement rather than the dog needing to be taught another trick at this point. All of these training sessions were based on trust. When you do something right you get a reward. Is it any different with kids? They make good grades, clean up their rooms, hang up their clothes and they earn a reward. They go to the movies, get an allowance or receive some other type of recognition for their good behavior.

The last two weeks of training I took Omar into the field to let him find and point his first bird. He did so with all the style and intensity of a completely finished gun dog, which of course by now he was. Up to this point he was stopped on the command "Whoa" and I threw or planted birds in front of him. By now all of the flushing, shooting the bird and him retrieving was a game that he had played many times before, although without him pointing it. Now he had to do it the right way, and he did. He was now upgraded from fair to pretty good.

When hunting Omar around the ranch he found and pointed numerous quail and a few pheasants, with very few mistakes. If he took a hop or two

when a wild bird flushed, I would scold him, but there was never a need to administer a physical correction. It was humorous to observe his reaction. He looked like a kid that got caught with his hand in the cookie jar. It wasn't a fear factor that stopped him from making errors. He wanted me to kill a bird for him. This didn't happen if he accidently flushed one. When he did it right he always got his reward, which ended up being only a head. A couple of quail breasts make a nice breakfast for a dog trainer. I have to eat too! A dog that has been stopped in the field and has a bird flushed in front of him doesn't identify whether he's pointing it or he's just standing there. To him it means the same thing. He just knows the end result of him being stopped and the reward it entails.

A short time after this Omar went home and to tell the truth it was a sad day for me. I really liked the dog. The client was very happy, as was I, over a complicated job well done. Omar went from being a pretty damn good dog, to a dog I wanted to buy and I don't buy junk. I needed another good quail dog in México and Omar was certainly a good bird dog. I made my offer, but the client declined. She decided to keep her dog in order to field trial him. She was told at the time, no e-collar, no release traps and no artificial training methods. The dog was perfectly broke, both on wild birds and planted game. When you rehabilitate a dog that was this bad he doesn't need to be reminded of previous traumas by going back to those old unsound methods. Those methods coupled with a heavy hand had put him into that predicament to begin with. I never heard anything more about Omar, but I'm hoping he made a mark in field trials. Read further, and at the end of this chapter I will walk you through the process of breaking a gun-shy, bird shy dog just like what was done with Omar.

Again, the purpose of telling these stories is so you understand that if a dog is considered hopeless, he is still redeemable. Dogs aren't born hopeless; men make them that way.

Judging by what you've just read you can appreciate the need to prevent problems rather than trying to cure them. You see what these last two accounts have in common is the use of hands, tricks and food as rewards when performing a chore. This is called behavioral modification.

Aquariums and zoos that specialize in animal tricks to amuse the paying public, have animals ranging from monkeys, elephants and water dwelling creatures such as seals, walruses and orcas. Yes, all of those animals that learn tricks and master complicated routines are conditioned on the principle of deed for feed. You accomplish the deed, you get the feed. This is a basic precept.

Gun-shyness and the cure: The first problem we will talk about is gun-shyness. When an animal has an irrational fear of gun noise, usually something went wrong in the training process. Earlier we talked about your dog having confidence in you. Repairing the damage done to a gun-shy dog is all about the confidence the dog has in you. He has to understand he's not going to get hurt, the trauma he's been suffering is over, and now the fun begins. When the dog trusts you his progress in conquering his fear of the gun noise will be accelerated. I will talk about various methods of remedying the problem of gun-shyness. Always when working to fix a problem with any dog, he should be hungry. I've written about this many times before, because that hunger always speeds up the rehabilitation process. When you cut back on the food he will be thinking about satisfying his stomach when you kill birds, and to him that means food. Usually problem dogs that are not cured of their phobias are sacrificed. If the dog suffers a little discomfort during this process, it's going to heal him, whereas death is permanent.

Method One: This is the quickest fix and is called *The Chain Gang*. This is where you have a long stakeout chain with a number of dogs hooked at intervals on it. I realize not everyone has three or more dogs to be able to use this system, although if you have access to one other dog that's not gun-shy, hereafter called dog *number two*, you can make it work.

Attach the gun-shy dog to a short stake out chain and make sure there is no escape. This is especially important, in that, if he breaks his collar or the chain, he's heading for greener pastures. Your work is then compounded. Now put dog *number two* on a stake out chain beside the gun-shy dog. This can be any breed of dog, a Labrador, a Springer Spaniel or a Poodle. It makes no difference as long as dog *number two* likes birds, is not gun-shy and will bark with excitement. The dogs need to be tied close, but with a space of at least three feet between them, so they are unable get to one another. This is necessary owing to the excitement you are going to generate. That excitement will cause a dogfight of immense proportions and this will happen once the gun-shy dog gets into the act. There should be enough room for you to walk between them without touching either dog.

"The Chain Gang"

Now let's start. One of the most important things to remember is, once the gun-shy is on the stakeout chain that's the last time you will pay any attention to him. Don't pet him, talk to him or wish him happy birthday, nothing! This is **critical**, so don't ignore this advice. Hook the gun-shy up first and take him off last. All of your attention is showered on the other dog. Everything that he does is great. During this process always have dog *number two* hooked on a check cord to maintain control and keep him away from the gun-shy. Plant a pigeon about twenty-twenty five yards away, but close enough so the whole proceeding is visible to the gun-shy. Now get dog *number two* to point the bird or flush it, whichever applies. It makes no difference at this point, but be sure you kill the bird for him. Use a .410 or a .20 gauge shotgun with light loads. Only fire one shot even if you miss the bird. That's why a bird bag is an essential part of dog training when working with planted birds and problem dogs. You are always carrying an extra bird or two for just this situation. When dog *number two* retrieves it or you go to pick up the bird, praise and make a big show over that dog. If you miss the bird, kill one from the bag and throw it up in the air so the gun-shy sees it. Part of this cure is about jealousy and excitement, and excitement like influenza is contagious.

At the sound of the gunshot the gun-shy dog will be flat on his stomach, and if he's really frightened he will dig a hole and try to hide in it. He doesn't want anything to do with this operation. "No Sir," this game is not for him! Wave the bird around after taking it from dog *number two.* The gun-shy should see the dead bird, but pay no attention to him. All the while you are praising dog *number two,* and if that dog will carry the bird in his mouth it's even better. The gun-shy can then see the bird he's carrying, and relate it to the praise he's receiving. Again I will caution you, have dog *number two* hooked to a check cord. It matters not if the dogs are pack members in real life, that won't apply once the gun-shy is cured. There will be a terrible fight caused by the jealously factor, if they accidently get together.

In two or three days dog *number two* will become excited and begin to bark when you go to plant the bird. Don't tell him to be quiet as this is exactly what you want. You are trying to transfer that excitement to the gun-shy. When the gun-shy realizes the other dog has no fear of the loud bang and is barking excitedly, he will begin to get enthusiastic about this whole process. This will take a little time, and depending on the severity of the problem, as to how long it will take. The gun-shy will start to get enlivened and begin to realize he's missing out on something. This is also a dangerous time now that the gun-shy is getting jealous of all the attention the other dog is receiving, and again, this is a recipe for disaster if they should accidentally get together.

Before you know it the gun-shy will start sitting up so he can better see the action, and shortly thereafter he will be standing to watch the show. In two or three weeks he will start to bark and show that he wants to join in. When this happens begin planting the bird closer to the stakeout chain, but don't take the gun-shy off the chain just yet, and not until he becomes really frantic to join the party. Have the gun-shy dog dragging a check cord when you first take him off the chain and *be sure* you kill the bird. This is very

important, but if you happen to miss, pull a fresh bird from your bird bag, kill it and drop it on the ground for the dog to retrieve.

Stop the gun-shy dog on "Whoa" some yards back, flush and then kill the bird. He doesn't need to smell it; he knows it's there. The dog will be more comfortable some distance away, for the reason that this is his first time actually participating in the process. In this manner the first bird that's killed over him is a source of pleasure. He doesn't have the pressure he might otherwise feel if he were closer to the bird.

When you've done this a few times you can actually let him point or flush it, whichever applies, and proceed from there. Let the dog go to retrieve the bird and if he mauls it as he probably will, don't scold him! This has to be great fun not another trauma situation. Pull him to you, pet him, make a big show and then take away the mauled bird. Give him a piece of it or all of it piece by piece. Pigeons are used as they are the best birds for curing the gun-shy. Later you can switch to quail, pheasant or chukar once the dog has progressed far enough. You can also start firing two shots when killing the bird. One shot for the bird and the next shot in the air. Dog *number two* is no longer necessary as the gun-shy dog is no longer gun-shy.

Method Two: This next technique of curing gun-shyness is a method that I've never explained to anyone before. I said at the start of this book I would hold nothing back, so here it is. When dog training professionally, you have to adapt to all situations that crop up. Clients are paying you for results, not your excuses. This method is for the person who owns one dog and that dog is gun-shy. Hunger is another factor you will want in your favor so maintain the dog in a hungry state. I've talked about this a lot, but it's one of the ingredients in effecting any cure, so reduce his rations.

You need to play the part of dog *number two* and the excitement you generate is one of the factors which will be instrumental in bringing about the cure. Follow the same pattern as the chain gang method, but remember you have a story to sell, so sell it with enthusiasm.

Have you ever seen a teacher reading to young children? The good teacher through her attitude and the excitement she's generating while reading the story, has all of the kids enraptured and sitting on the edge of their seats. They're anxiously awaiting to hear what happens next. The boring teacher who's reading the same story won't have the kid's attention and they will be talking and goofing around. You have to become that good teacher.

As before, take your dog to the field with some pigeons and after tying him, plant a bird about twenty-twenty five yards away. In this process use the same light gauge shotgun like a .410. Come back toward the dog, but ignore him, meanwhile talking excitedly. Turn back again and start walking to the bird that you have just planted and continue talking in an excited manner. Your vocalizing is the substitute for the barking dog. He will become curious and will wonder what you are doing walking back and forth. That will stir his interest.

As of yet he hasn't heard the gunshot, but he's trying to figure out what you are so excited about. When you flush the bird shout with excitement in your voice as you kill it. I like to say something like "Hey, Hey, Hey," and "Boom." When you go to pick up the bird you are still showing excitement, as you are walking back toward the dog. The dog won't be paying any attention to you at this point, but still go through the motions.

After returning with the bird, throw it on the ground within a few feet of the dog, but not so close that he's able to reach it. Ignore him as he's probably lying on his stomach with his back toward you, or trying to dig a hole so that he can hide in it. This advice about ignoring the dog is **crucial** to his cure. The stages of this cure are: your excitement which is transmittable if you are a good salesman, jealousy and also confidence, both in you and himself. The dog becomes excited due to you being excited and jealous of you because you're having all the fun. The last stage will be the confidence issue. The dog will begin to reason that if the loud banging is getting you excited there must be a reason for it. He's never associated any physical discomfort with the game you're playing, other than the displeasure that's connected with the noise of the shot. Now the game starts to get interesting.

After you have thrown the bird close to him, go to the house and have a cup of coffee. Ten or fifteen minutes later return to the dog. This coffee

break is very important as it gives the gun-shy time to process what just happened. When you return, hook him to a cord and lead him home. Again, don't give him any attention, and as this advice is of the **utmost gravity,** please don't ignore it. Save all the theatrics for when he's cured. Look for scratch marks on the ground that would indicate the dog was trying to get to the bird. That's a good sign, but it probably won't happen for awhile. Pick up the bird and dispose of it.

The first week or two of doing this daily, don't expect any dramatic results. There again it will depend on the severity of the problem, the amount of confidence the dog has in you and your acting ability. Don't get discouraged as this will take some time. Seeing scratch marks after ten or twelve days where the dog has been trying to get to the bird means you are advancing. If he's trying to get to the bird it means he's identifying it as food. This is a good time to pull the head off of the bird and throw it on the ground where the dog can reach it. By now he should be hungry enough to eat it.

Most canines are pack animals; although that theory is disputed by some scientists who say dogs aren't wolves and therefore aren't pack animals. By training and having close contact with countless dogs over decades, I can't agree with that assessment. When members of a pack do something that produces a reward, all members learn to do that as well. A pack of wolves will hunt to satisfy their stomachs. They're not hunting for fun. They have adapted to working together to produce an end result. What frightens one wolf will frighten all, and what excites one will excite them all. You are the leader of the pack and what excites you will also excite your dog. When he's unsure of something, he will learn to take cues from you to become nervous, or excited whichever is the case. This trait is what will help cure him of his gun-shyness, but if you are a boring teacher and can't put excitement in your voice and your actions, you are fighting a losing battle. This is the time you have to win an Oscar for your acting.

When your dog is turning himself inside out trying to get off of the chain, barking and jumping around, wanting to join in the action, he is cured of being gun-shy. You can now take the dog to the field and kill a bird for him.

Follow the example in the previous story. *"Whoa"* your dog some distance away and kill four or five birds on different days before you let him point or flush one. Be sure to offer him a reward of the birds head. This is important because the dog learns that after the loud report, he's rewarded for his participation.

I would like to offer a word of caution. The first hunting season you take the dog afield, use common sense when firing. Fire one or two shots and if you are hunting with a partner, caution him to do the same. After you've killed ten or fifteen wild birds you no longer have to be so cautious about how many shots that you fire.

Imagine what would go through the dog's mind now that he's accepted that gunfire means something good. On opening day you are hunting with two friends, a covey of quail is flushed and it sounds like World War II all over again. First three shots no problem, the next two shots the dogs starting to get a little concerned and by the sixth and seventh shot he's heading for the rhubarb patch. Don't let that happen.

Compare that with your friend who just got out of the hospital after being operated on for a broken shoulder. The shoulder is tender and sore and is just beginning to heal when you insist he go trap shooting with you. That doesn't make sense. Neither does firing numerous shots over a recently cured gun-shy dog.

Method Three: Another easy method of curing a gun-shy dog is to go dove or wild pigeon hunting with a friend and his dog. The downside to this method is it will take a long time if few birds are flying. Tie your dog and wait for the birds. Only shoot one bird at a time. To shoot a barrage at this time will defeat your purpose.

Your friend shoots a dove and sends his dog for the retrieve. When his dog returns with the bird, you make a big show over that dog. This will create jealousy between your dog and your friend's dog and it will speed up the process of the cure. Be careful the two dogs can't get together or a fight will ensue. Never pay any attention to the gun-shy as all the attention should be focused on the other dog. Don't try to assuage the fears of your dog, as that tells him he really does have something to be concerned about.

Depending on how much confidence your dog has in you and how many birds you are able to shoot, is how long this cure will take. This might take a week of shooting a lot of birds, or it might take two hunting seasons if you aren't able to kill enough birds to get the job done. After shooting numerous birds your dog will be going crazy wanting to join in on the action. At that point tie the other dog and kill a bird for your dog. Let him retrieve it, and don't forget to give a piece of the bird.

If you would prefer, you can do this by yourself. Go to a good location, tie your dog and start shooting doves or barn pigeons for that matter. The closer they fall to the gun-shy the better, but only fire one shot at a time. Show excitement as this will speed up the process of the cure. Throw shot birds close to him, but not so close that he's able to grab one. There again it's a matter of trust and how many birds you are able to kill. Lots of birds equal success. It won't take long before he's begging to get into the act. Once the dog is barking and lunging on the chain trying to get involved, he can be untied and allowed to make a retrieve. Give him his reward. Trust and jealously are the necessary ingredients to make this type of training a success.

Have you ever watched a Labrador go on a blind retrieve? He can't see anything, but every time his handler sent him on a blind retrieve there was something there. That's trust. The dog knows there will be an object for him to retrieve due to his handler telling him so. That's the kind of trust you want to instill in your dog. The means you employ in curing the gun-shy dog doesn't matter. What does matter is that you cure him of his gun-shyness. Whatever ordeal the dog has suffered; you can reprogram him into becoming a bold and competent gun dog.

Feather shy: Some species of birds such as doves have feathers that are easily removed. Pigeons that have been hit hard with the shot will freely slip feathers as well. The dog's tongue is wet and the feathers are dry, so consequently they will stick to the inside of his mouth. You could compare this to putting a big ball of cotton inside your mouth; it's disagreeable. Oftentimes dogs that haven't been force broken will become hesitant and even refuse to retrieve a dove or another gamebird due to the feathers slipping from the bird, and balling up inside their mouths. This is very uncomfortable for the animal. When you see that the dog is trying to spit out feathers, you must help. This is easily done by forming a **U** with your index or middle finger and thumb. Inserting those fingers into the back of the dog's mouth and closing them together while sliding them forward, will effectively eliminate most of the feathers stuck to his tongue. This simple action will prevent the animal from becoming feather shy and refusing retrieves in the future.

Bird-shy: Bird-shy most often goes hand and hand with gun-shyness. Seldom will you see a bird-shy dog that doesn't have issues with the gun. It's often difficult to separate the two as in all probability they were caused by the same action. Here's an example. A dog that wasn't broke to the gun chased a bird and the owner fired a barrage of shots over him. The next time in the field the dog wanted nothing to do with birds, due to identifying them as the source of his fear. Now the dog is both gun-shy and bird-shy.

A trainer friend of mine purchased a German Shorthaired pointer from another trainer. He came to me and asked if I could help him with the dog for the reason, he was bird-shy. We took the dog to the field and worked him on planted birds, and yes he was bird-shy. He certainly wanted nothing to do with birds, but I detected something else. When a bird was flushed the dog was giving off nervous signals as if waiting for a shot. I told the trainer the problem was that he was gun-shy, so first we had to address that issue. We worked the dog on the chain gang and in short order he was cured of his gun-shyness and became a very nice hunting dog. The point of this story is to make you aware that it's not always what looks to be the problem; it in reality might be something entirely different.

A bird-shy dog would be one which actually has an issue with birds and not from some other underlying problem. An electronic bird release trap could cause this problem if it smacks a timid young pup. It could also be something as simple as a wounded rooster pheasant spurring a shy puppy, or a retriever puppy getting pecked on the nose by a wounded goose. Both incidents would be something traumatic for a *timid* young dog. He smells

something nice and then he's hurt. Now it's a complication. Something as elementary as these two instances could have started this. Usually these types of problems will start when the dog is very young and will escalate with age if not addressed early.

So how do we fix a bird shy-dog? If you are absolutely sure it's only a bird-shy problem and the dog has no hidden issues with the gun, then the cure is pretty basic. Start feeding dead birds to the dog and then progress to live birds. The dog needs to identify the bird as a food item. This is another cure that can be completed using hunger as an assist. A bird dog that is scared of birds is worthless as a hunting dog, but he still has to eat. Reduce the amount of food you're feeding him, and on the fourth day when he's really hungry throw a freshly opened dead bird in his kennel. Coturnix quail work great for this due to their small size and palatability for a dog. He probably won't eat it so take it away and wait another three or four days. Then do the same thing by putting another freshly killed dead bird in his kennel. By now that bird should look good to him and he will identify it as food, but if not, you are still feeding him too much. I realize that withholding food is a tough thing for an owner to do. No one wants to starve a dog, and some will think this process is inhumane. You have a pet now, and nothing more. There are two options: look for another dog or fix the one you have. My suggestion is to solve the problem and rehabilitate the dog you have.

When you start this program give the dog a vitamin supplement every day to keep him healthy. He will lose some weight and that should be expected. When he's eating the dead bird it's time to put a live one in his kennel. After killing and eating that bird he is no longer scared of birds and is not considered bird-shy. He's made the transition from fear to courage through hunger.

Now, you have to take the lesson into the field. Let him catch and eat a few birds prior to you shooting one for him. In cases like these I use a clipped wing pigeon. Pull all of the wing feathers out of one wing, not both. Many strong pigeons are capable of flying away with the majority of feathers removed from both wings. When the feathers from one wing are pulled, the birds are off balance. They flop and struggle while trying to fly and this ignites the predatory instinct in the dog. It also helps if you show excitement and pretend you are trying to catch the bird as well. This puts your dog in competition with you. I'm assuming by now he's been introduced to the gun. If not wait until later in his training when he is actively chasing, before you fire over him. This is not a difficult cure especially if started as soon as you saw that the puppy was bird-shy. Luckily this problem is not a common one.

I can again hear the readers of this book questioning me over their dog eating birds, and thinking if they followed this program they would have a dog that's hard mouth and eats birds. Remember the story of Omar. If you have a bird dog that doesn't like birds, in essence all you have is an ill-adjusted pet and nothing more. Read on and I will tell you about hard mouth and how to cure it even though it was discussed in an earlier chapter on how to prevent it.

Painting by Edgar Alcántara

Finishing a gun-shy, bird-shy dog: Previously you've read the stories on how to prevent hard mouth in dogs! You have also learned how dogs were cured of their fears of a bird, the gun and other forms of training. If you talk

to ten bird-dog owners about how to accomplish some of these transformations, they will tell you it can't be done, or it's not worth the effort. The rehabilitation of most problem dogs is accomplished through awareness that a dog of this description wants no contact with birds or the gun and sometimes the owner/trainer as well. To the dog they represent an existential threat. The next question is why, and what is the solution?

It takes understanding of the thought mechanism of the animal, and knowing why an individual dog is like he is. In all probability something went awry during the training process. Now a determination has to be made as to how we are going to fix this particular problem dog. Once we have figured that out we can approach the problem logically and use the dog's fears to cure him. Many owners look at their dog, but don't really see him. Stop, look and listen apply not just to crossing a road. Observe!

Obedience and trust are the key ingredients in the healing process. Your dog will have to know the command "Whoa" and will have to respect it even if he's frightened of something you are doing. If you haven't worked the dog on obedience, now is the time to go back and get it done. The more you handle the dog the more he will be receptive about learning new things, and meanwhile his trust in you will be building. You must have a check cord attached to the dog throughout this entire process until he's completely finished.

First we will start with his fear of birds. We need to get the dog thinking birds are a source of food and not fear, and we do this by hunger. When a dog is hungry he will jump through hoops to satisfy his craving for food. Those persistent hunger pangs are a constant reminder that if he wants to appease his stomach, he has to cooperate with you.

As stated before I am not talking about starving the dog. I'm speaking about cutting his consumption of food to the point where he's always hungry. He will lose weight, but will be much more amenable to participating in his lessons after learning there's a food reward involved. I'm of course speaking about a bird head.

Some of you who are reading this book will think this hunger technique is cruel and won't want to do it. Again, let me ask you this; what do you have now? You bought a dog to be a hunting companion, but when you go hunting the dog stays home. For the dog's mental well-being you need to take him through this process until he becomes a bold hunting dog, without bird or gun fears.

Most dog owners have a kennel where they can confine their dog when they are absent. It's time to cut your dog's ration by one third for three or four days and then put a freshly killed quail or pigeon in the kennel with him. As time goes on and for his recovery to be successful he needs to look at the bird as food. It's pretty much the same process as rehabilitating a gun-shy, bird-shy dog. Leave the bird in his kennel for two days and if he hasn't made a move to eat it, take it away and reduce the quantity of his food even more.

Feed the dog a vitamin supplement daily to keep him healthy, and even though he will get thin, you have to think about the end result. You owe it to your dog to help him overcome these unfounded fears and by doing so you will remove a heavy burden the animal's been carrying.

When three or four more days have passed, kill another bird, open it up and put it in his kennel. If after one day he hasn't eaten it you are still feeding him too much, and it's time to reduce his ration even further. When six or seven days have passed your dog should be eating a dead bird. After he's eaten two or three birds on different days it's time to change the drill. Now he needs to kill a bird and eat it. Once he's done that his fear of a bird has been overcome, and he will consider it a food source. The quantity of food can now be increased although the dog should still be maintained in a hungry state.

Depending on the magnitude of gun-shyness in your dog, you can start with no gun or a .22 caliber blank gun. Whether you start with the blank gun or add it later will be your decision based on the degree of severity of the problem.

You will need access to pigeons to be able to do this. Kill a couple of pigeons, cut them into small pieces and put the cut up pieces in the refrigerator. Leave the feathers attached. Every day before you go training, take out two or three pieces and let them warm to room temperature.

Take the dog to a field where the inclination to run away is not too strong. You wouldn't do this within sight of his kennel. The reason is that

BIRD DOG TRAINING & PROBLEM SOLVING

after being made to "Whoa," he might escape and run back to his comfort zone, and then you have lost ground. In the field "Whoa" him, walk a considerable distance away, throw a bird and fire a blank. Be at least fifty yards away when you do this. If there is any doubt in your mind that the dog might bolt and leave his position, tie him. If you can't trust him to stay there, drive a stake into the ground and leave it. You will repeat this drill every day in the same place.

We are breaking this dog to wing and shot while curing him of his fear of the bird and gun. That dictates that you release a bird and fire the gun. After releasing a bird, fire and then bend over pretending you are picking up something from the ground. Have a piece of bird in your hand when you return. Give that piece to the dog for his reward. If he won't accept a piece of pigeon, you either missed the step of him killing the bird and eating it, or he's overfed. You will give him this treat while he's standing up and standing still.

When you have done this a number of times and the dog is starting to get comfortable in his zone, move a little closer and repeat the same thing. Do this over a period of at least a week or ten days, not all at once. At each training session you should throw at least three birds and on each released bird fire the blank gun, so this process will be expedited. After each shot return to the dog and give him a piece of the bird. Whether the dog is sitting or lying down is not important, but he has to stay there. When it's time to give him his tidbit; no treat unless he's on his feet.

Two or three weeks of this and your dog will begin getting comfortable with this procedure. A bird flies, a shot is fired and a piece of bird is given. Now it's time to start killing birds. As was stated before, use a .410 gauge shotgun if one is available, but if not a .20 gauge with light loads will have to do. When you start with the shotgun go back to your original distance of fifty yards in that the noise is quite a bit louder than the blank gun. Stop the dog, walk out the required distance, throw a bird and kill it. Pick up the bird and walk back to give him his head and two legs. He will eat it for the reason that he's still hungry. By now he completely understands the bird is food, and the food coupled with the gun noise is starting to make it a good thing. At this point you still haven't let him retrieve, but he's standing steady when you throw the bird and kill it. If he's still on the tie out chain take him off, "Whoa" him and continue the process. Remember what was said before about a gun-shy, bird-shy dog chasing a bird. I've never seen it happen!

It's time to up the stakes. Plant the bird on the ground where the dog can see it and observe his reaction. By now he should be anxiously awaiting for you to kill it, but if not you are moving too fast. If the dogs is giving off nervous signals don't ignore them. Remember when your training hits a bump, back up. Go back to being a little farther away where the dog is more comfortable, and then plant the bird on the ground; flush and kill it. Pick it up and take it back to him as before, but now you can let him mouth or chew on the bird prior to parting it out and giving the dog his rewards.

This will be the first time he's had a whole bird in his mouth. He will probably chew it like a Snickers bar, so it will be up to you to get the mangled mess out of his mouth. This is a natural thing for him to do. He believes a bird has caused his previous fears and by chewing it he's acting out all of his past grievances on that bird. After calling him to you, fish the damaged bird out of his mouth, tear it into three or four pieces and feed him the remnants. Remember; the treats have to come from your hand. That will be the secret of a tender mouth retriever in the future.

Now that he's actually sight pointing the bird on the ground you should kill fifteen or twenty birds before you advance to letting him find, point, and retrieve a bird. If you have followed this example your dog is no longer gun-shy, and or bird-shy. Now is the time to let him find and point his own bird. Using the same species, let him hunt freely instead of you stopping him in the field. You won't have to worry about him blinking it or chasing it after it flies. He's broke!

With dogs fitting this description of gun-shy and bird-shy that I've finished, most when sent for a retrieve were somewhat hesitant. The traumas that were associated with the gun and the bird have now helped you to break him. He's now completely happy to stand there, as that's his safe space. When you command him to make a retrieve, he has to leave that space, and It's a big step. Go to the dog and tap him on the head while calling his name. If he's still a little uncertain, walk with him if need be. Once

BIRD DOG TRAINING & PROBLEM SOLVING

he's picked up the bird, you should move back a few paces and call him to you before accepting it. As before be absolutely sure you give him pieces of the bird. This whole exercise is about winning the dogs confidence and then keeping it. Good work. You've done something everyone said couldn't be done and that's a big deal. After completing this process you can fix any problem in any dog. You are now a trainer!

"A Sucessful Hunt"

Chapter VIII

Complex Problems

Curing hard-mouth: Mistakes made in training, with the exception of force fetching a dog are the usual reasons why a dog becomes hard-mouthed. When you force fetch a dog, a small percentage of them will treat the bird roughly when first starting to retrieve. The dog has suffered some discomfort by being force fetched. When he finally gets a bird in his mouth he might take his frustrations out on said bird. This is normal, but that same dog when he's retrieved a few birds and gets a head of a bird after every retrieve, will soon be a soft or tender-mouthed retriever. That being said, there are some dogs which will refuse to eat a birds head no matter how much you insist, although most problem dogs will readily accept one.

Many sportsmen hunt with two or more dogs and the competition between dogs racing to a downed bird will often lead them to try and get to the bird first. This can lead to hard mouth or the eating of the bird, simply to keep it away from the others. I explained the concept of this in *Chapter IV*. All your hunter friends will tell you, don't feed bird heads as it will encourage your dog to start eating the entire bird. Don't listen to the cynics. Let us suppose I'm a vegetarian and drive a meat delivery truck; does that mean I'm going to start eating meat just because I handle it all day?

Many people think a hard-mouthed dog cannot be cured of chewing on or eating birds, and that's why this segment is included in *Complex Problems*. To start you will need access to about twenty five pigeons as they work the best due to their size. They are larger and physically denser than a quail, so it takes a dog longer to chew and/or to eat them. This system as mentioned before in preventing hard mouth is a food-based cure and this time the food is the bird. Have you eaten chicken for dinner two weeks in a row? Pretty soon you are sick of chicken and the same thing applies to a dog. It will happen to your dog after he's cured from chewing or eating the bird.

He will get tired of eating pieces of the bird and after making the retrieve, will just want to get back to hunting. Hunger is not used to help with this cure. It's better to have a well fed dog when starting this process.

Every dog training book I've read, and I've read many, suggested the method for curing a hard mouth dog is putting nails or tacks through a retrieving dummy. Other solutions offered included wrapping barbed wire around the dummy or bird, retrieving eggs, scrub brushes and even soda crackers. Either that or they omit any reference to a hard-mouthed dog in their story. When you advance to dead birds some authors suggest driving nails through the body of the dead pigeon, or game bird. In theory that sounds like an ideal solution. The problem with any of these theories is; you probably have never killed a bird in the field with soda crackers or a scrub brush attached, or for that matter one with nails driven through it. That being said, how can you make a tender-mouthed retriever out of a dog that chews on/or eats the birds you have just shot?

The majority of people when training a dog think like a human, because obviously we are human. If you want to have success training a problem dog, you will have to reason in the same manner the dog reasons. You will have to get inside the dogs head figuratively, and try to decipher just what makes him tick. In other words *read the dog.* The dog is not able to relate to you verbally (with a few exceptions) as to his needs, he can only do that through body language. Observe and try to understand just what his actions signify. The dog is able to read your body language instantly. He doesn't have the same level of intelligence as a human. You need to learn to read his body language as fast as he reads yours and this takes astute observation.

When dealing with a hard-mouthed dog, hunters tend to get really excited while the dog is making a retrieve and chewing on the bird. They scream at the dog and try to get the damaged bird away from him as fast as possible. That is the wrong thing to do! This adds pressure on the dog, exacerbates the situation and encourages more of the same behavior. He's retrieving the bird to his owner, and that person is shouting at him for chewing on it. The dog interprets this as the hunter being upset at him for bringing the bird. That's the kind of thing you want to avoid. This is why the dog should be rewarded with a head, or pieces of the bird for bringing that mangled mess to his owner. He begins to understand a fast prompt retrieve brings a quick reward, and what was a negative situation now becomes a positive one. The chewing will then stop as the dog is focused on only one thing, and that's to get that bird to his owner as fast as possible so he can collect his dividend.

Let me tell you about an interesting case. I received for training an English setter bitch from a Canadian client that was way beyond what's considered hard-mouthed. This bitch would gulp down the entire bird in a matter of seconds. She had to be finished steady to wing and shot, as well as making her into a tender-mouthed retriever. She was destined to compete in Canadian Kennel Club field trials. After finishing her basic obedience course we started on bird work. She always had a check cord attached which enabled me to have some control. The bitch would point the pigeon and I would then flush and kill it. She was sent for the retrieve with me running right behind her. As she picked up the bird I drug her toward me a distance of about six feet. That's all the time I had before the bird was completely ingested. She was pulled in front of me, and I would fish the mangled corpse out of her gullet. This is very rough on the fingers and I still have scars to prove it, not only from her, but from others as well. You can't discipline the dog for biting your fingers, but if this concerns you, wear gloves. It's time for positive reinforcement not for anything negative. You will have to suffer in silence. This bitch was totally concentrated on eating the bird. My fingers just happened to get in the way.

After fishing out the mauled remains, I started giving the dog parts of the bird piece by piece. In this manner I was giving the dog multiple rewards. Meanwhile I was praising her with each piece and telling her what a great dog she was. What I remember is that it took between twenty five or thirty birds to fix this bitch, and I was killing two birds a day for her. Over a period of time the dog started to return the bird as fast as she could run due to her being so excited about getting her reward. After a while she had no more interest in eating a bird head; she just wanted to continue hunting. The bitch became an absolute tender-mouthed retriever. Remember the story of your boss rewarding you in an earlier chapter!

Dogs that are cured of being hard-mouthed will oftentimes pick up the bird by whatever body part they can grab. In their haste to return they will sometimes drop it, and have to pick it up again. They are so focused on returning it to you they neglect getting a firm hold on the bird. This would be similar to a wide receiver in the N.F.L. who needs to concentrate on catching and holding on to the football, prior to running with it. Other dogs will mouth the bird by shifting it back and forth inside their mouth. They are not chewing nor clamping down on it. This is very common on a recently cured hard-mouthed dog. Don't get excited when you see a dog do this. The dog is now tender-mouthed.

That's basically all there is to this process. You kill the bird whether it was pointed or flushed, if you're training a flushing dog. When the dog picks up the bird, pull him to you by using a check cord, take away the bird and part it out for him. After a while the dog will be running back to you with the bird and the retrieves will be faster and tender-mouthed. When the hard-mouthed dog has completed a number of retrieves they begin to lose interest in eating parts of a bird. By then they are programed to retrieve the bird promptly and tenderly. They don't have time for you to part out the bird, or wait for you to tell them how great they are. That dog just wants to get back to business.

There will be a certain percentage of folks who are reading this book that won't be able to get their head around the fact that feeding bird parts will produce a tender-mouthed retriever. These folks are thinking like a human and not reasoning like the dog, so consequently they will probably fail in their attempt at curing the hard-mouthed dog.

I've heard numerous people including a veterinarian tell me the sharp bones of a bird's wing or leg can puncture a dog's intestine, but I have yet to see that occur. Theoretically I suppose something like that could happen, but I have fed literally thousands of birds, mostly quail, chukar and pigeons, and have never had a dog suffer any adverse consequences from eating one. However, if a pheasant was shot only the head was given due to the size and structure of the leg bones. Coyotes, wolves and foxes have been eating birds and other mammal's, bones and all, since their creation and seem to be thriving. If this concerns you, just feed the birds head and eliminate the leg bones.

I will mention one thing you do need to be aware of when feeding pigeon legs to a dog. Breeders of homing pigeons mark their birds with a seamless aluminum band, so watch for those bands, and pay attention so that the dog doesn't accidently ingest one.

Blinking: The blinking of birds is a man-made fault in almost all instances. It's also one of the more difficult problems to resolve. Usually it takes as much time as curing a gun-shy dog and the methods are similar. When too much pressure is brought to bear on a dog while he's working birds, and that pressure is applied at the wrong moment, the dog can easily become a blinker or even a bolter. The dog loses confidence in you, and what you are doing. He becomes confused and wants nothing more to do with a bird, in that the bird means trouble. The only other blinking problems I've encountered were young dogs getting hit on the nose with an electronic bird release trap.

There are various forms of blinking, but first what does the word mean? The term blinking can be used in different situations, but it involves a bird. The dog smells a bird, points, but then leaves it and continues hunting. Another dog will detect the birds scent, but give no indication of it and will carry on hunting. This particular form of blinking is the hardest to recognize, and the longer it persists, the more problematic it is to cure. Dogs can also smell the bird, point and then circle it a few times. That too is considered blinking. In all cases the dog considers the bird as something he would prefer to avoid.

A few years back a friend was working a field trial dog on horseback while at the ranch. I had a quail pen about a hundred yards from the kennel and had just arrived there to capture some birds for the mornings training. As I was walking to the door of the pen, a covey of about fifteen bob-whites erupted from the weeds besides the building. They flew twenty or so yards and settled into a small patch of grass. This was a covey that had established itself outside of the two callback pens which were in operation.

Four or five minutes later this man's dog came running by downwind of the covey, passed within six feet of those birds and kept right on going. He never even slowed down. By watching intently, a slight recognition was detected from the dog that told me he knew those birds were there. I was absolutely sure he had blinked the covey. The birds had been there long enough and the breeze was in his favor. The slight turning of his head in the direction of the covey gave him away. The dog also realized I was standing there watching him.

My friend caught up to me on his horse, and I mentioned that his dog had just blinked a covey of quail. He told me I was full of a certain malodorous substance and continued on to pick up his dog and put him in harness. When finished training for the day we went to the kennel to have a cold beer. I asked him if that dog usually found birds in a field trial.

He replied not too many, because the dog was short on nose. I told him his dog was blinking. He once again repeated his previous comment.

Will a blinking dog ever point birds? Yes, you bet they will on occasion. An example of this would be when no one is around when he finds a bird. People represent danger, but with no people in the vicinity it means no risk. This same man called me a couple of months later and told me I was right about the dog blinking. This dog was five years old and had been blinking birds for a very long time and the fault hadn't been detected. His lack of bird-finding ability was chalked up to a faulty nose. Next, we will learn how to cure a blinking dog.

COMPLEX PROBLEMS

The method I use to cure a blinking dog is complex in theory, but uncomplicated in practice. Use pigeons for this program as its probable the blinking started while training with that bird. The cure should be applied with the same bird that was used when the blinking problem began.

Before we begin, I will tell you how this process was discovered, as it was entirely by accident. When I first started training dogs professionally someone had given me a well-bred German Shorthaired pointer bitch that was a confirmed blinker. Having numerous pigeons to work with, I started planting them about twenty yards in front of her outside kennel door. I would then go and get her and of course she knew exactly where the bird was, as a result of seeing me plant it. She wanted to avoid that spot at all costs, but I wouldn't let her. I would stop her with a "Whoa" and then flush and kill the pigeon. After picking it up and giving it to her, I would let the bitch maul it for a while and encourage her to eat a piece before returning her to the kennel. After about twenty pigeons there was still no improvement other than her acquiring a taste for pigeon parts. She always wanted to avoid that bird planting spot, but I persisted.

One morning I had worked some puppies farther out in the field and a clipped winged pigeon had gotten away. When I went to get this bitch, the pigeon that was planted had also made its escape. I had not seen it fly away. After taking her to that spot I again stopped her, but couldn't produce a bird, so she was released to run and get some exercise. She avoided that bird planting spot like the plague. Her tail was tucked and she eased around the area as best she could. After a while she started hunting naturally and I was thinking, what's going on? The dog was making nice forward casts, and it looked like she was really enjoying herself, which struck me as odd due to her previous behavior. All of a sudden she detected that lost clipped wing pigeon and slammed into a point. I picked up the bird, threw it in the air, fired the shotgun and lo and behold she retrieved it to hand. She was then fed that bird piece by piece. The rest of the time I owned her she would avoid that blinking spot. She would point a pigeon or any other bird when away from that area. Eventually she was sold to a hunter as she was completely cured of blinking, and finished being a good bird dog that retrieved tenderly. That bitch taught me how to cure a blinking dog. It's not

always us teaching something to the dog; sometimes it's the dog teaching us something. We just need to pay attention to the signals the dog gives off.

Pick the place you will use for the blinking spot. The area should be where the prevailing winds come from. When you are leading the dog into it, he will have the breeze in his nose along with the birds scent. Make it a place with a little natural cover such as weeds or grass. Chose this area with care and close to the dog's kennel or close to his tie out where he can watch everything you do, including the planting of the bird. This is an important aspect of the cure. We know the dog wants to avoid finding birds in that he doesn't want the discipline associated with them. By watching you as you're planting the pigeon, he knows the exact place to avoid if he's given the opportunity. We won't give him that opportunity!

Plant a pigeon and bring the dog into the prevailing wind a decent distance, let's say around twenty five feet from the bird. If the wind is blowing from a different direction, you will still use the same spot. Don't worry if he can't smell it, he knows exactly where you planted it; he saw you do it. The dog needs to be hooked to a check cord, but at this point you don't want him too close to the bird. "Whoa" him some distance away and make him stand there. When dogs blink birds they are happy to keep a lot of space between themselves and a bird. Having to restrain them is usually not necessary, although, you certainly don't want him running back to the truck or his kennel.

Walk in to make the flushing attempt by kicking around the place where the bird is planted. Your dog won't be pointing as long as he's under duress, but that's not important now. Sometimes kicking the grass around the pigeon might generate some interest, but in other cases it might make him more apprehensive. This will be a judgement call from you as to how long you keep him in that spot. If he starts giving off signals of distress, flush and kill the pigeon immediately. Go to the bird and pick it up while talking excitedly to yourself about what a great shot you made. What you say is not important, but how you say it is very important. Remember the excitement; it's contagious.

Return with the bird and offer it to the dog to see if he will accept it, but don't try to force him to take it. He has to do it willingly. If he wants nothing to do with the bird, give it to your helper, and make a show over him, but ignore the dog. This is very similar to curing a gun-shy. We are trying to use jealously as one component of the cure.

If you are by yourself drop the bird on the ground and kick it around a few times while talking excitedly. The dog has to stay there in place, but you can't get forceful with him. Assuming that he doesn't want to stay there on "Whoa" and you don't have an assistant to help restrain him, drive a stake into the ground and tie the dog to it. You will do this in the same place every day.

We are trying to get your dog excited, and create envy over you or your helper getting the bird, and not him. Put the dog away until the next day. As mentioned many times before; my suggestion is to reduce the amount of feed you are giving him for the reason that a hungry dog will advance much more rapidly than a dog with a full stomach and is content. His focus changes when he has hunger pangs gnawing at his innards.

Repeat this same procedure every day until the dog starts showing some interest in the process. You are advancing if the dog is showing an inclination to get involved with the bird, but if not, don't fret. The majority of dogs won't want anything to do with a bird that's planted in the blinking spot. Now we will advance to the next step. After you have killed fifteen or twenty birds and your dog is still unhappy about being there, it's time to change strategies.

When the dog can't see you, walk out into the field at least two hundred yards and plant a couple of pigeons or have your helper do it. Dizzy the birds sufficiently so they will stay there for a longer period of time than what they normally would. Most excessively dizzied pigeons will remain in place at least fifteen minutes. You may also use a pigeon with the trimmer string attached as explained before. The dog mustn't see you plant these birds and **do not** use a release trap. Plant the bird upwind from where the dog will be approaching, if that's possible. That means the breeze should be coming from behind the dog. We want him to suddenly scent the bird when he circles around, in that when he does, he will most likely point it, but if not

you will "Whoa" him. Now that the birds are planted farther out, come back and let the dog see you bend over at the blinking spot like you are planting a bird, but today you won't be.

Today you're going to let him blink the blinking spot. Hook him to a check cord like always, but instead of stopping him at the same place walk right on by it. When he sees that you are continuing on through the area, he's starting to wonder, what's this guy doing? He's happy now that he's out of that evil place, but curiously some dogs will circle around to see if the pigeon is there. That's a good sign, but the majority of dogs are happy to leave the scene as rapidly as possible. Now that the dog is past that blinking spot you will see his demeanor change. He will relax and start to hunt normally due to the fact he's no longer in the danger zone.

Ideally he will abruptly come upon one of the planted birds. Prior to him finding the bird, do not caution the dog with a "Whoop" or any other means of telling him birds are near. You want him to abruptly come upon it. As said before you want the wind coming from behind the dog. Again, that's so when he circles around he suddenly smells and points it. This bird represents no danger to the dog. It's not in that dangerous blinking spot and as everything has transpired so quickly he hasn't had time to digest what's happened. You're not going to give him time to digest it.

When the dog points "Whoa" him with a normal voice, flush and kill the pigeon as quickly as possible. Don't forget the bird bag that you should always carry. If you miss the bird you can simulate a kill with a bagged bird. It's absolutely imperative you kill a bird in this situation. There's a good chance your dog will be steady due to the ground work you've done. He doesn't want to be too close to a bird, and this can work in your favor by you finishing the dog at the same time.

You have two options here. You can send him for the retrieve which is preferable, or you can go get the bird yourself. Don't be upset when he chomps the bird. He's been through hell and something has to pay for the anguish he's suffered. In this case it's the bird. You already know how to deal with this by having read the segment on curing hard mouth. Either way, feed the bird to the dog piece by piece, meanwhile praising him and telling him how great he is.

The next day skip the blinking spot, and don't plant the two hundred yard birds in the same place. He will now be actively searching for birds, so let him find one or two that you have planted in different areas. Make sure you kill those birds! This plan has never failed me and it won't fail you. I've cured quite a number of blinking dogs using these methods. There's no need to ever use that blinking spot again. Your dog left all his troubles there, and you've successfully buried them.

If things went according to the plan I've laid out, you have a dog that's no longer blinking birds. If things didn't go the way you wanted them too, you either skipped some steps or you didn't keep him long enough in the blinking spot. If that's the case back up and start over. There again, this, as in all training enterprises is about how much confidence the dog has in you.

False pointing: A Dog that false points, is showing too much caution on birds. This can be caused from over correcting the dog when he bumps a bird, or prematurely stopping him when he makes game. It can also be seen in some young dogs which haven't had enough bird exposure. It's frequently seen in timid dogs that don't have enough assertiveness to push into a bird. Dog trainers have a saying: *Point em or knock em.* This applies to dogs that continually false point.

This is one of the more troublesome problems to fix inasmuch as it depends upon many factors. First the age of the dog and how he's been handled, his timidity and genetic make-up could all be a component. It also depends on your ability to detect the fault when it happens. You will see this problem manifest itself on game birds such as pheasants, which run a lot when pushed. The dog will never drive forward and will always be pointing foot scent where the bird has passed some moments before. Nervous handlers who don't trust their dog will also "Whoa" him too soon. Then they're unable to produce a bird due to it having made its escape.

The solution to this problem is pushing the dog into the bird and stop worrying about him bumping it. When the dog does flush a bird from you pushing him into it, a correction needs to be made. Don't over correct him if

you recognize he didn't do it maliciously. The dog has the nose for detecting birds, you don't. It's up to him to learn just how far he can push a bird without flushing it. Too firm of a correction at this moment might result in the dog blinking birds or flagging in the future. It can even make the false pointing worse. This will depend on you, the trainer, to make an accurate assessment of what just happened.

For example: the dog is urged forward and he bumps the bird. At that point you have to determine if he feels guilty about the flush or he's pleased with it. Did he stop and take the attitude Oh Damn! I flushed that bird, or did he charge forward and intentionally put the bird into the air? Usually when a finished dog inadvertently bumps a bird he will assume a rigid pointing attitude. If it was intentional he will stand there wagging his tail or even chase the bird. By doing either, he's showing by his manner he believes he did a wonderful thing. That, my friend, means you have to make a rapid appraisal as to what happened. You will have to adjust your correction accordingly, from a jerk on the collar, to something a little harsher. By accurately assessing the situation and realizing the action wasn't done purposefully, a jerk on his collar and a sharp word will usually suffice.

The majority of false pointing dogs that I received for training had been mishandled for bumping birds. Due to those castigations they didn't want to get too close to the bird. By the dog unwittingly flushing it, they had been severely disciplined and consequently the false pointing started to manifest itself. They then became overly cautious. In my opinion this is a form of blinking.

Another reason for a false pointing dog is the genetic factor. This is easily seen in a young puppy. He will sight point anything that moves, from house flies to butterflies. They will often stand there for an indeterminable length of time. There are certain crosses of pointing dogs that professional trainers refer to as having too much point in them. As these dogs grow older they will point foot scent instead of body scent and this will result in unproductive points. Most times, but not all, these individuals will mature out of the false pointing stage. Others, when a little pressure is added to finish them steady to wing and shot, will revert back to being overly cautious.

The solution to this problem, like many others, is shooting a lot of birds over your dog until he gains the experience and confidence necessary to combat this fault. Don't caution him on game, but let him move up when he wants too and in time this unwanted behavior will stop. When he bumps a bird after all of his training, the dog doesn't need a heavy hand in the correction he receives. If a dog I worked had this problem, I would push him into the bird. I did this with a whistle or with the word "Alright" coupled with a tap on the head. If he flushed the bird I would "Whoa" him and then proceed to scold him. Dogs are quick to pick up on your displeasure. It's in the dog's nature to try and please you, so this method is very effective, especially for timid dogs.

Flagging: Flagging is usually a man-made fault with the exception of a tentative young dog that can't properly locate the birds. It's a lack of intensity and is demonstrated by the dog waving his tail back and forth or ticking it. This is easy to overcome if caught early and deciphered for exactly what it is.

Many five or six "month" old puppies that are starting to work on wild birds will know birds are close, but they can't always pinpoint exactly where they are. If the puppy is being overly cautious, he will exhibit this by flagging, or ticking the tail. When that happens the puppy should be encouraged to move up. Don't try to flush the bird until he points with intensity. He has to learn to point birds where they are, and not where they were. To encourage him to move up he should be tapped on the head and told "Alright" or "OK." If in the process he bumps the bird, that's fine too, as this is a learning process. He's a puppy and that's what puppies' do. This ability to locate and pin running birds comes with age and experience.

An older experienced dog that has been overly cautioned and/or sternly disciplined on game may soon start to flag. This is a common trait with a dog whose owner doesn't trust him. This creates pressure on the animal as he realizes he doesn't have the bird located, and wants to move up, but his owner stops him. It would go something like this. The hunter is after

pheasants. These birds are escape artists, and when the dog first starts to make game, the owner will "Whoa" him. Of course the dog isn't pointing a bird; he smells foot scent where the bird had passed a moment before. The hunter goes in to flush and produces nothing. Then he relocates the dog that's been standing there flagging. This is the fault of the hunter for not trusting his dog.

In *most* training endeavors you have to let the dog make mistakes and at that time you apply the correction, but don't overdo it. Remember the saying: *Either point em or knock em!* If that philosophy is adhered to, you will never have a dog that flags.

If your dog is flagging drive him into the bird. Tap him on the head and tell him "Alright," but keep him moving until he pins the running bird. If he accidently flushes it, a jerk on the collar and a verbal scolding is usually sufficient. If you get too rough with the dog and he receives too harsh of a correction, the flagging will get worse. Then instead of fixing one problem, you've created another. The same rule applies to a dog that false points continuously. As mentioned before; false pointing almost without fail comes from the dog being too cautious on game. Drive the flagging dog into the bird just as you would for the false pointing problem.

After you kill a number of birds over your dog this flagging will stop and so will the false pointing. The kind of mature dogs that flag have been under too much pressure and it's almost always caused by the nervous owner, who as mentioned before doesn't trust his dog.

Bolting or running away: This is a difficult problem to remedy inasmuch as it takes a fair amount of time and birds, but in most cases it's correctable.

There are two kinds of bolting we will discuss, and one is entirely different from the other. The first one is the dog running away to go have some fun and do a little hunting on his own. The second one is running away because of fear. If it's the second one, you have a long and arduous journey ahead of you. In both cases it's necessary to change the game plan the dog has been working under. Bolting to self-hunt is usually caused from not killing enough birds, and the dog learns he has more fun while hunting on his own. Bolting to run away from excess pressure is a fear factor, and is far more difficult to correct. A productive hunting dog is one who hunts for you and not for himself.

When the dog realizes he has more fun with you than without you, he will stop running away. *Trust and confidence* are other important factors when dealing with a bolter. When the dog trusts you, it means he likes and respects you. If he likes you he's happy to hunt for you, assuming you make it worth his while. You won't have a dependable dog until you make it profitable for him. So how does the dog profit, and how do you make it advantageous for him to stay with you in the field? We are dealing with bird dogs, so he needs birds to be killed for him and a piece of the bird to be fed. I've only rehabilitated a handful of dogs in my entire career that were bolters. Those dogs had a lot of pressure applied to them in the past and they thought the next county was a safer place to be. This type of animal is the most difficult to fix and make into a productive gun dog.

It's expensive for the owner to train dogs on planted game, as birds are costly. It's almost impossible to do this on wild birds owing to their scarcity. If you are one of the lucky few who have access to quail from a callback pen, or you club hunt for pheasant or chukar, you can get the job done. You won't be able to affect a cure on a runaway unless you kill plenty of birds. It doesn't really matter what bird you use to accomplish this objective. Pigeons are an attractive option to start with as they are good flyers and are the least expensive bird.

Now for the how too! Be sure you have the dog connected to a check cord. For a good test and to satisfy yourself it can be done, plant three birds in a small area and take the dog to one bird after another. When he points the first one, flush it, kill it and let him retrieve the bird. Part it out for him so he has his reward. It's not enough for him to just retrieve it. We discussed this in an earlier chapter. Dogs feel good about themselves when they're given a food reward and that's easily deciphered by watching how their attitude changes.

When the dog has found all three birds and you have fed a head or parted out a piece of the bird for him, take him home. The next day go to the exact same place you were the day before and plant three birds in the

same location. On this day the dog doesn't need to be connected to a check cord because he won't run away. After he's pointed all three birds, retrieved them and collected his rewards, it's time to pick him up and take him home.

Let's analyze what just happened. Why didn't the dog take off and go hunting on his own? I'm sure you know the answer to that, but I will confirm it. He stayed with you for the reason it was fun. The dog remembered where the birds were planted the day before and on that day he had fun and was rewarded with food. I appreciate the fact that it's not feasible to do this all the time. What I'm pointing out is the dog was quick to realize he had an enjoyable time *with* you and that's why he hunted for you, instead of running away or bolting. When you have done this three or four times with pigeons in different locations, it's time to change species of birds. If you don't have access to quail from a call back pen, buy a handful of bob-whites and plant them individually. This will also help put more excitement into your dog and create more desire to find and point birds. Dogs always respond to a gamebird better than a pigeon.

Over time, the dog will realize that he has great fun when he goes hunting with you, and as long as you are killing birds over him, he's going to hunt for you. When you start hunting wild birds approach it in the same manner. On every find the dog has, give him his share of the bird and in this way you will have a tender mouth retriever, plus a dog that's hunting for you and not for himself.

Like I've said before, this is a difficult cure, but mainly because of the time it takes and the amount of birds you have to kill.

Other ways to control your dog are as follows. You can put him in harness and have drag chains connected, or you can connect a short cord split into two parts to his collar with a rubber ball (tennis ball size) attached to each cord. The cord needs to be long enough so the balls interfere with his stride as he runs. They shouldn't touch the ground when his head is up. Another method to gain authority over the animal is to loosen his collar and put a front foot through it and retighten. When the dog gets tired of running on three legs, take that foot out and put the other foot in. Afterwards he will be worn out and become much more biddable, at which point you kill birds over him. These are all force conditions so the dog must be rewarded when he finds a bird, or you're just banging your head against the wall.

If you have a young dog I wouldn't recommend using these last three force options. You lose nothing by trying one of these solutions with an older dog that set in his ways. Follow the advice being offered here and it will keep your dog attuned to you. You can stop any dog from running away with force, but if he's not cured of this problem, at the first opportunity, it's Goodbye!

Knocking or bumping birds: This is not a common fault and many people have trouble understanding it when it happens. I've heard every excuse in the book, and I've also made a few, about why my pointing dog bumped a bird. The birds flushed wild, the dog was on the upwind side of the birds and didn't detect them, or scenting conditions were horrible. All of these are legitimate reasons why a dog could accidently flush a bird. Remember this; the dog is guilty ninety percent of the time that an incident occurs although sometimes this fault is difficult to identify.

When a pointing dog bumps birds intentionally, that's when a correction needs to be made. I've seen this fault various times in my career, but not often. Usually this, like most problems is caused by not killing enough birds for the dog. When you kill a bird the dog gets a piece which is his reward, so it's not logical for him to sabotage his own interests by knocking the bird.

If you're the type of hunter who shoots all flushed birds pointed or not, then your dog will deliberately bump birds. It's considered bad form for a sportsman to shoot birds his pointing dog has bumped. By doing this, the dog will never have proper manners. In making a determination whether the dog intentionally knocked birds, you need to be absolutely sure that no other circumstances played a part. Erratic wind gusts could be a factor, or the dog just wasn't able to distinguish their scent for one reason or another. It could be a respiratory issue or something less serious. Mostly this will occur on wild birds. The dog tries to crowd the birds and they flush.

An approach you can use to be reasonably sure whether your dog is deliberately bumping birds or not, is to use a planted bird for a test. Plant a bird and observe the dog when he scents it, but do not caution him. The dog

will realize immediately that he's not dealing with a wild bird, but he still shouldn't crowd it. Does he start creeping and moving up until he eventually bumps the bird or is pointing right on top of it? If he does this, then there's little doubt left in your mind that he's willfully knocking birds.

Some broke dogs will road up on a bird they have perfectly located and when the bird flushes, the dog stops and assumes an attitude of, who me? I didn't do anything wrong, it wasn't my fault! That bird flushed on its own! This is sometimes difficult to detect, but a couple of sharp jerks on the collar and a good scolding is usually in order. If this happens frequently, you are being played. This type of situation calls for more birds to be killed, but only when he handles the bird in the correct manner.

This is an easy cure; however, you have to be careful that you don't go overboard with your corrections as then the dog could become too cautious. You have to make the determination if a correction is called for when your dog knows exactly where the bird is, but keeps moving up anyway. *"Whoa"* him and grab his collar while lifting him up, thrash his legs a couple of times with a whip of some sort, but keep his back feet firmly on the ground. Move him back to the spot where he was first pointing. Keep your voice moderate and in control, and as you put him down, calmly tell the dog "Whoa." Flush and kill the bird. When he brings it back give him his reward of the birds head. Most dogs that have birds killed regularly won't demonstrate this misconduct, for the reason there's always a paycheck given them for their good work.

In the nineteen eighties I received an English setter to finish from a trainer who was having difficulty getting the dog completely broke. This dog had been whipped, shocked and who knows what other types of corrections had been administered. Evidently the dog would cleanly handle birds in one field trial, and break and chase in the next trial. This dog had a very strong character and wanted to do things his way.

I started by reducing his food ration and having hunger to help me train him. I then took the dog out working on quail, just to monitor him and think of a game plan. He was an animal with tremendous drive and bold to the extreme. When he pointed he would stay there as long as he felt like it, or he would bump the bird, although he would stop on the command "Whoa." As mentioned before, this dog had been trained with the electric collar and the flushing whip, all force methods. I made the decision he would have to be cured with boredom, hunger and reward by virtue of the fact that whatever could be done, had already been done.

At the time I was reading a pocket book about hunting in Africa. This paperback would be in my back pocket when working with the setter. Whenever he pointed a released quail, I flushed the bird and if he broke I would "Whoa" him, sit down and read my book. After about five minutes he would get bored and lie down. That was permissible, but I insisted he stay in the same place. When he had given up and forgotten about the abbreviated chase, I would put my book away, plant another quail (remember the bird bag) in the exact same place as the one he had previously chased. Watching me do this, he would stand up and point again. I then flushed and killed the bird, and sent him for the retrieve, and gave him the head. We would then go hunting for another.

The setter might have four or five finds in an hour and a half. When he did it right I killed the bird, he retrieved it, collected his reward and we continued on hunting. At the time I was using two callback systems and always had plenty of quail distributed around the area. This was an expensive cure for the owner due to the many birds that were killed.

Whenever the dog broke and gave a short chase, I stopped him and he had to stay in that same spot where the infraction occurred for a given length of time. Sitting down I would continue reading my book.

This went on for almost three months. Point it, stand there, a quail was flushed and killed, retrieve it, eat a head and go on to the next bird. I also had a flight pen full of pheasants slated for release on my hunting club, and the setter was worked on some those as well. Every time he did it right, there was an edible reward, but every time he bumped or chased a bird, I stopped him, sat down and read my book. As stated before, this dog had a lot of drive and it pained him to stay there that long after committing the crime! Most people think a dog can't tell time, and in our understanding of the word they can't. However, dogs do know when something unpleasant has happened, and they can relate that to the sequence of events which

BIRD DOG TRAINING & PROBLEM SOLVING

occurred. At the end of the summer you couldn't pay this dog to bump or chase a bird. And yes, boredom, hunger and reward cured him. By the way, I never made a physical correction on the dog, and I finished the book.

"A perfect retrieve"

Bird dogs pointing fur: Bird dogs are naturally inclined to point field mice, rabbits, deer or any four-legged critter that appeals to them. Anything fleeing from a dog will jump-start their predatory drive. Many gundog owners will shoot whatever the dog points or flushes, mainly rabbits. When a dog has a rabbit shot for him, it's a wonderful thing from his perspective, as it's a big mouthful and tastes good. These same owners may wonder why their dog finds more rabbits than pheasant or quail. Shooting a rabbit in front of a dog that's in full chase mode is dangerous for the animal, and every year dogs are accidently shot because of it. If you want to continue the practice of shooting rabbits, teach your dog the command "Whoa" so when the rabbit jumps out of hiding, the dog stops. This keeps him out of harm's way.

To break a dog of an obsession with rabbits, you can bump him with the e-collar while he's chasing and say nothing, or you can shoot enough birds over him that he loses interest in anything else. You may also express your displeasure with the dog by shouting a forceful "No" as he's beginning a chase. Teach the dog to come when called, no matter the circumstances and this problem can be easily resolved. You call the dog in and make him stand there for a short while before you resume hunting. This action redirects his mind off of the rabbit, and back on to you. Don't call the dog to you and start scolding , or making a correction as he will believe you are angry at him for coming. This is my recommendation. Shoot game birds over your bird dog, shoot ducks for your duck dog and shoot rabbits for your rabbit dog.

Trailing: The word trailing is used when one dog is chasing after another and not hunting on his own. This usually starts when a young dog is competing with an older faster and more experienced animal. The puppy watches the older dog cast off and he's right behind, while sometimes barking. This is an undesirable trait. The youngster also learns that the older dog finds the birds, and as he doesn't have any idea of how to or what to hunt, he becomes dependent on the older animal.

It's a bad idea to hunt two dogs together when they have a wide age gap. One's a rookie and the others a pro. Of course the rookie is going to follow the pro. This will encourage the trailing habit, and once the habit is established it becomes challenging to remedy. The juvenile then needs to be redirected so that he learns to hunt and find birds on his own, and not depend on the other dog. How is this done?

The best solution for this is to hunt the puppy by himself until he masters the technique of finding birds. Then when you put him to hunt with another dog he won't be dependent due to having learned where and how to find game on his own. That's my advice on how to prevent rather than trying to cure this problem.

If the habit is already established; the remedy is to hunt the young dog with a dog that's much slower than he is. The pup will soon get tired of following the slowpoke and start hunting on his own. He will learn to go and

BIRD DOG TRAINING & PROBLEM SOLVING

find his own birds and not depend on grandpa. When the puppy is competent at finding birds on his own, you can then hunt him with an older faster dog.

A well bred English pointer on a covey of quail

Chapter IX

Common Problems

Sitting or lying down on point: This is a common fault and is typically caused by too much pressure applied at the wrong moment. It's especially prevalent in pointing dogs which have been taught to sit or lie down prior to steadying them. Again, *it's easier to put em down, than to get em up.* Another reason why this bad habit could be established is when you the trainer bend over to flush a planted bird by hand. It's a short step from you bending over, to the dog lying down. The dog bows down as he's anticipating the flush.

I spoke earlier about getting a young dog to sight point a bird in your hand, but like any training exercise, don't overdo it. Sometimes having to flush a planted bird by hand is unavoidable, but don't let it become a habit. This bending over in front of the dog is setting a bad example. My advice is; don't do it any more than necessary.

In my career as a trainer I've had various field trial winners that were booked in for training needing to be reprogrammed, from lying down on point, to standing up. Although many of these cures aren't simple, some are. Let me tell you about an interesting case, and show you how the dog was rehabilitated.

A German Wirehaired pointer bitch that was a consistent winner in A.K.C. field trials was brought to me with just this problem. I remember her as being broke and around three years of age. She would point her birds, but when the owner approached to flush, she would lie down and would not get back up. If the owner stood her back up, she would promptly lie back down again. He showed this to me by using the pigeon pole apparatus. This is a counterfeit practice and personally I don't believe it should be used. The

temptation to overuse tends to create just these kinds of problems. For those of you who are not acquainted with this technique, I will explain.

A pole is buried in the ground or incorporated into a heavy base such as a tire rim that's filled with cement. It stands upright to eight or so feet in the air. On top of this pole a light line is connected to a swivel and that line then comes to the ground with an extra six to eight feet, or more. A pigeon is connected by one leg to the end of the line. When approached by the dog, the bird flies in a circle and then lands whenever it realizes it can't escape. This could be in front of as well as behind the dog, and there is nothing at all natural about this method. A lot of people in the past have used this system to break dogs steady to wing and shot. It's not realistic as the dog soon realizes. How many of us have seen a game bird fly in a tight circle and then plop back down in front of or behind a dog?

This particular bitch had been worked with other artificial training methods as well and that had paved the road for her in becoming a problem dog. A dog that lies down on point is worthless in field trial competition. These types of problems happen frequently with people who are too frugal, (I didn't say the word cheap) to shoot birds over their dogs. This alone becomes a recipe for failure. Dogs always respond to birds killed for them. Any fault can be corrected or prevented from happening when a plethora of game is killed. Bear this in mind! You can't have a dog that works day after day and doesn't get paid. It will show up sooner or later in the form of a fault. Not getting paid doesn't work for you and it doesn't work for a dog. They become less vigorous in their work and problems start to appear.

When starting to work with this bitch, she was recognized as a problem dog, so her feed was reduced. The first thing I needed to do was to gain her trust. She was taught two simple tricks. The first was the hot dog on the nose which I've explained before. The second one was to jump up on the feed table to clean up the spilled dog food. I would tell her this. I spilled a lot of food on top of that table, so would you mind cleaning it "Up?" Of course the word "Up" was the key and she would jump up on the table and eat the food that was left there intentionally. What she actually heard was "bla, bla, bla, Up."

This bitch was well schooled in obedience already. She would "Whoa," would come when called, and was a pleasure to work with. The only two problems that could be detected were lying down on point, and a little rough with the bird when retrieving. This told me she had never been rewarded with the head of a bird. I found out a short time later I was correct about that assumption.

Photo by: Meg Eden

I distinctly remember the first bird planted for her. It was a pigeon and was dizzied excessively when put down knowing it would stay there for quite a while. I wanted to see exactly what she would do using the same species of bird her owner had used when she flattened out. The wait wasn't long. She found and pointed the bird from quite a distance away. When I began approaching to flush, she bottomed out like the stock market at the beginning of the Great Depression. Going in to flush, I kicked all around the bird, but didn't flush it. After doing that for quite a while, she was starting to get confused.

I was talking to her all the while saying; "I can't find the bird, if you could show me where it is, I would kill it for you," etc.

BIRD DOG TRAINING & PROBLEM SOLVING

It was "jibber jabber" to her and nothing more. Finally you could see the bewilderment in her face. I was avoiding direct eye contact as I didn't want to intimidate her. She was trying to process this and must have been thinking that this guy is not very smart if he can't find the bird. At that point she decided to take matters into her own paws. She rose up and moved forward about six feet and pointed staunchly. I immediately put the bird in the air, killed it and sent her for the retrieve. When she came back the birds head was given for her to eat. She didn't know what to do with the head, but I persisted until she finally ate it. That was the last time the bitch ever refused a head and her retrieves became tender to hand.

That's the approach that was used the rest of the summer while training her to stand up. She had to stand up and point the bird with intensity. If she didn't do that, I couldn't find it, and if I couldn't find and flush it, I couldn't make the kill. She learned this was what you must do to get the reward. Actually it ended up being a pretty simple cure. This bitch went on to finish her career by winning over fifty field trial placements.

Dogs will get impatient with a prolonged flushing attempt and will react in one or two ways. The first is they will try to show you where the bird is by moving up and establishing point again or they will begin to melt and lose character. If they have already folded, then the only other way is to stand up, move up and point the bird correctly.

You make the sitting or lying down dog to indicate exactly where the bird is and then kill it while the dog is standing up. If you flush and kill the bird while the dog is lying down, you are sending the wrong message. The wrong message is; it's o.k. to lie down; I will still kill the bird for you. You are trying to get the opposite thought fixed in the dog's consciousness. Stand up and you get an immediate reward. Lie down and you get nothing.

You may need an assistant if your dog isn't finished steady to wing and shot. Ask a friend to give you a hand owing to the fact four hands are better than two. Make sure you have a check cord hooked to the dog's collar. If the dog is lying down, the cord will enable you to physically move him up on the bird, and still have control. When he's standing, you or your helper flush and kill the bird immediately. If you don't accept anything other than the dog pointing the bird while he's standing, the dog will start standing up again. This is the appropriate time to kill the bird and give the dog his reward. Don't neglect to do that. That's all there is to it. So kill lots of game over your dog and you will circumvent these kinds of problems.

Digging: I have heard numerous complaints from clients over the years about their dogs digging up plants and bushes they or their wives had planted. Some of those grievances were posed more as questions than actual complaints. I will answer them here.

The reason the dog is digging up the plants is he's watched the person doing the planting, and is convinced they are burying something to eat. There is a simple remedy for this. Lock the dog up so that he is unable to see when someone is digging and planting.

I remember the amusing story of a customer's wife who planted a dozen or so flowers in their yard. When she came outside an hour later, most of the plants had been dug up by her husband's hunting dog. Needless to say, that didn't endear the dog to the wife. Probably at that moment it didn't endear the husband either. When the man told me this story I found it humorous; however, my humor wasn't shared.

Dogs are quick to notice something different and new in the yard. If you don't believe that put a small white rock in an area the dog frequents. He will immediately notice the rock. That being said, a few dogs will still dig up a recently planted flower even though they didn't see it being planted. In this case put a small piece of the dog's feces beside each new plant. He won't dig it up, and after a few days you can dispose of the excrement.

If you have two or more dogs running around in your yard, do a test by giving them each a rawhide bone. A bone that is big enough so that it can't be finished in one setting. Soon after chewing for a while you will see one of the dogs start to sneak off to bury his bone. In his mind this is survival. The dog is hiding the bone so that when he's hungry, he can come back later and dig it up. This is basic canine behavior. When he sees someone digging, he assumes the reason is that they are hiding their own cache, so its self-preservation for him to dig it up and eat it.

Digging holes: Digging holes is a common problem, but one that's difficult to solve due to having to catch the dog in the act. The most popular method is to use an e-collar. The downside is you have to be there watching for long periods of time with the collar connected and turned on. You need to catch the dog in the act of digging and as soon as he starts to dig you give him a bump, but say nothing. He thinks the digging action produced the stimulation. This usually takes more than one lesson. If he's not entirely cured, in all probability he will dig again. You won't be around the next time, so in reality you have accomplished nothing. This always seems to be the go-to solution for most dog owners. Based on what was just discussed, the e-collar is not the best option for this particular problem.

If you have the type of dog that starts digging a hole and then abandons it; only to come back later to continue his project; you can try a mousetrap. Buy a four pack of the old style wooden type of trap. You'll probably use them all over time. Put the trap in the bottom of the hole and sprinkle a little dirt on top of it. When the dog comes back to finish his excavations he will set the trap off. This will startle him, but it won't inflict an injury. Usually that's enough to stop him from digging, at least in that particular hole. After that; on any hole that the dog starts to dig, use the mouse trap. On a soft or timid dog this will probably cure him of digging holes.

For a hard-headed dog, one that thinks he's related to a Case backhoe, you can use a wooden rat trap. If you decide to go that route you must glue stops under the U–shaped metal bar so that the bar doesn't close completely. That way the dog's foot won't be injured. This will scare him, but won't result in any damage. For the dog that thinks he's a landscaper and wants to redecorate your yard no matter how many times he's been disciplined for digging, please read on.

Another method which you can use successfully is to catch the dog in the act of digging, and wait until he actually has his head inside the hole and then sneak up on him. A dog can't see directly behind and the noise he's making while the dirt's flying covers up any noise that you may make. It won't require you to make a stealthy stalk. Grab the dog's collar and hold his head in the hole while shouting *"No"*, over and over again. I have found that the act of holding the dogs head in the hole to be a most effective measure. It has worked for me on numerous occasions with different dogs. It's very traumatic for the animal, and consequently makes a lasting impression.

Let me offer a word of caution. Make sure you don't suffocate the dog by holding his head too long in the hole. With his head stuck inside that hole he will have difficulty breathing. He will become frantic, so be careful or you might be looking for another hunting dog. You have to use common sense when estimating just how long you can hold him there without causing permanent damage, but while still getting your point across.

You should continue holding onto his collar for a while after letting his head out of the hole. Scold him with a tone that shows you are displeased with his actions. Believe me when I say, one time of using this method, he will have learned his lesson and you won't have any more holes to contend with. I have also had some limited successes using a slingshot for popping a dog in the rear end, and saying nothing while they were digging. Like the e-collar, it's only effective if it's on the dog and the slingshots with you when the infraction is occurring.

Before the advent of e-collars I was training a young English pointer in Canada, and this dog only wanted to hunt trash, which in that area consisted mainly of gophers. With every occupied gopher hole he encountered, he would try digging out its resident. A week of the same event happening during every workout, I'd had enough! The next time he was caught digging, I watched and waited until his head and front shoulders were inside the hole. This fellow was a serious digger. I reached inside the hole and grabbed him by the collar. Holding him in there for quite a while, and shouting "No," he probably thought he was fighting for his life. He was a strong dog, but I was an even stronger trainer. When he finally recuperated enough to continue running, that was the last gopher hole he tried to dig in for the rest of the summer. As with some dogs that love trash, he never amounted to much in the bird dog department.

If you have the dog on a chain, he's going to dig. This is done out of boredom and the need to use up his excess energy. When filling in any hole the dog has dug, put the dog's excrement just under the top layer of dirt. This effectively discourages dogs from digging in the same place, although it

won't stop them from digging another hole in another area. By keeping the dog well exercised, you will help curtail some of that digging.

Thunder and fireworks: Some dogs will dig before, or during a thunderstorm or fireworks. This nervous action results from the dog's fear of sudden noises and the intensity of that noise. Some scientists believe static electricity from lightning and the noise from thunder are actually painful to an animal. A good method to help your dog overcome this fear is to work with him on things he already knows. Give him treats for a task he performs all while the thunder is crashing. Make him perform a feat to get a treat. This is called distraction therapy. Do not console him! By doing that you are telling the dog he has reason to be afraid. Show him by your actions you are not concerned. A dog with these anxieties cannot be cured by using force. This phobia can start with a young dog and grow more intense as the animal matures.

Many fine hunting dogs that you can fire a howitzer over in the field never lose their fear of thunder or firecrackers. Gun noise in the field is something good, as it means a bird to retrieve coupled with a reward. Thunder and fireworks are loud noises with no benefits. If the loud noises mean perks for them, then the attitude of the animal will change. Sudden deafening noises scare most of us, but we have educated ourselves about the reason for it. We have learned thunder and loud firecrackers don't cause us any harm.

My suggestions are to create some diversionary tactics to be used when a storm is developing. This could be doing a trick, playing fetch or giving a treat. Anything you do will take the dog's mind off of the thunder crashing. As mentioned before, don't console the dog. Have a small box for the dog to go into such as an airline crate. Dogs are more comfortable when they are stressed, if they are able to curl up in a small space. Make sure something like a rawhide bone or chew toy is available for the dog inside the crate. A nervous or anxious dog will chew, so it's better for his peace of mind to have something to munch on. In all probability the dog will start going into the crate himself when he's frightened.

Excessive barking: A barking dog is a nuisance, and depending on where you live, it may cause a lot of problems with neighbors. It can also have legal ramifications as well. A dog will bark for long periods of time out of boredom or calling for attention. An example: you are playing with the dog in the front yard, but now it's time for him to go back inside his kennel. When you close the kennel door and start walking away, he starts to bark. He wants attention. You turn back and tell him *"No,"* but that "No" will only apply while you are in the dog's sight. Dogs express themselves by barking, whining, yodeling or with body language. The most irritating of course, is the continual barking for no apparent reason.

In the old days before the invention of bark collars, a sure way to stop the barking was to have a sprinkler system installed above the dog's kennel. When he barked it rained and when he quit barking the rain stopped. The downside to this system was the turn on switch to the pump was usually in one location, most commonly in your bedroom. If the dog started barking at night, you would flip the switch without getting out of bed. When you were working or were not in the house, the dog would bark. Your neighbors who were your friends, started to take a dim view of this situation and pretty soon the authorities were called.

The electronic age came galloping in on a white horse to save us from these types of problems. Now with a wide variety of bark collars from ultrasonic, vibrating and electrical stimulation to choose from, there is no excuse to have a barking dog. There are also collars using citronella spray.

Maybe we should have reservations about using a collar that sprays citronella every time the dog barks. My concern is this could affect their sense of smell. I'm not familiar with any research that's been done about the effects of citronella inhaled into a dog's nasal passage. We don't smoke in a car carrying our hunting dogs, so why take a chance on citronella when you don't have too? The dog's nose is what puts meat on the table, so we need to be careful about guarding this valuable asset. These collars might be perfectly safe, but it's your decision as to which to use. Citronella when sprayed on fighting dogs is usually effective, and I would limit its use for that situation.

When first introducing your dog to an electronic bark collar, make sure it's turned off. Wait at least three days, but preferably more before turning it on. By taking it off and putting it on a few times during those introductory days, the dog won't associate you or the collar with the stimulation he's going to feel when he barks. When turning it on, do so while it's still attached to the dog's neck. Following these suggestions, the dog won't connect you with the negative effects of the collar and won't learn the collar is the instrument that's biting him.

Dogs are quick to learn about e-collars and electronic bark collars, when they're not introduced correctly. They behave when they are wearing them, but they also learn they have the freedom to misbehave when they are removed. Done in afore mentioned manner, the dog won't learn that the stimulation he receives is from the bark collar.

A good type of collar to buy is one with an escalating feature. This is the type that starts on a low setting and increases in intensity when the dog continues barking. If the dog is a little timid, he's not hit with a heavy dose of stimulation the first time that he barks. If he continues to bark, the intensity increases and he soon learns to refrain from this unwanted behavior. The downside of these collars is that if you have an intruder prowling around on your property the dog won't bark.

Learning to kennel: Dogs should go into a kennel or box when ordered to do so. Nothing is more frustrating to an owner than having to chase the dog around trying to get him to jump into a box or go into his kennel. This seems to be a common occurrence. If something good happened to the dog every time he went inside the box it would change his perspective from a negative one, into a positive one. You wouldn't have to beg or force him to go inside.

In an earlier chapter I spoke about dogs that hate to ride in a dog crate as they get sick and defecate inside. They are a nervous wreck upon arriving at their destination. This is absolutely uncalled for. The dog should happily jump into his box, crate or truck, whichever is the case. It goes without saying that every hunting dog should kennel when ordered to do so. Usually the reason he doesn't, is the box is something fearful and the end results of his rides have been something unpleasant, like a visit to the veterinarian. We have to turn around this way of thinking so the box means something good.

First, we will talk about getting him into his box or airline crate on command. Put the box or crate inside the dog's kennel and put his food pan inside the box. Put the pan barely inside the door. Take the door off or block it open so it can't accidently close. Make sure the box is solid and stable. Lean it against the wire if need be, and if necessary put something heavy on top. You don't want the box moving or shaking. If on that first day the dog doesn't want to stick his head inside to eat, take away his food and do the same thing the next day. Make sure you leave the box inside his kennel. He needs to learn there is nothing terrifying about it. The dog after a few days will begin to realize that if he's going to eat, he needs to stick his head inside. When he is starting to eat, put the food pan deeper inside with each feeding, until he's entering the box as soon as you put the food inside. Now begin giving him the command "Kennel."

Start moving the box to different locations inside his kennel. By now he's beginning to see that torture chamber as a good thing. This is a good time to have some cut up hot dogs you can throw inside the box as well as his food. When he's eating the food inside the box it's time to move it. Put it in the bed of the pickup, or wherever you transport him. Physically pick the dog up and put him inside the box while saying "Kennel," but always have a couple of pieces of hot dogs or some other treat inside. When you have done this two or three times, connect a short lead to his collar and assist him inside using the command. It's a good thing if he tries to jump, but if not you should help him for the first few days. After that he will jump on his own. Sometimes the dog will have difficulty jumping into a box because of its height. If that's the case, when he makes his leap and is balanced on the edge of the box, put your hand on his neck and push. He's unable to lower his head to enter the box because of the angle. Pushing on his neck will help him to get inside. This process shouldn't take over a week.

Now that you have the dog jumping into the box on command, take him for a very short ride, work on some birds, kill one and give him his piece. Next time take him a little farther and again work on and kill a bird, and

make sure you reward him. As a result of all the preparation you've done, he's now happy to jump into the box, pickup, or whichever is the case, as he's learned the end result. Teaching a dog to go into his living quarters or kennel, use the same strategy by utilizing food as an inducement. A good system when going hunting is to load the dog into the truck, and then go back to put his food inside the kennel while leaving the door open. That way when you return from a day afield you can let the dog out of the truck and command him to kennel. He will make a beeline straight for his kennel and when you arrive later you can close the door. What you are doing is programming the dog. Doors open, food's inside, a command is given and in goes the dog. Later on you can dispense with the treats and go to caressing and sweet talk when he obeys a command.

The point I'm trying to make is that food is the great equalizer when training a dog, no matter what the situation is. Teaching a dog to kennel or to go inside a box is an easy task, if you follow the advice that's been given.

Preventing fights: Some dogs are more aggressive than others and those types of dogs have a tendency to start fights. This inclination must be nipped in the bud at once. No one wants to lose a valuable hunting dog in a fight. Some people think it's cool to have a dog that can whip another dog. There's nothing cool about it, and if you've ever lost or had a dog seriously injured in a fight, I'm sure you will agree with me.

When two dogs are together, look for posturing, tail straight up, lip curled back, teeth bared or one dog trying to mount the other. The aggressor is usually the dominant dog, and anytime this behavior starts, you need to quell it promptly. If not, it can and will escalate quickly.

There are many ways to stop a fight before it starts, but that depends entirely upon the mental make-up of the aggressor. When the dog is young and shows an inclination to fight, he should be disciplined immediately. Give the dog a smack with the leash, a flexible rubber hose or a rolled up newspaper. All are acceptable, but no hitting with the hands.

There is one exception to this rule. An effective method to use with two dogs that are posturing and getting ready to fight is to put your fingers straight out like you are going to give a karate chop. With these rigid fingers give a punch to each dog simultaneously right behind the rib cage. This is the exception to the hands rule. If the situation hasn't escalated too far it will instantly get their minds off of fighting. Sometimes a shouted "No" is sufficient and after that a good scolding is in order. The young dog has to understand this behavior is unacceptable and you won't tolerate it.

It's important to realize that dogs read our body language in an instant, so if you are excited they become excited. This was written about earlier, excitement is contagious, so remain calm and you will be able to handle any situation that develops.

Fighting: The most important thing when trying to break up a dog fight is to remain cool and keep your hands well away from the mouths of either of the two dogs. It's not a good idea to grab the collar of a fighting dog. This is a good way to get bitten. I will emphasize again. Keep calm; there are normally a lot of fierce noises, but usually not a lot of damage done in the earliest stages of a fight.

Observe which dog is the aggressor and go behind that dog, grab his back legs and pick them off the ground. This will usually make the dog release his grip or to stop fighting. You might need a second person to help you do the same thing with the other dog. If no other person is available and you have the dog on a leash, disconnect and loop it around one or the others abdomen and tie it to something. This will free you so you can grab the other dog's back legs. Dogs will seldom continue to fight if their back legs are off the ground. Cold water and citronella spray are also effective.

When you and the dogs have cooled down after the fight; start inspecting each one separately for any damage. Wounds to the ears bleed a lot, but are not serious, while the most dangerous type of wound is a puncture wound. These wounds get inflamed quickly and tend to get infected. They will scab over, swell up and need to be lanced. It's always best to wash wounds with soap and water and then sterilize with hydrogen peroxide, alcohol, iodine or any other suitable antiseptic. Where there are visible wounds, especially puncture wounds, an antibiotic should be administered. Now is when you will use the dog's first aid kit. You should

have all those health care items readily available, and it's also important that you have a working knowledge of these simple procedures, which were learned from your visit to the veterinarian's office.

Dominance: If a dog by his actions indicates to you that he is the dominant one, he needs to be reprogrammed immediately. This type of dog is dangerous to you or a family member, but especially to children. It matters not what breed of dog. It could be a poodle, or a mastiff. As I have said before, there is only one leader in the pack, there can't be two, although in a wolf pack there can be an alpha male and female. A dog that's dominant will show this by his behavior. For example he will growl and warn you he won't tolerate you sticking your hand near his food bowl. He can also try to push you away. Those warnings tell you that there's a problem and it needs to be addressed posthaste. A male that's continually bumping into you is also a sign of dominance.

Dogs won't always show visible demonstrations of dominance. Signs like the dog being headstrong, aggression if he's disturbed while sleeping, or showing aggressive behavior when given a command. All of these are considered an expression of dominance.

There are easy ways to assert your dominion over the dog. Of the many dogs this professional has trained, only a very few have shown this trait, although it's common in undisciplined dogs. It's carried over from the owners, by them letting the dog become the alpha in his family. When a client brought a dominant dog in for training, I couldn't advance until the dog understood that I was the leader, and not him.

The first three days were spent in making friends with the animal and afterwards the fun would begin. I went inside the dog's kennel and sat on his bed while starting to massage his ears. By holding both sides of the dog head with my fingers hooked through his collar (see photo), I would look him directly in the eyes and couldn't blink or avert my eyes for any reason. I held my gaze steady, while talking to him with a scolding tone. If this particular dog was intransigent and unyielding it could go on for up to a minute or more, but usually lasted no more than thirty seconds. A dog can't bite you in the face while you are challenging him in this manner. You have absolute control while holding his collar, and he senses this instantly.

When the dog averted his gaze that was usually sufficient to let me know he wasn't the leader anymore, and he would respect my position. If I felt I didn't accomplish anything with the eye gazing treatment, I would lay him down and assume a commanding position by lying on top of him. Obviously all of my weight wasn't put on the dog so that he was crushed. I was only showing him who was the dominant one.

If you have to lie on top of the dog make sure you hold onto his collar, so he can't escape or try to bite you. When the dog starts to relax and groan, that signifies he's had enough and has accepted you as the boss. The only dog I encountered that didn't respond to these first two treatments was a Jack Russell Terrier purchased for my sons. He, like many Jack Russell's was a cocky little bugger. After going through the program of eye contact and the laying on him, he still thought he ran the show. I then put him in the corner of an outside bathroom for employees, and urinated on him. That did the trick. After that treatment he grudgingly accepted me as his leader.

When working with a dominant dog you must be calm and assertive, but not forceful. If you are nervous or show anxiety the dog will pick up on those signals instantly, and you won't be able to take over as the dominant one in the pack. Be firm in your dealings with a dominant dog, but not aggressive, as that will only worsen the problem.

By following any one or all of these examples you will have the respect of your now ex-dominant dog. You are now the leader and you can successfully proceed with your training.

Poison proofing: I realize many people who are reading this book will not deem it necessary to poison proof their dog. Others who live in high crime areas might believe it's a necessity. From the thief's point of view, it's safer to poison the dog than to risk getting bitten while robbing a house. I will show you how to train your dog not to accept meat from strangers, and not to eat any other smell-good item he may discover in the yard or in the field.

Most people at some point have put out mouse or rat poison somewhere on their property. This can be fatal to a dog especially if he hasn't been taught to eat only from his designated dog dish, or tidbits given directly from your hand. Fortunately most poison manufactures now put green, blue or red dye into their products. This is readily seen in the dog's excrement after him ingesting poison and it gives you time to immediately contact a veterinarian.

First lock up your dog so that he's unable to see where you put the poison and try to make it dog proof. Not doing so is an invitation for him to find and eat it. It's best if you can have a stranger do this, but if not wear clean gloves so your hand scent is not prevalent on the poison. You give him treats by hand and your scent is on those treats. The dog finds the poison, detects your scent, and thinks it's acceptable for him to eat it.

When teaching a dog not to accept gifts brought by strangers its best to employ a person who has little or no contact with the animal. This is actually quite easy to do. First, have that person offer the dog a piece of meat and when he tries to take it, his nose is slapped and the meat is taken away. The dog will never accept any food from an unknown person after two or three different people have done this. It's important when the visitor calls the dog and tries to coax him into accepting the meat; he never uses the dog's name. It's also best if he does this in a place that's away from you. This way the dog doesn't begin to associate you with what's happening.

Taking this a step further and you want your dog to mistrust all strangers; the person who slapped the dog should act afraid and run away. The dog after three or four occasions of being slapped will begin to think he's tough, as a result of that fellow showing fear and fleeing. Your dog won't want any strange people close to him after that and will suspect all unknown persons of being treacherous. If you elect to go this route you must have control over your dog by having him tied. Many dogs will start to become aggressive toward all strangers after this training. You should take some time to think about this before you open up that can of worms.

To poison proof your dog not to eat anything that he finds outside of his dog dish, I will suggest two options. First is the e-collar. Second is the fence charger. The downside to the e-collar is you have to have your eye on the dog at all times. When you put out the meat you might have to wait hours before he discovers it. The first time he's shocked might not be enough and it might be days before he tries it again. That will usually occur when you've changed meats and locations. The second option is much more practical and therefore preferable.

Many hardware and pet stores will sell a pet fence charger with a continuous signal. That's unlike a fence charger for cattle, which is hotter and has a pulsating signal. These pet units are designed for keeping dogs out of the garden and flower beds. They are perfectly safe and won't harm the dog. I have been using this type of unit for years whenever I poison proof dogs.

When starting this program you will need to drive a steel or copper rod into a damp area for the ground post to be effective. Then you can hook up the ground cable from the charger. Use a hose clamp for a tight connection when attaching it to the post. The charger to function properly must have a good ground. Use however many yards of very light insulated copper wire that will go from the charger to anywhere in your yard. Once it's all set up, strip one end of the wire back about six inches. That's the part that will be wrapped around the meat offering.

It's important to wear clean gloves when you wrap the wire around the meat, or have someone else do it for you, otherwise the dog will detect your scent. Lock the dog up before you do this so he's unable to see what you're

doing, or he will eventually relate it to you. That's the wrong message. He's learned anything with your scent on it is good to eat. We are teaching him that anything that doesn't have your scent on it is dangerous.

Try to hide the cable back at least six feet from the meat. Put a piece of rubber or wood under it, so that it doesn't ground, otherwise it will make a crackling or buzzing sound. Cut the piece of rubber or wood just a little bigger than the piece of meat. He will try to eat the meat when he discovers it, but will drop it quicker than he picked it up. After a dog has been shocked by picking up the offering he will begin to notice the piece of meat on a large piece of rubber, or wood. He will also learn to be suspicious of the cable if it's not hidden. You will see the dog give that place a wide berth after he's been shocked by the meat offering.

When you set this up again after his first introduction to the electric treat, put different meats set in other places throughout the yard. By doing this the dog begins to realize whatever he finds in the yard is hot and he won't touch it. You should have a refresher course in six months and that's probably the last time you will have to do it. This program will only be effective if you always feed your dog in the same place and don't throw treats on the ground for him. Feed him either directly from your hand, or put the food in his dog dish, and that dish should always be in the same place.

The majority of people reading this narrative are hunters. As hunters, we need to be aware that in the fields where we hunt, there might be danger lurking in the form of poison which was put there for predator management.

Recently a poison called M44 which is a cyanide spray has been introduced in some states and planted in fields by governmental agencies to help with predator control. *This poison represents a serious threat to hunting dog's.* It has a stake for driving into the ground with a capsule attached to the end of it, and that capsule is smeared with scented bait. When a coyote, fox or your hunting dog pulls on the bait, a deadly spray containing sodium cyanide is emitted inside the animal's mouth. Death is almost instantaneous. It's a device that resembles a small sprinkler pipe sticking out of the ground.

By having an acquaintance disguise different types of meat he deposits in the field, you can train your dog not to eat anything he encounters. This is done so your scent is nowhere near the bait. You will need to know the exact location of each meat drop in order to act instantly. To do this the dog will need to be connected to the e-collar, and you will use it on maximum stimulation. This exercise needs to leave an indelible impression upon the dog, one he never forgets. When you see the dog go to any of the marked meats your ally has dropped, he's nicked *immediately* upon smelling it. You say nothing. This is very important! Ignore the dog and keep moving away from that site. Two occasions of doing this in different areas, he will avoid any strange items that he finds in the field no matter how good they smell. He's now learned anything without your scent on it is dangerous no matter where it's located.

That's why poison proofing your dog and disguising the meat offering with various types of designs, is essential in keeping your dog safe and away from the harmful things he will encounter while hunting. Obviously this takes a little more time, but the pain of losing your hunting dog to poison makes the extra effort worthwhile. Preparing for unforeseen events will keep your dog healthy at home and in the field.

Snake proofing: Every year many hunting dogs are struck by venomous snakes, and some of those bites prove fatal. This is a problem in many areas of the country. To teach your dog to avoid all snakes he needs to understand they are harmful. This is best done with a captured snake that's put inside a wire cage so the dog can plainly see as well as smell it. It should be done in an area with the same type of terrain you normally hunt. When it's done in the back yard the dog learns to avoid snakes in the yard, but not necessarily in the field. Your scent shouldn't be on the cage or in the immediate vicinity of the snake. This precludes you from setting it up yourself. Recall the poison proofing story where a stranger plants the meat? You can build the cage and capture the snake, but have another person actually plant it in the field. It should be dropped in an area where you would normally find a venomous snake, like near a bush or close to a rock pile.

This lesson will be taught by using the e-collar, and there again the transmitter should be set on maximum stimulation. It needs to leave a harsh message the dog understands. The message is; anytime he confronts a snake

it will hurt him. He has learned it's not safe to eat anything without your scent on it that he encounters at home, or in the field. Now he needs to learn a snake also falls into the same criterion, not necessarily to eat, but to maintain a safe distance from it.

When taking your dog to the field, don't try to encourage him to get close to the snake. If on your first walk by the cage the dog doesn't see or smell it, circle around and come back as many times as necessary until *he finds the snake. It's important that he sees or smells the snake.* You don't want him thinking the cage bit him. When he approaches the snake and smells it, *nick* him on the highest setting on the transmitter, say nothing and leave the immediate area rapidly, while showing fear. In this manner he thinks the snake bit him, and he identifies it as something harmful that he needs to avoid. By you showing fear and leaving hastily, he realizes that if the boss is scared of snakes there must be a reason for it. This avoidance training is usually needed only one time, and if it was done right the first time you probably won't need to repeat it.

Knowing that all dogs have different temperaments, there are a few hunting dogs which will try to kill any animal they encounter in the field. If you are the owner of a dog with such a disposition, be sure that you have a repeat lesson another time and in another place.

Porcupines: In many parts of the world, hunters and their dogs often encounter porcupines while afield. Many of these encounters lead to grief, both for the dog and his owner. While porcupines are not dangerous to humans they can certainly cause pain and suffering for an animal, making for lost hunting time and a costly trip to the veterinarian.

The same e-collar technique that was used in snake proofing may also be used to break a dog from trying to kill porcupines. Be aware, however, that in some dogs, ones with a strong killer instinct, it will make matters worse. When that type of dog is hit with a high level of stimulation, he thinks the porcupine is causing the pain and will attack it with more ferocity. Obviously this would be detrimental to the dog and the owner. That will be your decision as whether to nick him or not during a porcupine encounter.

Only you know your dog's temperament. It's not productive hunting with a dog that's always looking for porcupines instead of birds. These types of dogs usually get worse after every porcupine confrontation.

The only option I can offer here is, when hunting with this type of dog carry what I call a quill stick. A quill stick is a one inch diameter wooden dowel five-six inches long that has one eighth inch hole drilled through both ends. Into one hole a nylon cord about sixteen inches long is threaded through and knotted, while the other end is left free. After a hunting dog has a porcupine encounter the dowel is inserted into his mouth. The loose end of the cord is threaded through the dog's collar and back through the other hole, tied and secured. Now you have a dog that can't bite you as you go about the task of removing the quills. That quill stick should always be in your medicine kit.

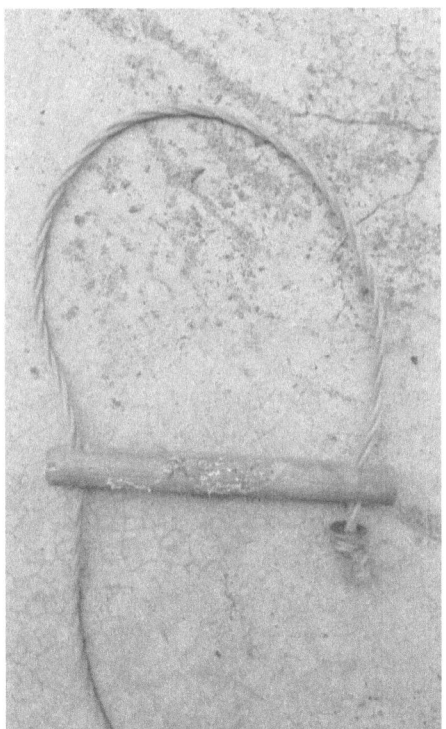

A well-used "quill stick"

Chapter X
Conditioning the Hunting Dog

Columbia Basin Herald photo

Building muscle and endurance: There are many ways to condition a dog you are trying to prepare for the hunting season. I will offer a variety of techniques and you should choose one which suits you and your situation. First you need a well-made harness with three D-rings. The harness should have a D-ring on each side and one on the top. These rings enable you to hook the dog to something, so he's encouraged to pull. That could be anything from a four-wheeler, a horse, pickup or chains. These harnesses can be purchased at any gun dog supply store.

The vast majorities of pointing dog owners who own all-terrain vehicles have made telescoping poles front and back on which to hook their dogs.

The dogs are then put in harness and worked for thirty minutes to an hour or more at slow speed on a gravel road. This not only builds muscle, increases endurance, but also toughens the dog's feet.

This can also be done on the back of a pickup truck, as long as the dog is visible in your side mirrors, but never on the front of a vehicle. A four-wheeler accidently running over the dog probably won't cause any permanent damage. Running over him with a truck is another matter.

By nature a dog wants to be ahead of you, and they exhibit this by pulling on the leash or harness. An effective means of conditioning a dog is by having him pull against a certain amount of weight. It increases the heart's ability to pump blood and to deliver more oxygen to the lungs and muscles. This in turn enables him to build muscle and to increase stamina and is one productive means of getting a dog ready for hunting season. I realize not everyone owns a horse or a four-wheeler, or has a place to use one or the other, so the following is an explanation of alternative methods.

Having a place to walk your dog, preferably on a gravel road, is all you will need. Go to a rocky field and walk him there if no gravel road is available. Don't walk him on cement or a hot asphalt road while he's pulling as he will surely slip his pads, and then you will have a footsore dog. Your dog doesn't need to run to build his endurance. He can walk beside you while pulling chains and the walking will benefit you both in preparing for the hunting season. For those readers who think a dog can't pull much weight, please read the following.

Dogs can pull an incredible amount of weight, as demonstrated by this next story which some of you may doubt. I was invited to an event to watch Pitbull's compete in a pulling contest. While there, they hooked up a well-muscled male with an elaborately padded harness, and secured him with a long rope. That rope in turn was fastened to the front bumper of a Volkswagen van. The van was parked on a concrete basketball court while the dog was in a grass field some distance away. The owner of the dog then asked some of the spectators to get inside the van. There were nine people inside that van, including me, and that dog pulled us across the court.

How much weight was involved? The van weighed well over a ton according to the statistics and the people weighed approximately fifteen

hundred pounds. A total of almost four thousand pounds or approximately eighteen hundred kilos would be a reasonable estimate. The Pitbull weighed somewhere between eighty and eighty five pounds or thirty seven kilos. He scratched and heaved, but once the van was rolling it was no problem for the dog to keep it moving. That dog pulled almost fifty times his weight. Our hunting dogs aren't Pitbull's, but all breeds of dogs are capable of pulling a certain amount of weight.

Now let's get back to discussing how much weight and how long those chains should be when hooked to the harness. Obviously you will use lighter chains if you have a smaller hunting dog, such as a Brittany or small English setter. A forty or fifty pound dog can easily pull twenty to thirty pounds, or more of chain. The idea is not necessarily having the dog pull a lot of weight, its having him pull the weight long enough to get into top physical condition.

My recommendation is to make two chains for a total weight of around thirty to forty pounds and that way you can use one or both. You will want a chain with heavy links so it doesn't have to be very long to get to the desired weight. A heavy anchor chain that's twenty four to thirty inches long and weighs between fifteen and twenty pounds is what you are looking for. Two of those will be needed. You can also use heavy rubber coated cable if no chains are available. The downside of using cable is the length they have to be in order to get to the desired weight.

Ch. Desert Gambler

Use a three quarter inch diameter cotton rope. Cotton is always a better choice if it's available. A cotton rope is not as abrasive as nylon on the dog's back legs. Connect a swivel snap to one end of the rope and the chain to the other. You want the rope to be long enough so all of the chain is dragging on the ground when the dog is moving, but make it no longer than necessary. The longer the rope or chain is will increase the dogs chances of getting hung up if you decide to work him in a field. Start with fifteen-thirty minutes of chain pulling on a gravel road and then go to a field if possible. This will stimulate the dog's interest, and you will be conditioning him at the same time. It's like us jogging in a different area. It becomes easier and more interesting by virtue of the new scenery. Plan your route carefully so that you finish at your starting point. That way you won't end up carrying the chains when your dog tires. When the dog begins to show signs of fatigue and his tongue is hanging out, it's time to quit. Be sure to carry a bottle of water and a small vial of a sugar additive like Karo syrup with you. This water will refresh your dog and the syrup will keep him from running low on blood glucose (hypoglycemia). Slowly build him up in increments of pulling from fifteen-thirty minutes until he's pulling an hour to an hour and a half.

Start the dog by using only one chain and that's hooked to the middle D-ring on his harness. The harness will slip to the side as he's pulling, but it shouldn't be too much of an annoyance. Connect both chains after working him a week with only one. He will start getting in condition that much quicker. Any time the dog balks on pulling the chains, connect a lead to his collar and pull him along with you. After a short time he will be happy to accompany you as he begins to enjoy the walks and the field work.

Hardening the dog's pads: You should condition your dog's feet prior to the hunting season, if not, your hunting trip may come to an abrupt halt when the dog slips his pads and becomes sore-footed. A sore-footed dog is usually out of action for three-four days or more. Hunting the dog on rocky terrain, such as what's found in the Chukar hills, before his pads are hardened can destroy them. You will never see a foot sore coyote, due to their feet being conditioned from the moment they begin to walk.

As mentioned before, the best thing to toughen your dog's pads in my opinion is gravel. There's nothing I'm aware of that creates tougher pads than roading the dog on a gravel road. By him walking on gravel, while pulling weight, the probability of losing pads won't be a factor during your hunting trip. For those of you, who haven't the desire or the time to do this, please continue reading!

Boots: To make a cheap pair of boots you will need a large bicycle inner tube. The tube has to have a circumference large enough to fit snugly over the dog's foot, however, when the dog is standing, his toes need sufficient room to expand. Cut the tube into six or seven inch pieces depending on the size of your dog and cut a V shaped slit down each side about two and a half inches from the top. The reason for the V is so that when slipping it on the dog's foot; you will bend the front flap down and tape with electrical tape around both the front part of the leg and the back flap of the tube. Without cutting the tape return the bent over flap to the front of the leg and continue taping around both flaps. These boots will hold for hours in rough terrain and save you from having to buy an expensive pair of custom dog boots. These homemade boots were used by me on numerous dogs while hunting chukars in the hills of eastern Washington. I've never had a dog blow their pads or the boots to come off if they were properly attached. These boots are very durable and can be used on various dogs for an extended period of time.

Eyes: After a day in the field, oftentimes we will find that the dog is squinting or scratching his eyes by using a front paw. Possibly the reason for this is he has weed and/or grass seeds caught in the pocket that's between the eyeball and the lower eyelid. Put the dog on an elevated platform and have your hunting buddy hold the dogs head while you do the necessary procedures. From your medicine kit take a Q-tip, insert it into that pocket and swipe it across while slowly spinning it. This will pick up any seeds or rubbish that's accumulated inside the pocket. Then use a saline solution and squirt it inside the eye to give it a good rinse. Be careful you don't touch the eyeball to avoid scratching it. That rinse will alleviate any discomfort he's feeling due to irritation from the debris. I've also used warm water to rinse the eyes on occasion, and there were no detrimental effects. After rinsing, put in an eye lubricant so the dog will be comfortable and will cease scratching, thereby possibly causing damage to the eye.

Food: Feeding a working dog calls for more protein and fat and a higher quality of dog food. A dog lying around the house taking up space doesn't need that high of protein or fat. A protein content of thirty percent or more and a fat content of twenty percent plus, should be fed to an active hunting dog. Dogs that are hunted hard all day should be fed twice daily. Feed a small ration two to three hours before going to the field and feed his normal ration upon arriving home. Consult your veterinarian for his opinion.

When hunting hard all day, a person should always carry a tube of something like Nutra-Cal, and should give the dog a spoonful every two hours or so. Products like this supply sugars, minerals, proteins, carbohydrates and vitamins to keep the dog firing on all eight cylinders throughout the day. The old cliché, you are what you eat applies to your hunting dog. He's an athlete and needs to be fed like one.

A recommendation: When *training* a dog, feed him immediately after the session. I believe this helps the dog to better retain what was just learned. This has been my observation after years of training countless dogs.

Chapter XI
Training Timid Dogs

Molly: An English pointer bitch was bred to be a falconer's dog. She was whelped from a litter that both sire and dam belonged to other aficionados of the sport of falconry. Kept in a kennel where the only human contact was at feeding and cleaning time, she was excessively timid and completely lacked self-assurance.

Dogs that are closed in a kennel for long periods usually become very apprehensive when exposed to the world outside of their realm. Often they are as brave as a lion inside their domain, but a nervous wreck when taken out of it. These dogs are much harder to work with than a dog that's been continually handled.

I was brought into the picture when Molly was nine months old. My ranch and kennel having been sold, I lacked the facilities to train dogs. Much like the old-time doctors, house calls were made, so in consequence Molly was trained at the owner's ranch. I will refer to him as Snake, due to his many friends calling him by that name.

Molly was very suspicious and wanted nothing to do with me for the first couple of weeks. Recognizing her as a problem dog her food intake was immediately reduced. By offering her small pieces of hot dogs she was slowly convinced I wasn't the devil incarnate. At that point I was able to pet her and attach a check cord. I also began to teach her the hot dog on the nose trick.

Exceedingly timid dogs are very difficult to work with as stated before. Sometimes, it's a genetic factor and not from human abuse. In Molly's case the problem was not genetic or from abuse, it was from being isolated. The professionals call this kennel shy. This particular bitch had spent too much time in the kennel and not enough time being socialized. Many professionals will tell you to get rid of that type of dog, due to it not being worth the effort to train them. They will tell you that you're better off starting with a new prospect. I strongly disagree with this perception, as a result of having successfully trained many timid dogs, and more than a few that were suffering from extreme panphobia, (fear of everything).

I'm going to explain how to make this kind of timid dog bomb proof. If you want to succeed, follow the examples given and the recommendations outlined. Don't stop due to feeling sympathy for the dog. It's very difficult to live with a timid or shy dog. You can't catch him when you need too, and you can't take him anywhere. He doesn't want to ride in the car, is a nervous wreck around people, and overall a pitiful specimen. Your friends will think you've mistreated the animal and that's why he's like he is. There's not much difference between this type of dog and a coyote; both are difficult to train, due to being frightened of anything new or different. If you own "or" are training a dog such as this and want to rehabilitate him, then tag along on this journey. By following the examples cited below you will learn how to reprogram these types of animals.

Molly was really frightened of me when I first started handling her. She was hooked to a check cord and we spent a lot of time just walking around outside on a gravel driveway. The first few training days she was becoming accustomed to me by hearing my voice, and learning my smell. She was always worked on a cord, for the reason that she wasn't trusted not to run away. I would call "Molly," pause "Come Here "and pull her to me, give her a piece of hotdog and then start heeling her, but with no pressure. When I stopped she was told "Whoa." When starting again I would tell her "Heel." The bitch had no concept as to what either of those commands meant. I only wanted to familiarize her with the words. At that point I didn't want the dog to associate me with anything negative. A week of this and it was time to up the ante by introducing the noisemakers.

Gathering together some soda cans I put two marbles inside each one of them. The marbles will just fit through the drinking hole by using a little force. I then punched a small hole through the rim of the can corresponding to that drinking hole, and attached a cold shut with a swivel snap on the end. If you decide you want to follow this program make a few extras of

these noisemakers. They will get banged around and eventually fall apart. For a dog that wants to chew, use a heavier can, something on the order of a condensed milk can.

I hooked one can to Molly's collar and the other one to her waist by using a light chain. A cord will get chewed, so you will need to use a chain. I then left the kennel. When you attach noisemakers to your timid dog you must leave the area immediately so the upcoming ordeal is not associated with you.

Molly went crazy and was bouncing off the walls, but after determining she couldn't get rid of those noisemakers, she sulked in a corner. It took three days before she learned it was just noise and it wasn't going to hurt her. She wouldn't eat those first three days, but started eating on the fourth, although gingerly, as the can on her neck would bang the metal food pan.

I took her out of the kennel after three days and walked her around the driveway, still attached to the noise makers. She wasn't too happy about the situation, but was beginning to accept it. Reluctantly Molly would take a piece of hot dog from my hand. That meant that not only was she very hungry, but she was also beginning to trust me.

A week later we began the obedience training. I put the "Whoa Strap" on her and started to tighten it around her waist, meanwhile putting emphasis on the word. I began to enforce the "Heel" and "Come Here" commands as well. She was handling the pressure, and I was happy with how well she was responding. Now we are about two weeks into the obedience training without having the cans attached. She was accepting the strap, was "Heeling" and "Coming" when called. All of this was done while Molly was still connected to a check cord. When she went back into her kennel for the night, the noise makers were reattached.

This was the time to introduce her to birds and gunfire. Her owner is a gun hunter as well as hunting with falcons. He also had a large supply of homing pigeons that were used for falconry training. Molly commenced chasing the birds thrown by hand in hopes of catching one. That began the shooting of .22 blanks while she was actively pursuing the bird. The gun noise had no effect at all. Molly was starting to gain more self-confidence and the trust was building between us. The bitch began to realize she wasn't going to be killed and eaten for lunch.

Molly began connecting me with all the good things happening. Now that she was gaining confidence, I began planting pigeons, letting her point and then chase them. I was starting too really like this young dog.

To get to the gravel driveway where she was receiving her obedience work, we had to go through Snakes workshop. This was always a hassle as she was apprehensive about going into that building. The different machines in the shop frightened her. To combat this she was taught to hunt dead while looking for pieces of hot dog and beef fat that were left scattered around on the floor. This helped her considerably. Molly started thinking about where she would find the next tidbit and forgot some of her fears about that machinery. She was also acquiring a valuable skill by looking for a treat and in the process was learning how to hunt dead. Finding those treats would eventually lead her to hunting for a dead bird in the field.

Learning to jump into the back of a four-wheeler was also a necessary part of her education, as she would occasionally be hunted from it. Molly would come through the shop door and there was the four-wheeler parked outside with a hot dog in the bed. By now, after about four weeks she was progressing smoothly and was starting to become relaxed about new things, until one morning she was confronted with the most ghastly and gruesome object one could ever imagine.

Now comes the amusing part of this story and it's worth mentioning by virtue of the shock it entailed, and the mental adjustments that were applied to get her thinking back on the right track.

Snake had killed a mallard duck with his falcon the evening before and had put the duck in a small cardboard box on the ground outside of the shop door. He had taken the duck out to clean it, but the box still had a lot of dried blood and feathers inside. When Molly came charging through the shop door on her way to the four-wheeler, she espied that box and smelled the duck's blood at the same time. She absolutely freaked out, ran back inside the shop and hid trembling in a corner. I went inside, hooked her to a check cord and literally had to drag her out through the door. She kept as far away from that bloody box as she possibly could. To this day it's difficult for me to understand why it scared her so badly, but this is where the story starts to become interesting.

To fully appreciate the humor of this event you have to visualize Snake's gravel driveway. It's rectangular in shape and about twenty five yards wide by fifty yards long. Small trees, bushes and grasses are planted inside the rectangle.

There was only one choice left to me after seeing Molly come unhinged over that box. My job was to cure this bitch of all of her unfounded fears, and train her to become a productive hunting dog. I started with that demonized box by tying it to a ten foot light cord and connecting it to her collar along with a short lead. Then we started walking down the driveway with the box dragging along behind. The moment she realized that horrible thing was chasing her, all hell broke loose. I dropped the lead and she took off down the driveway scattering gravel with every bound. That box was hot after her and for every jump she made, the box would bounce three feet in the air. I can't ever remember seeing a pointing dog run that fast. She made two loops around the driveway and one pass through the vegetation. I was able to intercept her before she made the fourth pass.

The box had fallen apart on the third go-round. Molly was frothing at the mouth, her eyes were as wide as pie plates and she was completely frightened out of her wits. Hooking the check cord to her, we started walking around the driveway. That had a somewhat calming effect. I did not try to console her because it would have sent the wrong message and defeated what I was trying to accomplish.

Snake was laughing so hard with that infectious laugh of his, and it soon became contagious. It began to affect me, and soon we were both laughing. I'm sure that laugh fest went on for at least ten minutes. It was and still is one of the funniest things I've ever witnessed while training dogs. As I'm writing this story I have a smile on my face.

I wasn't worried about the outcome from all of this in that I knew she would soon be adjusted mentally. After the initial excitement died down, Snake started to worry that the dog was ruined. I told him this wasn't my first rodeo. He calmed down and came to the realization he would have to trust me, just like Molly would have to do the same.

Gathering up what was left of the box; I taped it back together and put that horrible thing along with six other boxes in her kennel. Her food was put inside the duck box. If I remember correctly it was four days before she would stick her nose inside that box to eat. When taking her out of the kennel to work, she was given a vitamin along with her hot dogs and a little beef fat, so she wouldn't get sick. She lost a few pounds of weight during this process, but once she became adjusted to all the chicanery, it was gained back rapidly.

All the boxes that could be found were put in her kennel. It was really humorous watching her navigate around them. If she touched one by accident and it moved, she would jump two feet in the air. The neighbors wanting to help contributed several boxes after hearing the story. When Molly was finished working for the day she was tied outside and boxes were kicked all around her. Obviously this really disturbed her at first, but within a week she was becoming adjusted to it. Once she understood that the box wasn't going to eat her, a pigeon was planted underneath it. I would lead her toward the box and "Whoa" her about fifteen feet away. Then I kicked the box over to let her chase the pigeon as it was making its bid for freedom. While she was chasing, the blank gun was fired. I then went from the blank gun to the shotgun and killed a handful of pigeons for her. Within two weeks the box meant something good, so the box therapy was discontinued and the pigeons were planted in the customary manner. We then advanced to working on bob-white quail and those birds lit the fire in her furnace.

She was now turning into a bold confident dog. If she saw something new or unusual, she might give it a hard look, but it didn't cause any undue concern. By this time she had complete confidence in me. She realized I meant no harm, and I was the source of good things. As said before, a dog works primarily for their stomach, and when they are hungry you can do anything with them by offering treats. I was able to finish Molly into a broke gun dog as well as stand for the falcon kill. It was done in two different segments of two months in the fall, and two months again in the spring. I did it in that manner due to her age, timidity and immaturity.

By following the steps that were outlined in this story, from the cans to the boxes, and various noise makers with the final result of killing birds over your dog, you will be successful in your training. Schooling fearful dog's is all about taking away that skittishness, replacing it with self-confidence and them learning to have trust in you. When your dog trusts you great things can be accomplished. If you tell a four "year" old child that his grandpa is really Superman, he will believe you. That's trust! A parent has instilled that trust over a period of time, and the child has never had any reason to doubt. That's the kind of confidence your dog needs to have in you.

Boxes or any other type of noise makers are only *tools* that can help animals recover from their fears and become productive hunting dogs. It could be a cow bell, a bucket, or anything that frightens the animal. It isn't important what training aid's you use to accomplish this; it only matters that you do it. When someone is scared of heights, the only way for them to conquer that fear is to face it head on. It's the same thing with an animal.

People tend to freeze like a deer caught in the headlights when faced with a training dilemma. Usually it's from a lack of self-confidence that they can actually fix the problem, or from a dearth of experience and information on how to accomplish it. You now have that information, but the confidence issue is yours to resolve. The ball's in your court!

Again my point in telling you these stories of overly shy and sometimes mentally unstable dogs, is to make you realize that any animal can be restored, no matter how difficult it appears to be. Go the extra mile, and you will succeed. The methods that were used in the rehabilitation of these problem dogs will work on any breed of dog no matter how severe the issue is. The biggest factors are *trust and confidence*. The dog gains self-confidence and learns to trust you. You only need the confidence in yourself that you can actually accomplish this transformation. "You can!"

Tricks and Timing; how both pertain to timid and problem dogs: I have been debating with myself about incorporating this section into the book. I've been advised not to add it, but my feeling is this: A goodly portion of this narrative deals with timid and problem dogs and how to rehabilitate them, so I feel it must be included.

Tricks as mentioned before are only *tools* to help you get inside the dog's head to decipher just what's going on in there. These tools will help you bring a fearful dysfunctional dog back from the abyss, and aid him into becoming a functional hunting dog.

I've listened to criticism over the years about me misusing my time teaching tricks when they were not necessary. The criticizers say that teaching them is a waste of time and not necessary for a hunting or field trial dog. They say they will never be used in the field, so why bother? They're right about that, but be that as it may, the animal benefits and clients are always thrilled when their dogs have learned a few tricks. The reason is they just can't wait to show him off to their friends.

Using the theory that it's not practical to teach unnecessary things, why send your son to the university when it's not necessary? He can be a functional adult without going to college, but of course he would benefit from higher education. The same can be said for an animal. Teaching a timid or problem dog a trick will allow you to open a trap door that's been tightly closed and hasn't been pried open by another person. I'm talking about trust as related to a dog. *Problem dogs are just that. They're problems*! They have no confidence in humans, no trust in you specifically, and are skeptical about any training procedures. The longer this apprehension is ingrained in the dog the more difficult it is to remove.

The reason that I started teaching tricks to dogs was for my own amusement. Most of those were taught during television commercials after the day's training was finished. I would bring a dog into the house and start

teaching a trick. Dogs were taught to pick up various denominations of coins, play dead, bark on command, roll over, answer the phone, plus many more. When teaching these it became apparent my pupils were excited to learn more and their attention span had increased considerably. It's not about the tricks per say, it's about opening the dog's mind to accepting new things. In the process old wounds are healed and attitudes improve.

When deciding to try these tricks on timid and/or problem dogs and on the ones that were mentally unstable, the response was rapid and their learning was accelerated. I started having successes with the so called "incurables". Dogs that were so insecure, and so scared of people, they were deemed irreparable by others. My success in restoring problem dogs to sound mental health is largely attributed to the confidence the dog learned to have in me, and tricks coupled with treats. Sounds like Halloween! This being the case I would suggest if you are training a difficult dog that you first start with teaching a few easy tricks, accompanied with treats, in order to gain the dog's trust. If the dog has no trust in you, advancing with him is out of the question. Simple tricks are easy to teach, and with the teaching of each new trick the dog's confidence in you and himself will grow. Soon you're able to teach anything.

When starting this type of training have two or three sliced up hot dogs available and a fanny pack attached to your waist. Hot dogs are one of the best treats as they are easily handled and they can be trickled out over a period of time. You may also use your shirt pocket for quick access. With either, you are able to give an immediate reward. This is very important as a dog's attention span rivals that of a young child. In other words, short! Before we start, let's talk about timing.

Timing: When training a dog timing is everything. You can't make a correction, or give a treat thirty seconds after the fact. In either case the dog wouldn't understand why he was receiving one or the other. We have learned when an infraction occurs a correction needs to be administered immediately. Also when a reward is warranted, it needs to be given as soon as the task has been completed. *This is especially true with problem dogs.*

It's a common practice after the hunt to give the dog bird heads and intestines when cleaning the birds. This is a good tradition, but it doesn't take the place of giving the dog a bird head immediately after the retrieve. One is recognized as a reward, while the other is identified only as food. These are examples, but by reading this I hope you understand what was talked about earlier; the dog's attention span is limited. Act immediately whether it's for a correction or a reward. Timing!

Let's start: You've seen a few times in this text about teaching a dog the hot dog on the nose trick. Hold the dog's muzzle, place the piece of hot dog on his nose, call various names until you call your dog's name and that's called with emphasis. Let go of his muzzle. He will soon learn to flip the hot dog in the air and catch it prior to the piece hitting the ground. He can learn this trick in two or three days.

Another simple trick is for the dog to jump on command through a ring like a Hula Hoop. Start with the ring standing up on the ground and entice the dog to walk through by holding a hot dog on the other side. When he walks through it, say "Jump "and instantly give him a reward. Gradually hold the ring higher until he will jump through it at any height.

To teach the dog to play dead; make him sit, and then pull his front legs out from under him while saying "Bang." Keep him in that prone position while stroking him and repeating the word. When he stops struggling, let him up and immediately give an edible reward. Repeat that five or six times each day. When he has the command mastered and will do it without assistance, it's time to start pointing your finger at him while saying "Bang." He will lay down immediately, for the reason that he already knows the command. Next, for the amusement of your friends you can pretend you're screwing a silencer on the end of your finger. When you point that finger at the dog he will play dead. If you've followed these instructions you won't need to say anything. He will have mastered the dead dog routine.

These simple tricks lead the dog to having confidence in you. He also learns to have confidence in himself due to being rewarded instantly for his compliance. This is why the teaching of tricks, coupled with a quick reward,

is so successful in repairing problems. They are a great way to gain the dogs trust!

In field training it's more difficult to give an instantaneous edible reward. As mentioned before the dog's attention span is short. The time that you have to make a correction, or give a reward is measured in a few seconds. When teaching a dog tricks you will notice his attention span has increased considerably and now he's focused entirely on you. He's working for his stomach and a kind word, and this makes him eager to learn. When the dog is focused on you it means he's beginning to trust you, but also is gaining self-confidence. Now you can advance with other training. Take this information to heart; it's effective.

Tar: For those persons contemplating selling a dog, read the following story. Sometimes there is a financial reward involved in teaching tricks to a dog as shown by the story of Tar the Labrador retriever. In early 1974 while getting ready to go to summer training camp in Canada, I saw some kids playing in the street with a young black Labrador retriever. A very nice looking dog, so I asked the children who his owner was? They said he belonged to a Mr. M---. I went to see Mr. M--- and asked him if the dog was registered, did he have the registration papers and would he sell him? The answer was yes to all three questions, so I purchased the dog, and rather cheaply as I recall. It was a bargain that just couldn't be turned down.

After committing to buying the dog, I began to wonder what I was going to do with a Labrador in the Great Sandhill's of Saskatchewan. There is no water closer than ten miles other than a dugout that's made for cattle to drink out of, and I had a full consignment of pointing dogs. Well I thought, after the day's work I might have enough time and energy left to train Tar on obedience, dry land blind retrieves, "Backs" and "Overs." That plan didn't work out so well. A lot of his training ended up being done in the dark and on Sundays, as weekdays and daylight hours were taken up with training the pointing dogs. However, the job did get done.

When the summer training season was about finished, Tar was turning into a super performer. Thinking that he should be taught a few tricks due to the fact that I might decide to sell him. He was brought into the house and taught a couple of tricks under Coleman Lantern light. My camp was in a remote area and had no electricity. I would call the dog to heel, throw a coin, give him a line with my leg and command him "Back." This was done on a linoleum floor, so it wasn't an easy task for him to pick up the coin. He would bite at it until it stuck somewhere in his mouth and then return to heel. I then opened his mouth and took out the coin. I remember while teaching this trick a few coins disappeared down his gullet, but he always gave me back my change the next day.

He had already been taught "Dead dog" by me shooting him with the blank pistol. The blank pistol has a plugged barrel and when fired it shoots the wad into a pointed piece of steel in front of the cylinders where it breaks into numerous pieces. All of those pieces come out the side of the pistol, not the front. He had also learned the dead dog routine by me just pointing a finger and saying "Bang." When the dog had retrieved the coin and I had taken it from him, I would step away saying; that was the worst retrieve that I ever saw, and for that reason I'm going to shoot you. I would fire the gun, or point the finger and he would fall over dead.

Fast forward to late November; I was at home in Washington and decided to put an ad in a Seattle newspaper putting Tar up for sale at a premium price. If I couldn't get my price, I would be happy to keep him. Only one phone call was received. The caller arrived at the kennel a few days later. Gathering up some pigeons, the prospective buyer, Tar and I all went to the lake. I put the dog through his whole command structure, from taking a line, to blind retrieves and "Overs" and "Backs." He was flawless. On the way back from the lake we stopped at a cornfield and the dog went to work finding a pheasant. Within a few minutes he flushed a rooster, which I shot and Tar retrieved the bird tenderly to hand. His work that day was exemplary. Tar had a great day, and I was excited about the quality of his work, but the man was acting bored with the whole proceeding.

When we arrived back at the kennel I invited this gentleman into the house for a cup of coffee, and while in the house I decided to show him the dead dog routine. Calling Tar to heel, we went through the whole repertoire from retrieving the coin, until he was shot and fell over dead. When the dog

hit the floor the man couldn't reach for his wallet fast enough. No negotiating, he happily paid the price. He was more impressed with the trick than with the important field work.

That taught me the importance of adding a trick to a dog that I would sell, if the price was right. This man paid a premium price for the dog, not by virtue of his great field work, but for a trick that could be shown to family and friends. Tar was a well-trained animal, but the man could have bought any well trained Lab for the price that he paid. The trick was the difference and I never forgot it.

L-R Robert Pettit (Pettit Kennels), Jaime Lopez (Paraiso Kennels), R.J. Marquart (Quicksilver Kennels), Ron Bader (Baron Kennels). 130 years of combined dog training experience

Chapter XII

Pigeons and Game Birds

Pigeons: Having a ready supply of pigeons is essential in starting the puppy. Pigeons are one of the most practical birds due to their cost and availability. Bob-white quail, pheasant or chukar, can be used to finish the dog. If you have access to wild birds, or a quail call back pen, that's a good thing, but I will hazard a guess that the majority of people who are reading this book live in a town or a city. I'm betting you haven't seen many wild game birds running around the shopping mall, and even if you have, people frown on you shooting them.

Photo by: Kevin Pettit

As stated many times before, you can't develop a bird dog without an ample supply of birds. If you are an urban dweller you will have limited areas in which to work your dog, but there are always means. You can train on a ditch bank, a railroad siding or in a vacant lot as long as there is sufficient cover to hide a bird. You will be able to work on obedience even if you live in an apartment. The field work can be done when you run your dog in the country on weekends.

Homing pigeons: The best breed of pigeon to use is the homing pigeon which is readily available in most towns and cities. You can go to a farmer's livestock market for cull birds or contact a homing pigeon fancier who races birds. He will sell you his culls for a reasonable price, as long as they are for dog training. I say this because the racer doesn't want them back. If he sells you old birds, you will have to keep them captive all of their lives, or kill them when you are training. It will upset the breeder or racer, to have the birds he sold you return to his loft, especially if they are dragging a leg or have a similar injury.

A good plan is to buy un-banded young birds. Those can usually be purchased in late spring or early summer, and be used as fly-back birds after they have been conditioned to return to your pen. You should reserve any old homers or common pigeons that trap into your loft for shooting over your dog. Pigeon breeders, who like most of us, will sometimes get busy with other projects and will wait too long to band a squab. The baby has to be banded before its ten days old or the foot grows too big and the permanent seamless band won't go over the toes. That bird then becomes worthless to the racer, as no record can be kept of its racing achievements. Birds that race have to be banded with a numbered seamless aluminum band, which stays on the bird's leg for the remainder of its life.

If you have a small building in the back yard or a tool shed you can convert into a ten by twelve foot loft; that's all you will need for eight-ten pairs of pigeons. Those birds will produce enough young for you to be able to train one or two dogs. You should have a separate fly pen for the youngsters after they are weaned so they can exercise. This separate pen will keep the adults focused on raising their young and not be distracted with juvenile birds already out of the nest. If you live in a populated area you will constantly have cull pigeons trapping into your loft. That's a good thing as those birds can be used for training.

The four fundamental factors to remember when raising pigeons successfully are a balanced diet, good quality grit, lack of moisture in your loft and no overcrowding. The last tip about overcrowding is the most important. I have propagated well over a quarter million pigeons for shoots, and obviously a lot was learned along the way. Take my advice about those four recommendations.

For those of you who are interested in raising your own pigeons for dog training, you can find the most authoritative pigeon book ever written called "The Pigeon," by Wendell Mitchell Levi in most libraries, or it can be ordered through the online retailer Amazon.

Bob-white quail: For quail you will need a larger area and one free of feral cats, coyotes and other predators as the havoc these animals wreck on a covey of quail can be devastating. Bob-whites are a covey bird and you should have at least twenty five and preferably more, as you are going to shoot some of them. You can start with a covey of twenty five in your callback pen and have fifty more in an enclosure, in another location. This will give you enough training birds for two or three dogs. A hunting dog owner that only has one dog obviously won't need that many. A reminder; killing birds is what makes a good bird dog. Notice that I said, "Good bird dog."

Any outdoor hunting magazine will have quail advertised and you can probably find a breeder that lives near you. Quail are also listed on-line by many breeders. Bob-whites are a great training bird by virtue of their availability and their costs. You can use them over and over again, as they will call back into your pen. To establish a covey of bob-white quail on your friend's farm or your own training area, it's essential you have fields with some natural vegetation. This will enable you to develop your hunting dog. Any type of cover will work, but a variety is always best.

BIRD DOG TRAINING & PROBLEM SOLVING

Coturnix or Pharaoh Quail are generally much cheaper than bob-whites, but they don't covey and are poor flyers, so it's easy for a dog to catch them. That makes these birds not suitable for training pointing dogs; nonetheless, they can be used for retrievers, or as a food reward for non-retrieving field trial dogs. I will clarify. Your dog points a Bob-white quail; you flush the bird and fire in the air. That quail will return to the callback pen and you've saved it to work on later. When the Bob-white is out of sight, walk out and bend over to simulate picking up a dead quail. Have in your hand a freshly killed Coturnix quail, and take that bird back to the dog. You can give the dog his reward by letting him eat the head or the whole bird. This system can be used for field trial dogs that are not called upon to retrieve.

One piece of advice! Don't try to house coturnix and bob-whites together, as one or the other will all be dead the following day. This has been my experience when I released a number of Coturnix into a pen full of Bob-whites. Not only were they all dead the following morning, they were partially eaten. The birds pecked the newly introduced birds to death. Game birds like most animals are territorial and normally won't permit another type to be penned with them.

Callback pen: In the past I've used old rusty cattle watering tanks, and made them into callback pens. These steel tanks were used due to the many predators from bobcats to coyotes populating my ranch. This was before I learned about a deterrent. The smell of human urine absolutely deters bobcats and coyotes from nosing around your quail pen, but it's not

Painting By Alcántara

effective for feral cats or skunks. Those will have to be dealt with in another manner. By distributing absorbent urine soaked rags around the outside perimeter of your callback pen, coyotes and bobcats won't be a factor. Every time you go to the quail pen the scent should be renewed. You can find plans online about how to construct a callback pen.

When first starting your quail operation, don't release any birds for the first few days. Let them form a strong bond inside the pen and when you do start the release, let out only three or four at a time. This way they will find their way back and in short order you will have a productive working callback pen. Try not to fly the birds out of the pen the first few times you release them. They should walk out, and as long as they're not frightened, it's easy for them to find their way back. By doing that every day for a couple of weeks, it's safe to chase eight or ten out of the pen and they will generally return before night fall. Leave the majority of the covey, or one single male inside to call the others back. The more quail you leave inside the pen, the better success you will have with the other birds returning. Males are better callers than females, so bear that in mind. Spring time is when you have to be cautious as the quail will start to form pairs outside of your pen, and when they start to nest outside they're almost impossible for dogs to find. They lose their scent as this is nature's way of protecting nesting birds.

Once discovering a Bob-white hen nesting in a small clump of grass, I went to the kennel for my best bird dog. Thinking now I'm going to prove or disprove this theory; I worked the dog around that nesting quail for five minutes. At times he almost stepped on her, but never gave any indication there was a bird there. He passed within six inches of her numerous times, and from all sides, but detected nothing.

Quail can be used either out of a callback pen, or they can be used individually. When utilizing quail individually, use a pink or orange plastic surveyors ribbon about one foot long. These ribbons can be purchased at any hardware store. This will help you find the bird if it flies into heavy cover. Attach this ribbon to one leg only. This colored streamer not only gives you better visibility, it also handicap's the quail's ability to run. When you are at your training area walk away from your vehicle and give the quail a toss. If you don't do this most likely the bird will end up underneath it.

BIRD DOG TRAINING & PROBLEM SOLVING

Quail identify the shape of your vehicle as a structure, and if they are able to get beneath it, they are difficult to remove due to their feeling they are in a safe place.

Usually quail that were pen raised are weak flyers, and a fifty to seventy five yard flight is about the most you can expect. After that first flight let the bird rest for five or ten minutes before you go with your dog to work him. You can hunt the dog in the opposite direction and then circle back around. The first time the dog works a quail have him hooked to a check cord. You won't go wrong when the dogs connected to a cord, but you can sure go wrong fast if he's not.

When a planted quail is flushed, the dog detects instantly that here's a bird he can catch. The bird after a short flight will pitch into some type of cover. When you work the same bird again, his next flight will be much shorter. If the dog commits an infraction, discipline him in the previous manner as you have done on pigeons. If this is his first experience with quail, don't get too forceful as he still has to learn about this new bird. After making any correction and the dog is stopped, you should kill the quail and give the head to him.

Painting by: Edgar Alcántara

Chukars: I have used chukars in callback situations, but with limited success. There were some rocky bluffs on the ranch, so it was decided to introduce a small covey of chukars there. I installed a dozen birds in an open crate where they could see in any direction. After two weeks of feeding and putting in water, the door was opened and they were turned loose. They weren't chased away and were free to move in their own time. Also there were watering jugs and feed stations scattered around those bluffs. A callback bird was left in an open box six feet above the crate.

When the birds were no longer coming back to the crate it was removed, although the callback bird remained in the same spot. A male was used and he would actively call early morning and late evening, but when I started working dogs on those birds, within two weeks they had disappeared. Whether the coyotes killed them or they just decided to leave the area, I never found out. It wasn't effective for the money invested or the time spent in setting it up.

If you are going to use chukars individually, the best means is to dizzy one and release it in some sort of cover. You accomplish this dizzying by using the same method that you used on pigeons. Planted chukars tend to run and are often difficult to flush. For a young dog a running bird increases his desire to try and catch it. Keep this in mind when using chukars, in that sometimes your advances in training can be undone in a single incident. I have found that by using pipe cleaners to shorten the bird's stride, they will flush as a result of not being able to run effectively. This system will be explained next in pheasants.

Pheasants: I encountered a lot of problems when trying to raise pheasants, as oftentimes the mortality rate was too high to justify the time and money spent. If you are entertaining the idea of raising game birds for your dog training, do your research before starting. You may find, however, that buying pheasant hens from a game farm after the egg-laying season is finished, to be more practical. The cost of an old hen pheasant is usually comparable to the price of a bob-white quail or chukar. Another feature is that the birds are all wearing blinders, or have had their top beaks trimmed to prevent cannibalism. If the bird's upper beak has been cut back; they will have to be shot over your dog. Birds such as these can't survive if they escape during a training session, and that's due to them not being able to pick up food from the ground. It's a simple procedure to clip the pin holding the blinders on the hens that are wearing them. Those hens will have a sporting chance at survival should they escape.

Planting pheasants is done in the same manner as pigeons. Dizzy the bird by swinging it in tight circles; put its head underneath a wing and lay the bird in the grass head side down. If you decide to use a pipe cleaner instead, you can just dizzy the bird and release it into some type of cover.

Pipe cleaners can be bought at any store that sells tobacco products. They are about six inches long and made of light gauge wire wrapped with soft-absorbent cotton like material. The pipe cleaner is attached to both legs of the bird. First attach to one leg and then the other with no more than an inch of clearance between them. This will allow the bird to stand up and slowly walk, but won't allow it to run. Planting the bird in this manner will result in a flush and not the bird running. If the bird does escape, pipe cleaners will break and allow the bird to run normally before the days over. They will also rust off of the legs of the bird after a short period of time.

Is this what I'm supposed to point?

Chapter XIII

Dog Stories

GHOST DOG

I was a young professional dog trainer in the mid-1970s living in Washington State and training out of a large boarding kennel. The owner of the kennel was letting me use twenty kennel runs, all the training equipment necessary, truck and horse trailer, with the horses included. My job as the trainer was to produce winners for him. He enjoyed big running English pointers. Apart from the owner's dogs, he encouraged me to train other people's dogs from the outside as an extra source of income.

These arrangements were very common in the Deep South where large plantation owners would hire private trainers to train and compete with their line of English pointers, and English setters. Some of the most famous trainers in field trial history were the products of these types of agreements.

One of those outside dogs that was accepted for training was owned by a young banker who lived in a small town nearby. The owner registered the dog as Peter Pumpkin Eater, named after a childhood fable. His call-name was Pete and he was put in my charge to train and develop into an American Field trial contender. These types of field trials were mostly conducted on horseback, although now there are quite a few walking stakes, both amateur and open, that are sanctioned by The American Field.

All the rage in those by-gone days was to own a puppy from the A Rambling Rebel line of English pointers, as they were some of the big winners of that era. Ch. A Rambling Rebel was the sire of Pete and was a consistent field trial winner of major circuit all-age championships. The Rebel line of pointers crossed with Ch. Oklahoma Flush bitches also produced many field trial winners. This was Petes breeding. These dogs had big motors, and were difficult to manage as they had a mind of their own. The majorities of them, however, were good bird dogs and blessed with a lot of pointing instinct. They were also famed for having plenty of run. That eagerness they possessed often led them to search the far horizons for game, and this trait frequently contributed to their getting lost.

The dogs that I worked which were similarly bred didn't have a whole lot of "come-back" in them. Or to put it in the vernacular of my Cajun friend, "Dem dere dawgs jes dun wanna comes bac." If you could get these dogs to work with you, they were the types of animals that could be molded into field trial winners.

Such was the breeding of Pete who acquired more fame as The Ghost Dog than as a field trial competitor. When the dog was put into my hands for training, he was around a year old.

When first starting to work with this young dog I soon began to realize he was, to put it mildly, a hell of handful. For him a normal cast was measured in miles not in yards. There was no end of difficulties early on with his training, due to his proclivity to just keep on running. Often his eagerness to find birds overruled any desire to handle. No electric collars and Global Positioning System tracking units were available in those long gone days. Training aids were a fast horse and a flushing whip.

My first impression of Pete was that he didn't care much for people, and wasn't very tractable in accepting training. He was a morose type of individual, and you really saw this trait come to the surface when things didn't go his way.

A day that sticks in mind was when the dog wasn't responding either to whistle, or voice. He had to be ridden down, and have a bit of on the spot training on how to "Come Here" when called. That ended with a negotiated agreement. The negotiating was done by me and the dog did the agreeing. Afterwards, I tried to get Pete's mind off of that correction by playing with him for a little while. We needed to be buddies again, but he wasn't buying what I was selling, and wanted nothing more to do with me. In those early days of my training career, enough experience had been acquired to realize that if a dog ever quit the trainer, his training wasn't going to be successful. It was obvious Pete had quit me.

After training that day, the dog was taken back to his kennel. While trying to feed him, he stayed outside in his run and wouldn't come inside, where I was waiting in his sleeping quarters with the food. About twenty minutes later I went to the tack room to get a rubber ball we had occasionally played fetch with. Going back inside the kennel and sitting down on the dog's bed, I encouraged him to play a game of fetch, but he wasn't interested. While I was gone looking for the ball, Pete had come inside and had eaten a mouthful of food.

It's now been forty plus years since this incident occurred, but I remember it as clearly as if it happened yesterday. The dog was sullen and was feeling resentful toward me. He wouldn't forgive me for the correction he had received in the field.

Knowing that this was a do "or" die situation, I made myself comfortable while sitting on his bed, and played ball with myself. Pete had no intention of coming through that door to be with me. The thought occurred to me that I would stay there as long as it took, even if we both had to starve in the

process. Inside that kennel trying to get a surly dog to respond to my overtures, tired and thirsty, as well as dirty from working dogs all day, was not my idea of fun. Although needing a shower and being very hungry, there was no thought of giving up until hell froze over. Fortunately it didn't take that long.

Taken from notes I kept about this incident, it was forty five minutes before Pete finally stuck his head inside the door and decided to forgive me. He was hungry, and the hunger coupled with the dog food sitting on the floor, were the contributing factors that finally brought him inside. That spectacle so many years ago taught me a lot about hunger and the use of food as a training aid. He was hungry, but couldn't eat without confronting the bogeyman plopped down on his bed. Reluctantly he finally stuck his head inside and I was able to pet him a little. He didn't want to play ball; he only wanted to eat. It was decided if he wanted to eat, he was going to have to take the food out of my hand. Finally he did, and he was fed all of it, piece by piece. At the time this was going on I was talking to myself, because sure as hell the dog wasn't listening. When it was realized that we were once again pals, I left for the night. Up to that point, this was one of the most difficult training dilemmas I had ever been faced with.

I appreciated the fact I would have to be very careful with Pete due to his temperament. It didn't leave me a whole lot of options on how to advance his training. He obviously wasn't responsive about accepting any type of correction, even if it was called for. I was at a loss about how to train a dog without some form of discipline. This was one of the turning points in my career in training timid and/or resentful dogs. It was also my introduction to using food as a training aid. It wasn't a new concept; I understood it well enough, but hadn't practiced it.

I decided to finish Pete steady to wing and shot in view of the fact he was pointing staunchly, and didn't have a whole lot of chase left in him. The owner knew enough about the dog's temperament to let me do it my own way. Normally I wouldn't break a dog when he's fourteen months old, as most aren't mature enough and lack the experience to be able to cope with the pressure. Having already given Pete basic obedience by this time, I anticipated I would have more control over him if he was broke. Immediately the breaking process was started, but it was done in a slow gentle manner. Retrieving was something that didn't concern me, as dogs competing in American Field trials at the time didn't have to retrieve; they only had to be steady to wing and shot.

By reading the previous statements you realize Pete wasn't a dog that would submit to a lot of pressure. He was bold in the field, but timid and fearful around people and didn't accept new things easily. In those days I hadn't educated myself with some of the techniques I now use with problem dogs. By taking it slow and easy and advancing one step at a time, by the age of sixteen months he was pretty well broke. He could also be caught when we were finished with a workout. Sometimes it involved a long ride, but when I was within shouting distance, he would come to me. When running Pete in a derby competition, I could ride to him when time was called, get off my horse and call the dog to me. This was a huge improvement and if memory serves, I believe he gained placements in a couple of derby stakes.

It was July, and it was time to start heading north to the Great Sandhills of Saskatchewan as my dog camp was located there. With two helpers, a load of dogs and four horses, plus all of the sundry equipment; I had everything necessary for a three-month sojourn to the prairies.

The Great Sandhills in southwestern Saskatchewan is a wonderful place to train dogs. There is an abundance of game of all species, such as whitetail deer, antelope, rabbit, fox, coyote, but unfortunately skunks and porcupines as well. It's an absolute mecca for sharp-tailed grouse. The sharp-tailed grouse when young is not as wary as the older wiser birds. This helps the trainer to develop the natural pointing instincts of a novice dog. As the season progresses the birds become craftier and often flush prematurely, making them more difficult for the dog to point. This works well for the dog, as he becomes more proficient in the art of handling these birds.

The Great Sandhills is an area made up of rolling hills and valleys dotted with chokecherry trees, wolfwillow bushes and many other types of vegetation. Some of the larger sand hills are barren without vegetation, and appear to be pushed up from underground. They form a spherical shaped

mound of pure khaki colored sand. Kids from the surrounding towns would occasionally come out to the hills to play and slide down those dunes.

Grass is also abundant for livestock, but there's a species of grass which presents a peril for dogs and that is Speargrass. That grass called Speargrass, unfortunately, is plentiful as well. This grass has barbs on the point of the seed with a two to three inch long tail. Late in July most of these seeds are dry and have fallen to the ground where they pose no danger to a dog. However, there is still a need to be vigilant, as there are always a few seeds remaining.

A dog that's running through the country with his mouth opening and closing will attract Speargrass seeds, which will stick to the saliva. It's mandatory when calling a dog in to give a drink of water that those seeds are removed from inside of the mouth. Luckily, most of the remaining seeds still have the tail attached and this makes their removal simple. Failure to do this can result in the dog swallowing the seed and it migrating throughout the body and possibly lodging in a vital organ. That could result in the death of a dog.

Pete was one of the dogs sent north for summer training. In his workouts he was doing a good job of pointing and handling the sharp-tail. I was able to keep him in contact with me, but it was always under duress. The feeling was there he would have been a lot happier being somewhere else running his own program. I didn't trust him not to bid me farewell, at the first opportunity. Pete was a true all- age dog and was a difficult dog to handle. Normally with a dog of this nature you can keep him working for you by killing a lot of birds. He will then start to become more subservient to the gun. During the training season in Canada, trainers are not allowed to kill game for their dogs as it would result in the forfeiture of their training license. Obviously that option was off the table.

For those folks who aren't familiar with what an all-age dog is, I will explain. A true all-age dog is the type that's very independent and will run to the limits in his quest to find game. A shooting dog is a wide hunting dog more in sync with whoever's handling him. All-age dogs were developed for horseback hunting where game was scarce and the terrain was open.

Sometimes it would be a half mile or more between bird contacts. Oftentimes an all-age dog will be lost on point, or get lost when he runs too wide and loses contact with his handler. Most of these dogs will find their way home, but not always. Pete happened to fall into the latter category.

In late August the Rocky Mountain Derby Classic is run near the town of Cardston, Alberta and is judged on all-age standards. This mean the dogs must run a wide searching race, but they don't necessarily have to show finished manners on birds. This is due to their age as they are still considered juveniles. I thought Pete stood a better than even chance of winning the derby stake, as he was finished on birds and always ran a wide sizzling race. This competition was run entirely on wild birds, the principal bird being the sharp-tailed grouse.

The field trial venue was located on the Blood Indian Reserve near the aforementioned town of Cardston, Alberta. The Blood Tribe (Kainai or First Nation) is a member of the Blackfoot Confederacy. The Blackfeet were named for the habit of dying their moccasins black. The Blood Tribe had a formidable reputation for protecting their lands and resources. The Lewis and Clark expedition (May 1804-September 1806) was forced to skirt the perimeter of these tribal areas which at the time extended well into Montana. Lewis made a mistake when he told some Blackfeet warriors that he would give guns to their enemies if those enemies would agree to a peace plan. Due to that, the Blackfeet became bitter foes of the Americans.

The town of Cardston itself was formed and settled in 1887 by members of The Church of Latter Day Saints who had traveled north from Utah Territory. The church members were being persecuted for their belief in plural marriages. In order to escape fines and jail terms they searched for sanctuary outside of the United States.

After making the four hour trip from my dog camp to Alberta, I arrived on the reserve and again saw my old friend Big Melvin. A book could be written about him as he was and still is a personality like none other. He could ride anything on four legs and proved that to the field trailers on numerous occasions. He measured about six feet six inches tall and was a very imposing man. As a First Nation person and a member of the Blood Tribe, he lived on the reserve and the point where we cast off the dogs was

practically on his front doorstep. To give you an idea of just how large this reserve is, it covers approximately five hundred and fifty seven square miles. It's one of the finest places in North America to show a wide running dog.

Starting time was usually eight a.m. and as I remember it Pete drew the second brace in the morning. In late August in southern Alberta, with summer ending and fall beginning, leaves are turning, the air is pure and crisp and it gives you the satisfactory feeling of just being alive. Competing with bird dogs which is my passion was just icing on the cake.

The first brace cast off directly in front of Melvin's house and on all the courses we ran you could see for miles. These were contiguous courses and after one brace was finished we would continue on with another pair of dogs. This required a dog truck which would carry the next two braces of four dogs, to meet us at a prearranged spot. Visible in the background were some parts of the Rocky Mountain range, and they were almost always covered with snow. Absolutely stunning!

The part of the Reserve that we were entrusted with for our field trials was mostly rolling prairie land with swales and coulees, some with water, and a range covered with a rich prairie grass. It's also dotted with wild rose bushes that produce a fruit called the rose hip. The red-orange rose hip berry is packed with vitamin C and is consumed by birds, deer and other prairie dwelling mammals. Saskatoon berry bushes are also prolific throughout the area. They produce an edible purple berry that's greatly valued by Native Americans. The tribal people have used this berry for hundreds of years to make a sweet soup, and it's also used for religious purposes. The seed is put back into the ground to feed Mother Earth for future generations.

This prairie grass is used to pasture cattle and horses, although you could ride for hours without seeing any domestic livestock. When you did see stock, it was usually a band of eight to ten semi-wild horses that had free access and could go anywhere they chose. There were few fences to hold these animals or hinder the field trailers who were on horseback.

The courses went on for many miles, and the field trailers never came close to the boundaries, when running their bird dogs. The distance any object could be seen, was only limited by the size of that particular object. A dog could be seen at tremendous distances.

When Pete was turned loose that day I didn't realize he was about to make bird dog history with one of the longest casts, if not in distance, then surely in time. It was measured in many months. The dogs opening cast lasted almost nine months, from the latter part of August until late May the following year. It went on through a bitter cold winter with six to twelve foot snow drifts and temperatures as low as minus 25° to minus 30° Fahrenheit.

How a domesticated shorthaired dog could survive and thrive for that length of time is still an unsolved enigma. He was thought to have sometimes slept in haystacks, but that was speculation as no one knew for sure. What he ate is anyone's guess, but all indications were, he survived by catching mice, birds and innumerable other small prey. If he ever stole food from any of the tribal dogs in the area, he was never caught in the act. Anything a coyote would eat, he had to have eaten. The miracle was, he never tried to tackle porcupines, which are prolific in the area. If that had happened he would have succumbed to infection and hunger.

When Pete made his first cast that day he was heading south, and I began getting nervous due to him not responding to my whistle. He's going to be difficult to finish I remember thinking, and I was right! He stayed to the front and was handling for about ten minutes and then faded into the distance. When he couldn't be shown to the judges after twenty more minutes, they counted him out.

I rode around for another hour watching and waiting for Pete to appear, but never caught a glimpse of him. Going back to camp I began preparing my other dogs for the competition. At that point a lost dog wasn't a reason for concern, because if he was heading home to Washington, he had a long trip ahead of him. Upon arriving back at field trial headquarters, a.k.a. Melvin's house, the dog still hadn't returned. I spread the news to all of the field trial people that he was missing and asked if they would watch out for him.

Field trailers on horseback generally carry extra water, check cord and a harness. If a lost dog is discovered, they will catch him and bring him back to camp. This is a courtesy everyone adheres too. Usually what will happen with a lost dog, is either he will report back to camp on his own, or will join

another brace that's running. With the whistles blowing and all of the shouting it attracts the errant canine's attention and he will be picked up by someone in the gallery that's not actively running a dog.

We had lunch and there was still no sign of Pete, but that wasn't too worrisome as there was a lot of daylight left. I continued running my dogs and rode every brace looking for him. When the trial ended around five p.m., I was starting to get a little worried, so after taking care of the dogs and horses, I saddled up again and went out to search for the dog. It's a real dilemma trying to find a dog in that wide open country. That is surely comparable to looking for the proverbial needle in a haystack.

Unbeknownst to me at the time, a friend of Evel Knievel (the famous motorcycle stunt man) was at the field trial that day having driven up from Montana hauling his dirt bike. After the trial was finished for the day and all the dogs were run, Mr. X-- decided to go out for a ride. What a great place to ride, few fences, no distractions and a variety of different types of terrain to test his riding skills.

This next anecdote was told to me by another friend of Knievel's, so I can't personally vouch for the veracity of it, but logic tells me it was true. The bike rider came across Pete and having heard about the lost dog he decided to have a go at trying to catch him by riding him down. From me writing this story you are able to determine his plan wasn't successful. After that incident Pete turned into a wild frightened animal.

When a dog is lost and has been running for hours they begin to run low on glucose and some become hypoglycemic. This affects their already limited powers of reason. Some dogs begin to get nervous with muscle tremors, incoordination and become agitated, while others show fatigue, appear lethargic, dazed and confused. When this advances beyond a certain point, they can have seizures and possibly die. From what information I was able to obtain at the time, I believe the dazed and confused part was Pete's state of mind when the biker discovered him.

The trial finished two days later and once again I made a horseback search, but to no avail. After speaking with Melvin and giving him the phone number of Pete's owner, he was asked to spread the word about the dog. I explained the dog also had a name tag attached to his collar with the owner's telephone number. I couldn't lose any more time searching for Pete; I had to get back to camp.

While competing at the trial my helpers were taking care of the animals back at dog camp. We didn't have cell phones in those days, so of course I was worried about how everything was progressing. My helpers weren't permitted to work the dogs in the field, but they had been trained to teach simple obedience and also how to condition the dogs using a motorless buggy.

On my way to camp, I stopped at a gas station to call Pete's owner and explain the whole story. I erringly told him that when the dog got hungry enough, he would put into someone's house on the reserve and they would contact him. I had no idea that call was nine months down the road. When arriving back at camp everything was in order, but I had to get busy as there was still another month of training with the other dogs. Pete out of necessity was put on the back burner.

After having a successful training season with no other major mishaps, it was time to head south and return the hunting dogs to their owners. Most of the field trial dogs would remain with me for the fall trials. This return journey was in late September. When leaving Saskatchewan I decided to swing through Alberta to see if there was an outside chance someone had captured Pete. Obviously that hadn't happened, so I continued on to Washington State.

Having finished with the fall trials and settling in for the winter, my thoughts would drift north now and then, and I would wonder if Pete could possibly still be alive. Around late November and early December I started hearing rumors about a brown and white dog the tribal members were calling the Ghost Dog. I had friends who lived in Lethbridge, Alberta and would speak with them occasionally. They would train dogs some weekends on the reserve, and were able to keep me updated on the Ghost Dog as he was now called. Examples of the stories received were; he was spotted north of a farmer's place, he still had on his orange collar, anyone who tried to approach him was not successful. He was completely wild and would run

away when he saw a vehicle, or a man on foot or horseback. Pete had become as wild as a coyote and as almost as wily.

The dog was gaining a modicum of fame in the surrounding area and a local pharmacist decided he would make it his hobby to try and catch the dog. He spent many weekends trying to make contact with the Ghost Dog, but to no avail.

In January after a fresh snowfall, a doctor from Lethbridge thought he would try tracking the dog by using a snowmobile, and then try to run him down. The doctor's plan didn't go too well. Late in the afternoon he picked up the dog's tracks and followed them. After coming across Pete he decided to run him down and try grabbing his collar. If he had been successful this story would never have been written and that would have been the end of the Ghost Dog saga, except for one little detail. The dog had already been through that ordeal with the man who had chased him on a motorcycle. He promptly turned on the threat which was for him the snowmobile, and promptly took a bite out of the seat. At that point discretion became the better part of valor, and the chase was abandoned.

Now any hope of capturing the Ghost Dog was put on hold, and as far as I know, was never tried again. If anyone thought the capture of this dog was going to be simple, they had learned there was more to this enterprise than just coaxing him with a pan of dog food.

The bitter cold of January and February on the reservation coupled with deep snowdrifts, and strong winds, made me give up any hope the dog would ever be found alive. The Ghost Dog was pretty much put out of my mind. When on occasion I did think about him, I just couldn't fathom how an English pointer with short hair and no survival skills could withstand that bitter winter. Even if by some remote chance he were caught, it didn't seem logical he could be useful in field trial competition, or as a hunting dog. He was as wild as a coyote and wanted nothing to do with humans. He ran in the coulees and other low areas and would never skylight himself, much as wolves and coyotes do.

In the months of March and April the deep snow was melting and the prairies were greening up with new life, so maybe it was natural that a young dog's sentiments turned to things other than survival. Those instincts would end the reign of one of the longest surviving domesticated dogs in one of the harshest environments in the history of bird dogs. In late April the Ghost Dog would occasionally be seen hanging around human habitations. As this was an unusual activity on his part, it was thought maybe the time was approaching when he would finally be caught.

The latter part of May I received a phone call from the owner stating that the dog had finally been captured! That news came as a definite shock to me even after hearing the numerous stories about him being alive. I just couldn't get my head around the fact he could survive that harsh winter. On my part it was always assumed he had perished.

This is the story I was told about his capture. The dog had entered into a barn where a bitch in season had been tied, and at one end of the building the door was closed. The farmer's young son was walking inside to feed the animals when he saw the Ghost Dog, and knowing the story about him, immediately closed the open door. When approaching the dog both were nervous, but the teenager told me personally, that once he laid his hand on him, he was as docile as any other domesticated dog. The young man walked to his pickup, Pete followed and when he opened the door the dog jumped onto the seat and was driven to an animal clinic. There he was given a complete physical. The following week he was shipped by air to Spokane, Washington where I received him in the cargo bay at the airport.

I was really curious about just what was coming back nine months after losing him, but I was apprehensive as well. Approaching the dog crate, I was talking to him and unbelievably Pete started wagging his tail when he heard my voice. When we were back at the kennel I gave him a thorough going over. There were quite a number of scars on the dog's head that appeared to be from fighting, along with a scar on one front leg. His heart beat was really slow indicating he was in superb condition, and after the vet had checked his stool, incredibly no parasites were found. The dog was thin, but not emaciated and appeared to be happy and content now that he was finally home.

Calling the owner, I asked him what he wanted do with the dog. He told me to give him to anyone who would want him as a pet. Before that

happened my curiosity had to be satisfied as to what Pete would do on a planted bird. What was expected I really can't say, but I surely didn't expect what did happen!

Going to the field I planted a pheasant, and then came back to the truck to get the dog. I had a check cord attached to him; with that cord I would have control. When he scented the bird, he slammed into a point and the thought occurred to me, Yeah! Right! You lived on birds, mice and who knows what else, and you expect me to believe you pointed them all?

I played the game with him by saying "Whoa." Flushing the bird, I killed it with one shot. Turning around, there was Pete still standing steady to wing, shot and the kill. I remember exactly what I said to him. I told him he was a lying s.o.b. I knew damn well he had chased and caught game or he wouldn't be there with me, he would be dead. That's pretty much what was expressed to him, but what was really said was riddled with expletives.

This was all so implausible for me to believe what I had just witnessed with my own eyes, but like the old saying goes, "seeing is believing!" His training was so ingrained that he hadn't forgotten any of it during the time he was running wild.

After that Pete was quick to adapt to civilized life, and seemed to be better adjusted mentally than before he got lost. He was eventually given to a friend who being an avid bird hunter was able to hunt the dog on foot. I never thought I would see that day! The same person told me that "Ol Pete," as he was now called, was an exceptional bird dog and lived in the house with him. I specifically asked my friend if the dog handled his game in the correct manner. He told me he had never had a dog as broke as "Ol Pete" was. The dog was completely attached to my friend, and when they went hunting he always wanted to keep his owner in sight. The last thing the dog wanted to do was get lost. I assume that nine months of running wild gave him a new perspective about handling and staying in touch.

I was later told that when Pete lived with my friend and his family, much of that time was spent in the house. When let outside to do his business, he would scratch at the door to be let in when he was finished. He lived a useful life with my friend and his family until he died at the age of eleven.

Bob Pettit, Saskatchewan Whirlwind, Col. W.G.A. Lambe
Columbia Basin Herald photo

THE REJECT

This story about The Reject was almost never written and if I had my way about accepting this dog as a gift, it wouldn't be written now.

Getting ready to go to Canada to train for the summer, and having a full consignment of dogs, I didn't want to accept any more. The day before leaving, a professional trainer friend came to visit and to wish me a successful summer training season, or at least that's what I thought. In reality he was on a secret mission to get rid of a one "year" old English pointer bitch that neither he, nor anyone one else wanted.

After pleasantries were exchanged he got down to the real reason for his visit. He showed me a heavily marked white and liver bitch which he assured me, was just the most wonderful prospect he had ever seen *"bla, bla, bla."* He had gotten her as a gift from someone else, and I could only speculate as to how many someone else's had given away this pitiful looking specimen prior to him getting her. The bitch was a sorry looking dog. She

was exceedingly thin, her coat was rough, and she was cow-hocked, barrel-chested, terribly under shot and fearful of everything, especially humans. At least she didn't have mange, distemper or parvovirus, so that was positive. The only thing good thing about her was her breeding. According to my friend, her pedigree had Ch. War Storm and Ch. Riggins White Knight within two generations. Later when I received her pedigree I saw that this was true. Riggins White Knight was the sensation of the early 1960s winning six major circuit championships including the National, and War Storm which was also a well-known major circuit winner. Both of those dogs were prolific producers of quality puppies. That was the only reason she was finally accepted, or at least that's what I told myself.

I argued for an hour while telling my annoying friend that the dog trucks were full. There was no time to work with a personal dog. She was so ugly that even if the bitch was made into a competent hunting dog, I probably wouldn't be able to sell her to recoup the time and money that would be invested. The bitch had been in a kennel all her life with no socialization and was scared of her own shadow. She had no idea what a bird was and had never even heard a gunshot. In other words, a one "year" old reject that neither he nor anyone else wanted. They obviously felt the bitch wasn't worth wasting time on, and at that moment I felt the same way. This friend was on a mission and he was more determined than I, so finally not being able to say no, she was accepted. An interesting fact was that he just happened to have a current rabies certificate which would be needed to cross the border into Canada.

The trip to summer camp in Saskatchewan is expensive counting transportation, rabies shot for dogs, blood test for the horses, all of which make up only a small part of the total costs. Someone has to pay for human food, wages for assistants, gas, horse and dog food and all the other numerous expenses which are incurred with a three-month training trip to the prairies. The dog owners take the responsibility for this, so extra non-paying dogs don't fit into the agenda. That's the principal reason why trainers don't like to take their own dogs. It's just too expensive and your time belongs to those who are paying the freight.

After making the tiring trip, including the border delays to clear customs, we finally arrived some fourteen hours later. When dropping anchor at summer camp, it was always in the wee hours of the morning, but there is no rest for humans until the animals are taken care of. Feeding, watering, putting out individual dog houses, driving stakes into the ground to hold the dogs; its daylight before the work is completed and everyone is physically exhausted. The Reject was turned loose to run wherever she wanted to go. The trainer who gave this dog to me called her Judy, so the same name was continued with. Judy wore no collar, ate and slept on the front porch of the camp. The bitch was completely free and if she wanted to run away the opportunity was there to do so. She had to come back to camp if she wanted to eat. I didn't have the time to worry about her, as my hands were full with innumerable other responsibilities.

Fortunately she hung around, but sure made a nuisance of herself. She was always getting in the way of the dog trucks as we were leaving to go to the field to work dogs. She came very close to being run over on a few occasions. When arriving back at camp after the days training, she was there waiting for the trucks to stop so she could eat the grasshoppers stuck to their grilles.

Around camp there were sharp-tailed grouse, which professional trainers call chicken, and every other kind of bird and animal one could think of. Throughout the first couple of weeks I would notice Judy on point in the fields around camp, and would see her flush sharp-tail and chase them. Well, at least she can find a few bird's now and then, I thought, and she looks pretty good while pointing. The helpers and I were too occupied with the paying dogs to worry about her. Any clients who came to camp to visit, and to watch their dogs being trained would go home without Judy. I guess my mistake in trying to get rid of her was, not enough money was offered for someone to take her.

In mid-August it looked like the bitch was here to stay, so it was decided to give her an opportunity. I put on a collar and taught her to tie out with the other dogs. She was then started on basic obedience. Judy was exceedingly fearful and was difficult to work with, so she began spending evening hours with me after the days training. I would take her into the

house for short periods to feed treats and to just handle her. She was taught to jump up on a chair to get a treat. After a few weeks of this hands-on treatment, Judy accepted the fact that she wasn't going to be barbecued on the pit. The bitch had even started to come when called, but as always, crawling on her stomach and sometimes urinating.

It was time to take Judy to the field and have a good look at her. She started riding in the dog truck three times a week with other green broke young dogs. While running a promising derby dog, she would tag along. Pretty soon I started to notice that if a derby dog had two finds on sharp-tail, she had three. If the other dog was on point and Judy saw him, she would honor him. She would run an acceptable race and was very competitive with the other dog. When the other dog would point a bird and look like a million bucks, Judy would point and look almost as good.

Maybe it was time for me to reevaluate this situation! I was starting to fire the blank gun over her while she was chasing birds, and she never paid the slightest attention. When switching to the shotgun she was oblivious to the loud bang. Judy was still a timid and fearful dog, but was starting to gain a little self-confidence and was beginning to trust me. When it was time to go to the field she would jump into the dog truck unassisted.

At this point I'm starting to think: maybe she will make a decent hunting dog after all. She can sure find birds, looks pretty good on point and doesn't want to get lost. Having no personal dog at the time to hunt chukars with, I decided to take her with me to my home in Washington State. When wanting to bird hunt I would be able to work with her after the fall field trial season.

As mentioned before she was very timid and when someone walked toward her she would squat and urinate, or just completely lie down on her stomach. This is an attitude of submission and when you break a dog steady to wing and shot it involves the dog standing up when you approach them. These types of dogs take a lot of time and understanding to get them right. If I ever wanted to enter her in competition, obviously she would have to be standing.

I continued working her with other dogs and by the end of the summer; she was starting to impress me. Judy's physical structure was all wrong, but she had a big heart and a competitive spirit. Her desire was such she wouldn't quit no matter how long she was run, and she was always focused on birds and not fur. Point them, flush them and then chase the hell out of them! That's exactly what a young dog should do, and she did plenty of it.

With the Canadian summer training season drawing to a close in late September, it was time to head back to the United States. I needed to show and give back the hunting dogs to their owners, hoping they would be happy with the progress that had been made. The field trial dogs remained with me in order to enter them in the upcoming competitions.

By late November my field trialing had ended for the season and I wanted to get in a little chukar hunting. To describe the chukar hills to those people who have never hunted them. They are a series of high rolling hills with canyons, some with trickling water and most are sparsely covered with cheat grass and sagebrush. Commonly called hills when horseback hunting, but usually referred to as mountains when hunting them on foot. On top of these hills you will often find wheat growing, the seeds of which make up a goodly part of the fall and winter diet of chukars. They also consume grass seeds, insects and tender green cheat grass shoots when they are available in the spring. A most interesting winter food source is a type of root that I've never been able to identify. If the ground is partially frozen, they are still able to scratch that root up and eat it. Another intriguing fact about this wonderful game bird is they are able to survive in a hot, dry environment during the summer and a frigid, wind-swept area in the winter. In addition to chukar in those hills you will find California quail, mule deer, coyote and a sprinkling of sage grouse.

Most of the time I foot hunted both to get my exercise and to give the horses a much needed rest after the long hard training and field trial season. Judy would really stretch out in the chukar hills even when hunting her on foot. At times I wouldn't see her for five or ten minutes, but would often find her on point. She was learning how to find and also how to point and handle chukar. On numerous occasions she showed me that she wanted to hunt with me, even though she hunted at extreme distance for a foot hunter. I

didn't feel the need to restrict her range and shorten her, because I really enjoy a dog that hunts according to the terrain on which they are searching for game. Open terrain, bigger race, restrictive terrain, shorter race!

I'd learned many years before; only a few dogs made good chukar dogs and even fewer were outstanding. In my lifetime I've been fortunate to own and/or train three exceptional chukar dogs and Judy ended up being one of them. On most of the hunts that were had with this bitch, she would find five or six coveys of chukar, and one or two coveys of California quail. Occasionally a covey of Hungarian partridge would be found although it was a rare occurrence. I was able to kill a quantity of birds over her that first hunting season. It wasn't time to think about finishing her yet, as she was still too immature.

After the hunting season and during the winter quite a bit of obedience work was done with Judy and she was responding well. My opinion was beginning to change about the dog I called The Reject. She was certainly a physical disaster as stated before, but the bitch didn't have any quit in her and you can't buy that drive and desire. You can certainly build on it, but a dog either has it or doesn't. I was learning about that old adage: "Never judge a book by its cover." That winter when Judy was about eighteen months old the decision was made not to run her in field trials due to the fact she had no owner. It's never a good idea to enter in competition a dog the professional trainer owns. This can create a conflict with the owners who are paying you to compete with their dogs. Consequently the following year she wasn't entered in any contests.

When the spring field trials were over and after securing enough dogs to make the trip viable, it was time to head north to the prairies once again. This time I took along two helpers who had grown up around dogs. They weren't totally ignorant about animals and both had some dog knowledge. This is very helpful to the professional due to him not having to take the time to teach them every little thing they need to know. Those same young men had learned from their exposure around dogs, some of the basic points of dog training.

It's a common practice for some owners to send their teenage sons to summer dog camp with the trainer, so they learn about hard work and mature a little faster. It's a hard life, but the young men develop faster with hard work, more responsibilities and no television or other distractions to occupy them.

Dog camp had to be well organized to make it run smoothly, and everyone had a role in keeping it functioning like a well-oiled machine. For example; I would wake up at four a.m. and start breakfast for the crew. Fifteen minutes later they would be rousted out of their beds to come and eat. We had no electricity, so all the cooking was done with gas and even the refrigerator operated on gas. When breakfast was finished the boys would head out to clean up after the dogs and take care of their personal needs.

Each dog had his own individual house and was staked to the ground using a thirty inch chain. The dog houses were situated along rows of shade trees which protected them from the afternoon sun. Every two weeks the houses and the stakeout chains were moved to virgin ground to prevent parasite infection.

Working the dogs on obedience took until seven a.m. I would help the boys harness and hook up twelve dogs to a motor-less buggy that the dogs would drag in a circuitous route going eight miles out and back. These were field trial dogs and were worked on the buggy one day and in the field the following day. With that schedule they were in excellent condition when the fall field trials rolled around. Judy became one of those dogs.

It was time to break Judy as now her age and maturity levels predicated that she be finished. This was done in a short time due to all the preparatory work that had been done. I recall an incident which happened when we were running her in a workout. I saw her pointing near a grove of chokecherry trees, but didn't call it to my scout's attention. He was daydreaming and wasn't paying attention to what was going on. This young man was enamored with Judy, so he was often let to handle her and be in on the breaking process. We rode on for another quarter mile when I asked him;

"When was the last time you saw that bitch?"

He replied that he had seen her back a ways from where we were. I informed him maybe he had better take a ride to the rear, to see if he could find her. Judy, by this time, was pretty honest on her game. It didn't worry me that she would break and chase the birds. I wanted my scout to discover her for the reason he would be excited about finding her on point, and it was good training for him to start paying attention. It wasn't long before the call of "Point" was heard. I went riding back to where she was pointing and Judy handled that covey of sharp-tail in excellent fashion. The young man was absolutely thrilled with the fact he had found her on point, she showed finished manners and he had a hand in helping me to break her.

It was late August and time for the first prairie field trial to be run near Cardston, Alberta. We packed up the dogs that would be competing in the trial with Judy being included and made the four hour drive to Cardston. Judy was entered in the shooting dog stake where she would be competing against some very good dogs run by other professional trainers. I competed with all-age dogs and had no other shooting dogs belonging to clients, so I was absolved of any culpability should she win. A prairie shooting dog is expected to run a wider race than a shooting dog that's run in more restrictive country. The prairies are more open topography where you can see a dog at remarkable distances. Judy ran a nice race, but wasn't as wide as one would expect a dog to be in that type of terrain; however, she did have a nice find on a covey of sharp-tail and placed third.

The Canadian training season was over in late September so it was time once again to head south to participate in the West Coast field trial circuit. After sending the hunting dog's home I hit the road with a handful of dogs to compete in the fall trials. Judy was left at the home kennel and due to the fact that she was ownerless, she was not run in any trials that fall.

Upland bird season generally opens in September or October in Washington State and finishes in late January. Due to prior field trial commitments, I wasn't able to begin hunting until early December. Judy was my go-to chukar dog by now and she had developed into a good one. I hunted her on pheasant as well, but was not happy with her performances as she was too cautious. A good pheasant dog has to push the bird until it hides and stops running. That caution Judy exhibited was learned on the sharp-tailed grouse. In the fall of the year the sharp-tail are flighty and will flush for any reason, and that is why a dog learns to show caution. That tentative approach doesn't work so well on native pheasants. I had a better pheasant dog to hunt with, so after those experiences with Judy; she was retired from the pheasant fields and used exclusively for chukars.

While chukar hunting on a long downhill slope on a cold breezy December day, I saw Judy go on point about a half mile farther down the hill. There were some power lines running through the area so I was able to accurately mark her position by using those poles as a reference point. Walking through a depression I lost sight of exactly where she was pointing, but those poles guided me. Judy was well broke at this point, so I didn't need to be worried about her breaking and chasing birds no matter how long it took me to get there. She was an honest bird dog and wasn't prone to having an unproductive. All her points produced birds. After arriving at the spot where she was pointing shortly before, Judy wasn't there. I knew I was in the right place because I'd counted the power poles on my way down the hill and marked a patch of sagebrush she had been pointing in front of. I was there, but the dog wasn't. Suddenly five or six Hungarian partridge flushed; my reflexes took over, and I shot one. I don't usually kill birds unless the dog is pointing and the work is satisfactory, although at that moment I did.

After picking up the dead bird I started to worry. Why would she blink that covey of Huns? She had to have blinked them! There was no other explanation. I was in the exact same spot where she had been pointing shortly before, and she sure as hell wasn't there. Judy was under no pressure from me, and she had never blinked a bird prior to this incident, so now I'm confused. I started calling and blowing the whistle, but she didn't respond. I'm really worried now. Did she run further down the hill chasing birds and have a heart attack? That didn't seem to be a logical explanation either, as she was well broke and appeared to be healthy and in good physical condition.

I continued walking down the hill as there was no reason for me to remain in the area. After covering about a hundred yards or so, I entered into another little depression and there discovered Judy pointing behind

waist high sagebrush. The thought was running through my mind, how could she blink a covey of Huns and then point another bird a little farther down the hill? At that moment a covey of six or seven birds exploded twenty or so yards in front of Judy. I was able to drop one. I sent Judy for the retrieve, and when she returned with the bird I saw it was a Hungarian partridge. That gave me pause. It was something I needed to think about for a while. I knew from hunting this area for many years that to find a covey of Huns was not common, but to find two separate coveys within a hundred yards was not possible. Calling Judy in, I made her to lie down and take a rest while I sat on a rock and thought about what had just happened.

Finally I came to the conclusion this was part of the original covey she had pointed back up the hill where I had first seen her. The covey was spread out feeding, and she had pointed the birds on the outer edge. For whatever reason, that part of the covey moved farther down the hill with Judy following along behind them. It's possible they were spread out feeding or were nervous about her, and due to that they moved to another location. Obviously they knew she was there and recognized her as a predator. She wasn't pushing them hard, so they elected to run and not fly.

From what looked to be a very poor showing, coupled with a major fault exhibited by my best chukar dog, it turned out to be an exceptional piece of dog work. That was the only reasonable conclusion that could be drawn from the preceding event. All the calling, whistling and firing the gun had no effect as she stayed pointing those birds. From a very concerned trainer moments before, I went to being a very happy one. That taught me to stop jumping to conclusions and learn to analyze situations for just what they are.

After that hunting season Judy was registered with the *Field Dog Stud Book*, as Saskatchewan Whirlwind. The name was applicable due to the way she dashed from here to there and everywhere, just like a whirlwind. She now became my go to personal hunting dog and gained a lot of experience on how to find and handle chukars.

Judy's following years were spent hunting with no field trialing, until one day Col. W.G.A. Lambe a retired military man from Canada, expressed interest in buying her to campaign. The deal was concluded and she was run in the Pacific Coast Championship and the National Chukar Championship. She placed in neither, but did a creditable job in both.

The following year was 1980 and Judy was coming six years old when the tables suddenly turned in her favor with her winning the National Chukar Championship against a record field of forty entries. Her win was so decisive that no runner-up was named. My scout Lou Phillips was a big factor in her winning the Championship. Owing to his eagle eyes and fast riding, we were able to finish this hard charging all-age dog. I will quote some of what the field trial reporter wrote about her performance.

"Saskatchewan Whirlwind stole the show in winning the 21st renewal of The National Chukar Championship. She has come on strong this year, performing well in the Pacific Coast Championship and capturing The National Chukar Championship in no uncertain terms. Her conditioning was superb, permitting her to run beyond the limits. She is a knowledgeable chukar dog and is beautifully broken on her birds. Her first find was incredible, beyond the boundaries of a fence, off course and involved her standing a little less than twenty minutes. It took a hard ten minute ride and when arriving Bob Pettit and the judge had to dismount and walk another two hundred yards to flush the three chukar from where Judy was pointing. Her manners were impeccable. She was brought back through the fence, watered and cast off on the flats above a canyon heading west. Halfway along, she dropped over the rim and point was subsequently called. Handler dismounted, flushed chukars about fifteen yards directly in front of her. After the shot was fired she remained rigidly on point. As Pettit returned to collar her a single chukar flew from directly under her nose. She did not move. A shot was again fired and the gallery was buzzing. Judy was then brought back onto the course and as she continued across the flats she again struck game. Her third find was not as spectacular as the first two, but was perfectly handled at the conclusion of her hour."

After that great win and with her winning another regional Championship, she was retired and given to me. Judy remained my personal hunting dog until her death at nine years old. In her retirement years, and in the off season, she was allowed the freedom to run loose on the ranch. She spent a

lot of time chasing birds, digging holes and generally making a nuisance of herself, but she had certainly earned it.

This was a story about a great little bitch that no one wanted. She had the fires of a bird dog burning brightly within her, and those fires couldn't be quenched despite her many physical defects. She was all heart, and she showed that each and every time she competed.

L-R, Robert Pettit-handler, W.G.A. Lambe-owner, Lou Phillips-scout, kneeling with: 1980 National Chukar Champion "Saskatchewan Whirlwind"
American Field photo.

Nine time Champion Ronco Traveler

THE RUNAWAY

The litter that was bred from my winningest derby dog Triple Play x Ahtanums Georgia Girl produced an orange and white male that would later make headlines across the field trial world. Whelped on January 10th, 1976 he was in my opinion the standout puppy of the litter. Of all the puppies, both male and female, that particular male caught my eye. Little did I suspect at the time, that squirming voracious little puppy would set the West Coast field trial circuit on fire, and would become widely known throughout the bird dog world.

That plump little puppy would propel himself into field trial fame and drag me and others along with him. I had been training dogs professionally for about six years when the litter was whelped.

When the puppy was about three months old he was sold to a Canadian man who started running him in the logging slash on Vancouver Island while looking for blue or dusky grouse. The youngster was starting to, as we say, get some legs under him. The owner was losing him every time he was put down in a workout. That obviously wasn't working out well for the pups new hunting partner, in that he believed the puppy was running away by virtue of the fact he wouldn't be found for hours.

The logging slash on the island is very rough and restrictive and any dog that wants to travel will soon be lost from view. To successfully hunt terrain such as this, you have to be half mountain goat and half horse to navigate over the cut logs and thick brush, but it's one of the types of topography that appeal to the species of grouse previously mentioned. This young dog was classified as a runaway and sent back to me.

I was left with a washout that had started gaining fame as a runoff dog. His call name was Pete, but he became known as The Traveler to the many admires who knew of the dog. After bringing the puppy back to Washington, I began going to the field to work him on horseback, where he was able to highlight his running skills. He moved with style and grace, but didn't have a clue as to what he was supposed to be looking for in the way of birds. He was spending his time chasing and yipping at meadowlarks and other small birds. Showing very little desire to handle, he was also erratic in his pattering, but I liked him and had a good feeling about this youngster. The puppy wasn't scared of tackling the country and would really stretch out, but he had no contact with wild birds. The area where he was run was very spotty with game birds, and they were only occasionally found by other more mature dogs. At the time that was the only area available to me for training, and all the older dogs were worked on planted birds.

It was late June of the same year 1976, and it was time to gather dogs that would make the trip north with me to the Canadian dog camp. It would be a shame to leave such a promising puppy in the kennel, as a result of not having an owner to pay his fare. Picking up the phone I dialed (they didn't have pushbutton or flat screen phones in those days) a client whom I had previously trained a few dogs for. Mr. Ron Bader a California field trial enthusiast was the recipient of that fateful call. While I was describing the physical attributes of the dog he asked me how he looked on point. I replied that I had never seen him point. He then asked if he found a lot of birds and I told him I had never seen him find a bird.

Mr. Bader then exclaimed: "Well, what the hell are you trying to sell me then?"

After telling him this would have to be a case of trust owing to the fact there was no picture to send him, only a physical description and that was related verbally. I mentioned the pup was bold and built to have endurance, with a deep chest and a long fluid stride. I told Mr. Bader I felt this puppy was going to develop into a really nice field trial dog. Telling him that if he didn't buy the pup he would have to be sacrificed as there was no one to care for him in my absence. I thought that would be a good sales ploy, although it was somewhat duplicitous. The justification to myself was; that exceptional puppy needed to go north with me, no matter what it took. It worked! Relating to him the cost he decided to trust me and agreed to refund the original purchase price to the previous owner. When hanging up I was ecstatic about having a new owner. In the excitement I had neglected to ask him whether he would send the dog with me to Canada, or if I needed to ship him to California. Another call was made and after a lot of grumbling on the other end of the line, Mr. Bader agreed to send Pete to the prairies. He emphasized he wanted the puppy to get into a lot of birds and to let him develop in his own time. He had nothing to worry about in that respect.

After the fourteen hour trip from Washington State to dog camp in Saskatchewan, Canada, both man and beast are stressed. When you are carrying almost fifty dogs, two rigs and four horses there's a mountain of work ahead of you upon arriving. We started the trip that year in the early morning hours of July 2nd.

The following day was a day of rest for the dogs and horses, but not for people. When you are training that many dogs, it's difficult to get more than a few hours' sleep at any one time. There is always something to be done.

The responsibilities are heavy and you constantly have to be attuned to what's going on in camp. The dogs will always let you know by their barking if something is amiss. This often means getting up in the middle of the night to go outside and put things right.

Field training would start on July 15th when the majority of Speargrass seeds have dropped to the ground and the recently hatched sharp-tailed grouse chicks are old enough to fly. That would give us at least ten days, twice daily of obedience training the dogs.

Taking Pete to the field was an experience. An affable pup, he was a pleasure to work with, but was fascinated with deer and antelope and loved to chase them. I didn't try to discourage this because, like sharp-tail, he had to learn he couldn't catch them. He wasn't hunting for birds as much as four footed animals and had pretty much a free rein as long as he handled and stayed with me. He was worked entirely on horseback. There were only a few instances of check cord work when he was close enough to me and I saw some sharp-tail alight. When he actually found a covey of sharp-tail on his own, he would chase them out of the country. When he found a herd of antelope he would do the same. He had no inclination to point, only to chase. That plus obedience was pretty much his summer training. He was developing his running and hunting instincts as the summer wore on. The pup had great fun that summer, but so did I while watching him develop.

If Pete had belonged to a foot hunter he would have washed him out as being a renegade. He was anything but! The owner had instructed me to let the dog mature and advance at his own rate, and that was exactly what I did. Pete was the only dog out of that group of dogs that went north that summer to never point a sharp-tail.

When summer training was over, it was time to head back to the United States and return the trained hunting dogs to their owners. The field trial dogs stayed with me in order to run in competition. Pete, however, was shipped to California where the expectant owner picked him up at the airport. Mr. Bader was thrilled upon seeing the dog and talked about what a fine specimen he was. At that point he probably had close to a thousand dollars invested in the dog without even seeing a picture. This would be the equivalent of almost five thousand dollars today. It doesn't sound like a whole lot of money now, but this was the mid-1970s and the purchasing power of the dollar was strong.

The following spring the dog was entered in and won the Pete Cunningham Puppy Classic, one of the premier puppy stakes on the West Coast. He was then registered as Ronco Traveler. A number of other people who had a close association with the dog always referred to him as Traveler. Many never knew his real call-name. So from now on in this story I will refer to him as Traveler.

When Traveler was around sixteen months old the owner called me. He told me that he had put the dog with another professional trainer in order to work him on both wild and planted birds for a couple of months. After evaluating the dog the trainer told Mr. Bader the dog would never point a bird, as all he wanted to do was chase. The trainer said he had no pointing instinct. When Mr. Bader relayed that conversation to me, I told him to jump in his truck, bring me the dog and I would have him pointing in twenty minutes. I sure didn't think he would do it, as he lived eight hundred miles south of me, but he did. Two days later he was there with the dog, so now having made that bold claim, I had to live up to my word.

Gathering together about thirty homing pigeons used for training, we took them to the field, along with the dog and the old style pull string release trap.

Mr. Bader was told he had one job. As soon as the string on that trap was pulled he needed to immediately put in another bird.

I led Traveler up with a check cord attached and as soon as he scented the bird he enthusiastically charged the trap. I pulled the string and dropped the check cord. Traveler was in an all-out chase and it was three-four minutes before he returned. He charged the trap as before and that bird was also thrown. This went on with about ten birds before he came back with his tongue dragging in the dirt and started sneaking up on the trap. Each chase was shorter in duration. Whenever he took a step, out went the bird and away went the dog.

To say the dog had a lot of chase left in him would be putting it mildly. By the time fifteen birds had been thrown; he was in a pointing mode and

was very intense. I then started pushing him into the bird, and he was pushing back. That was the bird which we killed for the dog. The elapsed time was about twenty eight minutes. I had mislead the owner when he was told the dog would be pointing in twenty minutes, but I don't remember him complaining about it. That was the start of something great, as from then on Traveler pointed most if not all birds, both planted and wild.

The next training trip to summer camp was coming up and of course Traveler was included, as this was the time he needed to be finished on game. I remember well that summer as there was an abundance of sharp-tail. It was a great year for finishing both field trial and hunting dogs.

Mama sharp-tail and her young brood are very cooperative on the hot days of July and early August. During the summer months in the mid-day heat you will often find the hen and her chicks in wolfwillow or buffaloberry bushes owing to the shade they offer. When you flush the birds, they only fly a short distance and right into another bush. You are able to work them numerous times before they tire of being chased and make longer flights. This characteristic enables a trainer to have multiple finds on the same covey, and in short order the dog is finished. When the cooler fall weather is approaching the chicks are older and they become flighty.

Traveler was having numerous game contacts each time he was run and was showing a proclivity to handle birds. He had given up chasing four-footed game as they had lost their appeal. I believe this was due to Mr. Bader and me killing numerous game-birds over him. Now the dog's attention was focused only on birds. This was all good news as he was developing into a fine young field trial dog. The day that stands out most in my remembrance of that year's trip to the Sandhills was Traveler's great limb find. It's still etched in my mind.

A limb find for those who are not familiar with the terminology, is a find that's a considerable distance from the handler. It indicates a find on birds that were dug up and didn't come by the dog just happening to stumble across a covey. Of course these types of finds from an all-age dog are quite thrilling in that it involves a wide searching race with a productive find on birds at the end of a long cast.

It was the middle part of August and Traveler was running free with no handicaps such as chains or check cord. On this particular day he made a long cast to the front searching the bluffs on his way out, when all of a sudden an unmoving white speck was seen on the horizon. I started riding and when I was within one hundred yards of the dog a covey of sharp-tail erupted from the bluff and started flying away. Traveler stood and handled the covey with intensity and assurance. This young dog was very exciting; he was developing into a phenomenal prospect.

When the training day was over my excitement couldn't be contained any longer. I drove into Sceptre which was the closest town from my camp at thirteen miles away. There at Doc Brown's Esso station was a public pay phone. Calling Traveler's owner, I told him the exciting news that our boy was finally broke. Mr. Bader was ecstatic now that he had a top all-age contender capable of winning any field trial anywhere.

With the summer training season in Canada over, I shipped Traveler back to his owner in California so he would have the opportunity of competing in The Quail, Pheasant and Bird Dog Championships. That was the last training trip the dog took with me as there was no longer any need for it. I was able to run him in a few field trials over the years when the owner wasn't available, and under my guidance the dog gained two National Titles. When neither Mr. Bader nor I were available, Traveler was sent to certain trials with other professionals and amateurs alike.

The phenomenal thing about The Traveler was the fact he knew his job well enough, and went out and did it. It didn't seem to matter if a stranger was in the driver's seat. This type of dog is a rarity and the fact that he could win nine Championships while running under five different handlers was a testament to his character. There certainly aren't many dogs which could have achieved that. Traveler, besides being adaptable was a very competitive dog and always gave his best effort whenever he was entered in field trial competition.

The following is a story I wrote about one of Traveler's best performances at The National Chukar Championship.

The year was 1984 and it turned out to be a special one for Ronco Traveler, his owner and trainer by the dog winning the twenty fifth renewal

of The National Chukar Championship held at Prosser, Washington. The course on which Traveler ran was number three, which of the three courses is the most difficult for an all-age dog and his handler to navigate. Some areas of this course are covered with dense patches of tall sagebrush and in many places the visibility is near zero.

The topography of the Anderson Ranch where the National Chukar Championship is contested yearly is made up of steep rolling hills dotted with clumps of grasses, sagebrush and deep canyons. Most places, however, are accessible on horseback. In the spring of the year when this field trial is held, the sagebrush is starting to bloom and the smell in certain areas is sometimes overpowering. It was always a wonder to me how a dog could actually scent a bird with that aroma wafting through the air. No handler wants to draw course number three due to the complications involved in trying to finish a dog. If a dog didn't want to handle, that course presented him with many opportunities to elude his handler.

Traveler wasn't that kind of dog. He hunted with every jump, was full of exuberance and totally dedicated to finding birds. His long easy stride would carry him to the limits of any course, and he would sometimes get lost in his search for birds. Those times were infrequent, as he was a dog that liked to go with whoever was handling him. That trait was attributed to the fact he was hunted for pheasant, quail and chukar both on foot and horseback. When we were foot hunting, he worked at hunting dog range.

Traveler was allowed to compete in fun trials that were shoot to kill competitions, but was not allowed to win a placement when competing against hunting dogs. This was an education for those who believed you couldn't hunt over an all-age field trial dog. Those fun trials were an opportunity for everyone to see just how versatile a field trial dog was. It was also a good training exercise for the dog. When a bird was killed he received his reward of the birds head after the retrieve. From those appearances he acquired more fans that were added to the growing list. At weekend trials wherever he competed the lid came off, and he ran true all age races.

When Traveler was turned loose that day there was no reason to be nervous; I knew what kind of dog he was even though we had drawn the most difficult course to finish a dog on. Having raised Traveler from a puppy and had broken him on sharp-tailed grouse in Saskatchewan, we were pretty well attuned to one another and had great rapport.

His first cast was straight to the front and at around the ten minute mark I could see a non-moving white speck far in the distance. It was Traveler standing there on point. Having ridden course number three many times before, I had never seen anything there that could be confused with a pointing dog, so I called point.

When the judges arrived the dog was standing like a statue with a high head and tail. He was a beautiful dog and always drew people's admiration when he was pointing. With an orange head and a luminous white body he was fine example of English pointer breeding.

After flushing a pair of chukars, I fired my gun and sent him on. Now the terrain was starting to open up and Traveler was seen devouring large portions of the country and looking for more. He was a fast dog and in his quest for game no country was too big. He would be absent for about ten minutes and then show momentarily far to the front. It's almost uncanny how true all-age dogs can be aware of their handler's location, even if that same handler has no idea where his charge is.

Disappearing and showing frequently, he was putting on a thrilling show. The riders in the gallery behind me were vocalizing and the noise was rising to a crescendo as we were all witnessing an electrifying race.

At around forty five minutes my scout Dave Lachance (a professional trainer from California) and I had just given Traveler a drink of water. When released, the dog was heading to the front when misfortune almost reared its ugly head. The bird planter had tossed a chukar which flew over the top of the dog and landed about twelve or so yards in front of him. Traveler was running full throttle when this incident occurred. The bird planter was saying, "I'm sorry, Bob, I'm sorry." It happened so fast that I didn't even have time to caution Traveler, but he was up to the challenge and had already slammed into a point. The spectators were heard to exhale in relief. I got off my horse and flushed the bird, fired and sent the dog on.

When the judges called time Traveler was pointed out far in the distance looking for more territory to conquer in his quest to find more game. It was quite a long ride to go and get him. I felt that it was going to be very difficult job for any dog to beat the show Traveler had just thrilled the spectators and me with.

I had previously run a bitch named Blackbelt's Net and thought that due to her performance she had a very good chance of winning. As good as her race and bird work had been, in my opinion Traveler had beaten her. He gave a thrilling exhibition of a blistering all-age race, ran to the limits of the course, but still maintained contact with his handler. To top that off, his bird work was perfect under trying circumstances.

While Traveler was in harness and I was roading him back to camp, field trial regulations were broken by me killing a chukar that he pointed. Following the exhilarating performance that was just witnessed I felt the dog needed to be rewarded. After killing the chukar, I sent him for the retrieve and then parted out the bird piece by piece so he could eat the evidence.

Two days later he was named National Chukar Champion and Blackbelt's Net was named Runners-up. Traveler's final win record stood at thirty three wins, nine Championship Titles including two National Chukar Championship titles under my direction. End of story.

Another remarkable fact about this dog was that he won seven out of nine Championships while competing with only one eye. He lost an eye in a fight as a three "year" old. I remember an incident where he came running near a dog on point in the California Pheasant Championship. The judge told Mr. Bader to pick him up owing to the fact he didn't honor the other dog. Mr. Bader whistled and Traveler swung around and as soon as he saw the other dog, he immediately honored. A dog can't back what he can't see. If I remember correctly it was Traveler that won the Championship.

Traveler was a wild pheasant dog supreme. He was one of only a handful of dogs that I've trained that could time after time pin a running native pheasant without flushing it. Anyone who has had experience with wild pheasants, that are continually harassed by dogs and field trailers, knows exactly what I'm talking about.

Included is an article written by Dr. C. A. Hjerpe, an acknowledged bird dog expert, as an endorsement for the Field Trial Hall of Fame. Dr. Hjerpe followed most of Traveler's career. Quote: "I cannot remember ever seeing him knock birds, chase or show any evidence of intimidation around game. In addition he was the best wild pheasant dog I have ever seen. Ronco Traveler had a knack of pinning a pheasant in such a way that it would stay put until you got there to flush it. It didn't matter how long that might take, and/or how tall and thick the cover might be." End of quote.

Using this opportunity I will insert another quote from a client whom I once took pheasant hunting with Traveler. He was also endorsing Traveler for the Field Trial Hall of Fame in his article. It was long and descriptive, but I will only use the part that pertains to this story.

Quote: "Bob asked me if I wanted to go pheasant hunting behind The Traveler. I had previously watched Ronco Traveler at several field trials and was very aware of the gigantic races he put down every time he was cast off. I remember being completely amazed that he was able to be foot hunted on pheasants." End of quote.

The Traveler had limited opportunity at stud and was never bred to top producing bitches, yet he was able to produce three champions out of twelve bitches bred. Most of the puppies resulting from those breeding's were sold to hunters and not field trialers. The number of winners that he produced was twenty and those winners had a total of eighty eight wins. All in all a remarkable percentage of winners for the few times he was bred.

Ronco Traveler was retired at nine years old and was allowed the free run of the Bader dairy farm. He passed away peacefully in his sleep at age fourteen in 1990 and was given a burial place of honor in the Bader animal cemetery.

This dog taught me more than I taught him. I will always be grateful for the opportunity Mr. Bader accorded me in being able to train and run Traveler in various field trials. I was able to ride the dog's coattails on the road to fame and recognition for his championship wins and for that I'm grateful. Here's to you! The Runaway!

QUESTIONS AND ANSWERS

These were questions that were submitted to me over the years. They all pertain to common training problems. The solutions are offered in the answers.

Two questions were submitted by Sr. Victor Dominguez, Morelos, Mexico

Question # 1- "My English pointer bitch is steady to wing and shot and I sometimes run her in weekend trials. In training sessions when she points a bird, I flush and fire, but when I walk back toward her she loosens up and loses all character. She looks great on point, but as soon as I approach, she folds and looks like she's been beaten. This is not a game changer, but I realize it looks bad. How can I prevent this?"

Answer: Sr. Dominguez, I'm taking two questions from you as both of them apply to common problems. From your description, I'm sure you have a somewhat timid or recessive bitch, and she's probably been overcorrected around game. These types of dogs naturally show submission when you approach them head on. You didn't mention anything about killing birds over your bitch.

To cure a dog with this problem I use several methods, but the best method by far is to kill birds. Shoot the bird, pick it up and bring it back and give her a piece of it. As you are approaching, have the bird held around chest level and jiggle it, so as to keep her attention focused on the hand that's holding it. You should only give it to her when she's standing on her tiptoes. After you've shot so many birds and brought them back to her, she will stand up tall; she's anticipating a reward, which is a piece of the bird.

I trained and competed with a bitch called Saskatchewan Whirlwind. She was a very recessive animal. After she had a find and the shot was fired, as I was walking back to collar her, she would fold completely and lay flat on her belly. Your situation sounds less severe than my problem was with the Whirlwind.

I was able to solve that dilemma by killing a lot of birds, and by me picking them up and delivering them to her. She was always fed the head and usually both legs of whatever species I was hunting. I used the same tactics I suggested earlier. I would bring back the bird while twitching it to keep her attention focused on my hand, which I held at chest level. Over time she stood up like a statue while licking her lips in anticipation.

Another method is to approach your dog obliquely. Don't approach directly from the front. When you are walking back and are parallel to her stance, turn slowly and walk to her side. If after you've done this eight or ten times and have seen no improvement, try walking backwards towards her while quartering and pretending to flush another bird. It also helps to flush more than one bird in front of her while she's pointing. This will keep her intense if she believes that there's always more than one bird in the bush. Use a bird bag to carry an extra bird or two.

A human is quite a bit bigger than a dog and to a recessive animal or one that's been harshly treated, you represent a possible threat. When your back is turned to an animal, you don't represent the same threat. Over time the problem will fix itself if enough birds are killed.

Question # 2- Submitted by Sr. Manuel Azcona, Mexico City

"I have a three "year" old English pointer bitch I hunt quail with and she is an excellent retriever with the exception she eats the first two or three quail that I kill. How can I fix something like this?"

Answer: To answer this question we have to think about the cause and effect factor. We know the effect, so let's try to figure out the cause. Often times when we discover the cause and eliminate it, the effect will disappear by itself.

My guess is you hunt with multiple unbroken dogs, and the first dog to the bird gets to claim it, and in this case eat it. I have rarely seen a dog start eating birds that wasn't either extremely hungry, was encouraged to eat one, or didn't have a lot of pressure exerted on him. They will chew the bird, but seldom eat it on their own. This problem could be caused by owner pressure, like hurrying to snatch the bird away, shouting at her for mauling the bird or pressure from the other dogs to get to the downed bird quicker.

Have you ever watched a wild animal documentary about lions, where the male is dominant and chases away the females from the kill until his

hunger is satisfied? I believe the same thing is going on with your bitch. She is first to the bird and to keep it away from the other dogs, eats it and eats enough of them until satiated after which she will retrieve the quail. This is a survival mechanism and you will see the same thing with all of the canine species. When have you heard about a wolf or wild dogs sharing their meal with another, if the meal is only a small portion? A wolf or wild dog will choke it down so that the other members of the pack don't have access to it. They will share with their young, but normally not with another adult unless it's a large kill, and that took a pack effort. It's just not nature's way.

The three things that I suggest are: feed her a goodly portion of dog food before going hunting, hunt her alone with a short cord for control. After killing a bird and while she's chewing on it, pull her to you, fish it out of her mouth and feed her all of it piece by piece. Every retrieve she completes, feed her as much of the bird as she will eat. Her retrieves will also begin to be faster. No competition from other dogs equates to no hurry to gulp down the bird, and no pressure from you as now you are rewarding her for bringing the bird instead of snatching it away. The taste for quail will soon disappear and she will stop eating the birds. You should also be talking to her in an approving manner as you are feeding the bird. This way she begins to understand her actions are sactioned by you, her leader. If this is an engrained habit in your bitch, it will take longer to reprogram her.

Years ago I cured a quail-eating dog in Mexico. This particular bitch belonged to a friend and had been hunted with other dogs all of her life. As I remember it, she was about five years old. The competition to retrieve was the reason she learned to get there first, and eat the bird so the other dogs couldn't have it. I hunted with this friend almost every weekend and we would hunt my dog for a couple of hours and then his dog for about the same length of time. What I recall is; it took between fifteen and twenty quail over the period of a couple of months before she was bringing them back with a tender mouth.

As soon as the other dogs were taken out of the equation an improvement was seen almost immediately. She mauled them when retrieving, but when the bird was brought to hand, it was parted out and given to her piece by piece. She began to realize that when she returned with the bird she received multiple rewards, a head and two legs, and it quickened her retrieves. She ended up being a tender-mouthed retriever and after a time had no more interest in eating a piece of quail, even when it was offered.

A year later the phone rang and it was my friend telling me the bitch had reverted back to her old ways of eating the birds. I then questioned him as to how many dogs had been hunting with her that day.

He then asked me: "How in the hell did you know that?"

Pretty simple logic when you think about it. Cause and effect! Competition with no reward was the cause, and eating the bird was the effect.

If you want to continue hunting your dog's together, my suggestion is to break all of them steady to wing and shot. In this manner you have complete control over any situation which may develop. For instance; when one dog points and another is backing, kill the bird and give the pointing dog the head and the backing dog a leg. In this manner both dogs have been rewarded and by doing so you've effectively eliminated any rivalry between them. Read the chapter on, finishing the Gundog.

Question # 3- Also submitted by Sr. Victor Dominguez.

"I have just finished running my English pointer bitch in a shoot to kill field trial competition using quail. It was a timed event and the dog with the most birds pointed, along with the most birds shot and retrieved would win. She did really well on the first six birds, but on the seventh and last bird, I shot too quick and destroyed it. She went for the retrieve, picked up a piece of the mangled quail and then spit it out. Should she have retrieved what was left of the bird? Should I have made her retrieve it? Is this going to be a factor with future retrieves?"

Answer: This is the first time I've been formally asked that question in fifty years of dog training, but it's an easy one to answer. Like you, I have on occasion done the same thing and yes, a dog will refuse to retrieve it, no you shouldn't insist they do, and no, it won't be a factor with her future retrieves.

First of all your bitch is accustomed to bringing back a complete quail. Imagine what's going through her mind at the time, as she's never been presented with a case like this before. You indicated to me you were worried about creating a problem. You also told me that was the last bird you shot in the competition. Well I will make this simple. I've seen this crop up a few times with hunters I have guided using my personal dogs. When that happened my dog would not be sent for the retrieve, as the same thing would have transpired.

You destroyed the bird and the dog went for the retrieve, but instead of finding a whole bird she found a few grams of minced meat with feathers. Obviously, the bitch then became confused as to what she was supposed to do with the mess, so she dropped it. I'm happy you didn't try to force her pick it up for the reason she would have become even more confused.

A dog that has retrieved many birds before, when confronted with this hurdle will usually not make the retrieve. You shouldn't insist they do, by virtue of the fact the animal is confused. The next birds that are shot will be retrieved normally.

Question # 4- Submitted by Sr. Jose Benito Garcia, Canary Islands.

"I hunt Barbary partridge and would like to know if its o.k. to feed my dog the guts of the dead bird?"

Answer: Absolutely Jose, I have always preached the need to reward a dog *immediately after* the retrieve. A retrieve in itself is not a reward, it's a chore. Read in the retrieving section about the boss rewarding you with money for a job you did well. Everyone will tell you the reward should be in the retrieve itself, in as much as the dog is happy to bring the bird to you. Here's an example.

You go about your work with a good attitude, but you receive your paycheck with more happiness than you receive another assignment. You will do that task with a smile, for the reason it's your job and you've been programmed or trained to do it. It's the same thing with the dog. That's why *immediately* after your dog preforms a chore, you should give him his paycheck in the form of an edible reward. A head is suitable compensation or as you have indicated the bird's guts or intestines. You can never go wrong by doing this. It will increase the speed of the dog's retrieves. It will make him hunt for dead or crippled birds with more enthusiasm, in that he's learned what the end result will be. I will say again: The reward should come promptly after the retrieve not two hours later when you clean the birds.

Question # 5- Submitted by Sr. Antonio Larre, Mexico City, Mexico

"When hunting my German Shorthair male he points wild quail with a lot of intensity and with fast retrieves of the dead bird. When I train on pigeons he's slow on retrieving, and points with less intensity. Why is my dog showing a lack of intensity, and why such slow retrieves with pigeons? What's the difference between one bird and the other?"

Answer: Sr. Larre, you have almost answered your own question. You said when you train on pigeons and hunt quail. Training and hunting are two different things. You also didn't tell me the age of the dog in question. I'm confused by your query in as much as why would you train on pigeons when you have a game bird to hunt and train on? When your dog is handling quail in an acceptable manner, there's no need to work on pigeons any longer.

The dog is bored with the pigeon game and it couldn't be any clearer than if it was written in stone. Your hand scent is on the pigeon and probably most of the pressure you applied early on was done on pigeons. Wild quail don't have your hand scent. If you never hunted quail again, but twice a week shot planted pigeons for your dog, fed him the heads and then put him away, this story would eventually change. Your dog would start getting excited about going to the field and finding pigeons. In short order the dog would be showing more intensity and more excitement with the pigeon game. If you decide to continue working on pigeons, start feeding a head and both legs to your dog for every bird killed and retrieved. In time this will pick up his interest and also the speed of his retrieves. No it won't make him hard mouth.

Question # 6- Submitted by Mr. Jared Whitaker, Hartline, Washington.

Bob, how old should my pup be before I force break him to retrieve? He naturally retrieves, but sometimes he wants to play keep away and chew on

the birds. I didn't let him retrieve for a month as I thought that would help. It didn't. What should I do?

Answer: Jared, you don't work for free so why should your pup? Whenever you kill a bird, feed him the head. It will make his retrieves faster; he will bring them tenderly and will put more effort into finding crippled birds as he's learned the end result. The end result is his premium. Read the part written about retrieving and how to prevent hard mouth.

Question # 6- Submitted by Darrell "Bunky" Oldridge, Moses Lake, Washington

"I bought a bark collar for my young setter bitch to shut her up. She was barking continuously and I was fed up, so I put the collar on her. She quit barking for eleven days until I had to take off the collar to charge it. A few hours later she was barking again. What should I do? Do I have to keep the collar on her the rest of her life?"

Answer: Mr. Oldridge you messed up to put it bluntly. When putting an e-collar or bark collar on a dog its necessary to leave the collar on the dog for at least three days before turning it on. During that time you should remove it and put it back on the bitch a few times. By doing so, she will become acquainted with the bark collar and not put any significance to it. This accustoms the dog to the collar and there are no consequences, such as a shock. After that amount of time go to the dog and massage her neck to distract her and turn the collar on while still leaving it attached. When done in this manner she doesn't equate the collar with the stimulation she will receive later when she barks.

My best advice is to start over with the collar turned off. Leave it on her for a week and then activate it while it's still on her neck. After it's hot for a few days, turn it off and then back on for a few more days. This way she will never know when it's activated. Don't take the collar off the dog's neck when activating or deactivating it. Dogs are quick learners about electrical stimulation. I'm hoping this will work for you. If not, yes; she will probably wear it the rest of her life. Be careful the electrodes don't irritate or make sores on her neck. Depending on the length of those electrodes; this will sometimes happen when it's left on the dog's neck for an extended period of time. Good luck!

In Conclusion

This book was started in June of 2008 and finished eight years later. It has been a long arduous journey, but also a labor of love. My hope is that I was able to explain training techniques clearly and precisely, but especially the methods that were used in rehabilitating problem dogs. If I've accomplished those two important goals I will feel I've contributed to the understanding and betterment of dog training. Throughout my long career with dogs, I have come across many serious problems and some which were almost insurmountable. I would retire for the night with a training problem weighing heavily on my mind and when I awoke, I had the answer. I've always felt that God gave me the solution to these mind-boggling problems and to Him I give all the credit. Thank You for reading the book.

Columbia Basin Herald photo

Acknowledgements

All paintings featured in this book were painted by **Edgar Alcántara,** who is a self-taught artist that has worked with pastels and oils for over thirty five years. The practice of hunting and his relationship with wildlife have greatly influenced his work. Edgar paints many different subjects, but wildlife, dogs and hunting themes hold special meaning for him. He may be reached at: aleewildlifeart@hotmail.com

Authors note: I wish to thank the people who donated pictures for this book. Without their work and dedication in obtaining many of these photos, this publication would be imcomplete.

Photo contributors: Meg Eden, Columbia Basin Herald, John Sullivan, Oscar Chavez, The American Field, Jose Benito Garcia, and Kevin Pettit.

People who influenced my decision in writing this book, and to them I give a hearty "Thanks."

Bob and Leslie Griggs

Bob Jamison

Ron Updegrave

Sandy Anderson

Robert Pettit may be reached at: bobr-consulting@hotmail.com

Glossary

Blinking: A blinking dog has an unfounded fear of finding a bird, usually brought on by harsh punishment around game.

Brace: In a field trial; its two dogs competing against one another while running under judgement at the same time.

Breaking: Meaning to finish a dog steady to wing and shot, or the dog pointing and then chasing a bird.

Bolt: The term bolting applies to a dog running away to self-hunt for a variety of reasons.

Broke: The word broke applies to a finished dog.

Bump: Bump means to accidently flush a bird, but more than likely intentionally flushing one.

Cast: A cast is usually referred to a dogs heading toward an objective while searching for game.

Check Cord: A rope used for controlling the dog under trying circumstances. All dog trainers must have a check cord.

Crowd: Crowding birds is the term used when a dog habitually pushes into birds even though he knows exactly where they are located.

Dropper: Is a English pointer- English setter cross.

Find: This word is used when a dog searches for and then *finds* a bird. To most professionals that word is used to describe a game contact.

Finished: Breaking and finishing mean the same thing. When a dog is broke or finished, he is steady to wing and shot.

Flagging: Dogs that flag have a tail which is waving back and forth or ticking. It's caused by a lack of intensity on game.

Hacking: This usually refers to a person continually shouting at a dog trying to keep them in shotgun range. Besides being very irritating it's counterproductive.

Handle: This refers to a dog that has been taught to hunt for you and not bolt to go self-hunting. This is called handling.

Knock: Knock means a dog flushes a bird and does so intentionally.

Limb find: This is a dug-up find on birds which would normally not be found by a closer working dog.

Range: When speaking about range, it means the distance the dog is from the gunner. A dog that ranges wide should still be under control, and when finished on game there is no reason to shorten him. Most dogs will hunt close in heavy cover and then open up in an area that has little cover. This should be encouraged, not discouraged.

Roading: This can mean two different things. One is exercising the dog in harness while he's pulling against an object, and the other is roading a bird. That means the dog smells the bird and is cautiously easing up on it while in a pointing attitude. Depending on the terrain and conditions, some dogs can road birds from unbelievable distances.

Stop to flush: When a dog is hunting and a bird or covey of birds flush that the dog didn't know were there. He then stops and usually in a pointing stance. That's called stop to flush.

Trailing: This refers to one dog trailing or chasing after another. This is usually brought on by hunting an inexperienced youngster with an older faster dog.

Whoa post: A whoa post refers to a pulley system attached to a rafter or tree limb in order to control a dog, and to teach him the *"Whoa"* command.

Whoa strap: This is a two inch wide strap that's used around the dog's waist or flank in teaching him to stand still on the command "Whoa."

Yard training: this term is used loosely to mean training you dog anywhere, but in the field, whether actually in the yard or the driveway for that matter.

www.ingramcontent.com/pod-product-compliance
Lightning Source LLC
Chambersburg PA
CBHW020225170426
43201CB00007B/319